POUND **FOR** POUND

THE MODERN GLADIATORS OF MIXED MARTIAL ARTS

BRIAN J. D'SOUZA

THRACIAN PUBLISHING

Pound for Pound: The Modern Gladiators of Mixed Martial Arts

Brian J. D'Souza

Thracian Publishing
Copyright © 2012 Brian D'Souza
Published by Thracian Publishing
Toronto, Ontario
www.BrianDSouza.com
Thracian.Publishing@gmail.com

Library and Archives Canada Cataloguing in Publication

D'Souza, Brian J., 1981-
Pound for pound : the modern gladiators of mixed martial arts / by Brian D'Souza.

Includes bibliographical references.
Issued also in electronic format.
ISBN 978-0-9881493-0-4.--ISBN 978-0-9881493-3-5 (US)
ISBN: 978-0-9881493-2-8 (Kindle, PubIt!, iBooks and Kobo ebook)
ISBN: 978-0-9881493-1-1 (Smashwords ebook)

1. Mixed martial arts. 2. Martial artists. I. Title.

GV1102.7.M59D86 2012   796.81   C2012-908272-4

Editor: Jeff Evans
Paperback Designer: Jonathan Scott
Cover Designer: Ananiy Vasyura
Cover Photo: Brian J. D'Souza

Printed in the United States of America

THRACIAN PUBLISHING

For Jeff Evans
Who showed me the way forward

And Romeo D'Souza
Who gave me the drive

Contents

POUND FOR POUND

Introduction

From the white belt in jiu-jitsu who wants to earn a legitimate black belt to the young boxer who thinks about becoming the undisputed champion, there is something primordial and fierce inside of every participant in combat sports. Yet that initial fiery intent often fades when time passes and other commitments divert focus to paths of lesser resistance. You see it in the people who make New Year's resolutions to get fit—gyms without a single parking spot in January, then with a nearly vacant lot come February. Even among the most gifted prospects, there always comes a time when their eyes glaze over and they really begin to feel the mental fatigue set in. Over the course of years, the turnover whittles away the crowd until just a tiny fraction of the original dreamers is left.

To be ranked at the top of the "pound-for-pound" list in professional fighting means more than to stand among the best. It denotes ability of the highest caliber, true character in the face of adversity and the will to win no matter what the circumstances.

The general public walks away from their flat-screen TVs after having a laugh at what they watch, whether a rerun of *Friday Night Fights* or the latest season of *The Ultimate Fighter*. It's entertainment, a diversion to be consumed and forgotten. But for the fighters, there's much more going on beyond what the audience sees. Achieving the pinnacle of winning a title, and holding that status against all challenges from top contenders, takes relentless dedication and work.

As mixed martial arts (MMA) has emerged from the fringes to become known as one of the fastest-growing sports in North America, it's important to make some truths about the nature of MMA understood. What lies at the heart of a sport that some view as barbaric, a throwback to the ancient gladiatorial days of Rome? To answer this and other questions, I traveled throughout the US, Canada and Brazil to speak with the fighters who make the existence of MMA possible. The information and insight gleaned from my interviews with Georges St-Pierre, BJ Penn, Anderson Silva, Maurício Rua and Fedor Emelianenko—as well as their teammates, managers, coaches and other insiders who invested incredible amounts of time and energy into helping the fighters achieve success—are a valuable resource for anyone seeking to understand what it means to be on the "pound-for-pound" list in mixed martial arts.

Perhaps Muhammad Ali, destined to hold a place forever in history due to both his legendary career and the explosive political and social changes that intersected with his era, understood it best when he said "Champions aren't made in gyms. Champions are made from something they have deep inside them—a desire, a dream, a vision. They have to have the skill and the will. But the will must be stronger than the skill."

For the fighters, stepping into the ring, the octagon, the cage—whatever the arena—is a chance to prove to the spectators, and more importantly, themselves, that they belong. In the fighter's minds, they are providing far more than just sports entertainment—they are risking their pride to achieve something of lasting merit. The journey may be costly if measured by broken bones and bruised egos, but no matter what the price, the line-up of potential contenders continues to grow, with no end in sight.

MMA fighters often find themselves on the short end of the stick in financial matters, most often being woefully underpaid or ruthlessly exploited. Their desire to win and prove themselves works against them as they risk their health and ease of body for executives and an audience that is all too eager to move on to the next big name. Not every fighter reaches pound-for-pound status, but whether limited by internal or external factors, there's something unique about each story.

What keeps us watching beyond the entertainment value? There is something redeeming at the core of all combat sports. The qualities that draw us in are what we believe the fighters represent: that unconquerable place inside, the spirit that tells us to continue when we can't.

A fighter's win/loss record tells but a sliver of the true story. It's what the public can't experience firsthand that makes the sport of MMA and its participants so remarkable. There is more at stake than whether they won or lost—but how it went down. What were the circumstances? What really happened? And even if I try to explain, will you ever understand without stepping in there and doing it yourself? You'll never know the complete truth—but that's part of the appeal.

The mystique of watching a spectacle where either participant can be severely damaged makes it compelling right up to the end. Yet the audience can get up and walk away when the fight is over, while the people who performed as the main attraction are entrenched in an all-consuming lifestyle that they have sacrificed nearly everything for.

Most MMA fighters wouldn't have it any other way.

SECTION I: CANADA

GEORGES ST-PIERRE

1

FALLEN ANGEL

When young Georges St-Pierre first talked about his dream of becoming a great mixed martial arts champion, people around him ridiculed the idea. He was too small, came from the wrong environment and was otherwise unsuited to challenge for supremacy in the octagon. From the way he carried himself, shy and insecure, it was painfully obvious that he was talking nonsense.

The criticism cut straight to the bone, and instead of bowing out in agreement with the naysayers, St-Pierre worked his way into contention as an MMA fighter and won the Ultimate Fighting Championship (UFC) title on his second attempt, in 2006. What was the turning point? Where were the critical nodes where St-Pierre made decisions that would shape his life forever?

Said Georges on encountering the UFC on rented video cassette tapes as a teenager, "I knew right away it was going to be a very popular sport some day."[1]

MMA was a cult sport back in the '90s, gained mainstream popularity in Japan in the millennium and then exploded in North America around 2005. The waves powering careers were awe-inspiring and treacherous, as business forces and politics shaped achievement almost as much as skill and talent. Throughout the boom in North America, St-Pierre had ridden those waves, surging past opponents and cementing his claim among the pound-for-pound best fighters of all time in MMA.

There were many others who had worked hard, sacrificed and had martial arts credentials that far surpassed those of St-Pierre. Yet as 2008 came around, it was St-Pierre at the center of attention, both a recognized dominant champion and a commercially successful fighter.

Two UFC records were broken for the Georges St-Pierre vs. Matt Serra rematch scheduled for April 19, 2008, at UFC 83 in Montreal: fastest sell-out, with all tickets gone within a minute of sale to the public and a new UFC live attendance record of 21,390 people at Montreal's Bell Center. St-Pierre, the main attraction of the event, was swarmed by fans on the streets, eventually comparing his plight to that of heroes being chased in a zombie film. Meanwhile, outside the public eye, St-Pierre waged his private battle over the doubt and fear that had clouded his psyche since Serra first smashed him to pieces in 2007.

In the weeks preceding the Serra contest, there were two promotional UFC posters, one of St-Pierre and the other of Serra, hanging side-by-side on a wall at Tristar, the Montreal gym that St-Pierre called home. Over his poster, Georges had inscribed a promise, '*19 avril au Centre Bell à Montréal, je vais battre Matt Serra et redevenir Champion du monde.*' In English, "On April 19 at the Bell Centre in Montreal, I will beat Matt Serra and once again be World Champion."

St-Pierre's injuries and physical wounds could be salved with sports medicine, but the mental scars from Serra's fists, as well as other bad memories, were not so easily treated.

Taking back the welterweight title and everything that the belt symbolized to him was the action St-Pierre believed would make him whole again. Becoming champion and staying at the top was about sustaining the high of victory—the thrill of being the number one welterweight—and all of the rewards that he could accrue with such status.

Ready as he was to roll the dice of his life, fear and anxiety pervaded his mind as the fight drew closer. Was this going to be it? The turning point where his rightful place as champion was restored to him?

Every fight is a challenge, a maelstrom of danger that has to be navigated on conditioned instinct. The question going forward was not just whether St-Pierre would go in balls out and give it his all, but also whether he would survive the dark forces that existed outside the UFC octagon.

Georges was a small-town kid with no previous experience that could have prepared him to deal with stardom. When he was growing up, he worked as a garbage man for eight months to help pay for his post-secondary schooling and did other jobs—flooring, bouncing, working with delinquent youth. St-Pierre even claimed to have earned a diploma in kinesiology at Edouard-Montpetit College.

Underneath his muscle-bound exterior, he was naïve and placed his trust in the wrong people repeatedly throughout his career.

"I got screwed," said Georges in a 2008 interview. Speaking of his management at the time of the first Matt Serra fight, St-Pierre was upset because, as he put it, "A lot of people were stealing money" from him.[2]

St-Pierre had also dealt with problems due to taxes he owed the government, a typical problem among athletes and entertainers who transition to a dream world of wealth that they barely understand how to manage.[3] Even though St-Pierre knew how to deal with the deadliest forces inside the octagon, he was as vulnerable as a babe in the woods outside of it.

Georges St-Pierre was a special piece of the puzzle when it came to the mainstream acceptance and popularity of mixed martial arts in North America. To industry insiders and educated fans, St-Pierre was a quantum leap forward from the one-dimensional brawlers, wrestlers and submission experts who had often previously defined the UFC in the public image.

His fighting style itself was akin to a smash-and-grab robbery where opponents were shown no quarter. Even though the rules permitted a wide number of techniques and styles of fighting, St-Pierre's opponents almost never had the opportunity to mount sustained offense. Georges was simply a dominant, all-conquering force of nature who didn't allow his opponent the chance to fight back. Early in his career, Georges had earned the nickname "Rush" because of the speed in which he trounced his opponents.

When St-Pierre made it to the top of the heap, the lights of the big stage just weren't as bright as they'd seemed when it was his martial arts heroes, be they Jean-Claude Van Damme or Brazilian Royce Gracie, kicking ass on the television screen. Now there was pressure from all sides—top-down from the UFC management that viewed St-Pierre as a tool to collect revenue; across the octagon from opponent Matt Serra, who taunted St-Pierre at every opportunity; inside George's camp, due to lawsuits related to his management; and within St-Pierre's own family that endured its own tumultuous cycles of dysfunction.

Despite all the pitfalls that tarnished the golden opportunity of being champion, St-Pierre realized that his path was worth taking. It wasn't hard to understand why the risks were worth the reward: our era is one in which individualism has been submerged by the herd-like mentality of a society where conformity, mediocrity and lowered expectations are the norm. The film *Fight Club* captured the growing sense of meaninglessness and powerlessness that pervades modern life—but the real-life sport of MMA provides an organized model that allows its fighters to act as an enduring symbol for the freedom, pride, honor and respect that society seems to have lost touch with today.

All the same, St-Pierre was aware of the medical facts regarding the brain damage caused by mixed martial arts, accounting figures on the revenue he was losing to the leeches around him and the direct correlation between his growing anxiety and his involvement in the fight game. But all this information was repurposed and filtered by those around him and his own cognitive dissonance, keeping him in the fight game. There was also that intangible thought process—the idea that there was something noble and virtuous at the heart of the fight that trumped other concerns. St-Pierre was driven to compete because he could make it happen in the moment where it counted—and he was more than willing to stick his hand into the fire over and over to get to the prize.

2

TRISTAR

"Boxers don't know ground games and MMA guys don't know how to box."

—*Freddie Roach*

New York Times, January 7, 2012

Early in his career, Georges St-Pierre was as unknown as an MMA fighter to Canadians as the UFC itself was to the mainstream. As his career in the UFC progressed, the UFC itself had breakout success thanks to *The Ultimate Fighter (TUF)* reality series, on which St-Pierre would do a guest coaching spot in 2006. Launching in January 2005, *TUF* had been the same vehicle that had showcased some of the best emerging talent in the sport to a voracious audience that ate up the mix of semi-staged reality drama and fighting.

While many people have tried some form of martial arts as a child or in their teens, the difference between such recreational training for a hobbyist and what St-Pierre—and other lesser-known but equally hard

MMA fighters—endured was the difference between driving on a busy highway and racing in the Indianapolis 500.

The main facility where St-Pierre practices his trade as a professional is the Tristar Gym, founded in 1991 by Conrad Pla, Michel Lavallee and Ron Di Ciecco, who were the three "stars" the gym takes its name from. Situated just off the Decarie Highway at 5275 Ferrier Street, the building housing the gym is surrounded by unattractive strip malls, such as are common to the outskirts of cities across North America. As much as the Quebecois have character and spirit, this area represents the cheap suburban sprawl and bargain-basement ambience that defines portions of Montreal.

Gym members walk up a flight of stairs that is well lit by wide windows; enter through doors on the third floor, where a sign politely notifies people to remove their shoes (status quo at every MMA gym in the world); and step into the entrance lounge of Tristar. The lounge consists of a counter, juice/protein bar, merchandise area and walls covered with laminated articles from all the gym's stars—boxers, kickboxers, Muay Thai champions and, of course, MMA fighters. On the right entrance corridor are the words "TRI" and just below, "STAR" graffiti-sprayed in blue on a brown background with purple fringes. Beyond that are the cardio machines, with a beautiful mural on the far wall of Muhammad Ali standing defiant over an emasculated Sonny Liston, blue aura surrounding "The Greatest." In the left corner of the 15,000-square-foot facility is a boxing ring. Further down are yet another boxing ring, an octagon and a large matted area. In the far right corner of the gym is a dojo with a hardwood floor, a Japanese flag (to honor the roots of karate) and various trophies.

Teammate and training partner David "The Crow" Loiseau dates Georges St-Pierre (GSP)'s involvement with the Tristar Gym back to 2001, when he saw him compete in an amateur event.

"I went to see him to congratulate him. I told him he should come train at Tristar gym," recalls Loiseau.

Georges remembers his roots at the gym starting later: "I started very late to train [at Tristar]—it was just after my fight against Justin

Bruckmann, where I became World Champion—eh, Canadian Champion."

The fight with Bruckmann was in June 2002, with St-Pierre winning via first-round armbar.

"I always come from South Shore," said St-Pierre of his commute from the suburbs of Montreal, so-called because they were located on the southern shore of the Saint Lawrence River opposite the Island of Montreal. "At the time, I was trained by myself."

The introduction between St-Pierre, by this time in his late teens, and Brazilian Jiu-Jitsu black belt Wagnney Fabiano was critical. Without Wagnney's instruction at GAMMA, a facility in competition with Tristar, St-Pierre might have become a mediocre fighter due to lack of ground training. Many other fighters would succumb to geographical hurdles, unwilling or unable to move to where they could get better instruction, then finding themselves repeatedly out-positioned or submitted in fights.

"He never trained with people like our level," said Fabiano of St-Pierre's inexperience.

The typical initiation into a BJJ class involves a short period of "rolling," or grappling while looking for a submission. It was a humbling experience for St-Pierre when the 145-pound Brazilian submitted him several times over the course of just a few minutes. The humiliation and loss that come with such an experience usually convince most initiates to quit BJJ—but the dragon within a true competitor like GSP simply roared to a fully-aroused state.

"Soon, he trained with me, he fell in love," says Fabiano of their first meeting. "I knew, I knew, I knew he [was] going to be a big star, because I saw his style shine."

Fellow GAMMA student Ahmad Zahabi, brother of Firas Zahabi, concurred with Wagnney's assessment, saying, "You could tell that he was a very talented guy—and a very humble guy, as well."

"The first time I met Georges, Wagnney told me something which never normally happens—'Go check out this new guy,' " says Ahmad.

Most Brazilian Jiu-Jitsu beginners are unremarkable and forgettable, but Fabiano—who was hard to impress—knew there was something special about St-Pierre from day one.

This was also the early era when neither BJJ nor other comparable grappling arts were disseminated widely, even in martial arts circles. The expectation that St-Pierre would be easy meat for other, more experienced students to handle proved incorrect.

Said Ahmad, "You could tell he was really exceptional on his first day, he was really difficult to roll with: smart, technical, athletic—just incredible on day one."

Georges earned his blue belt—the first rank in BJJ—within six months.

"Back then, getting your blue belt was a big deal," says Ahmad. "To do it in six months from Wagnney—was a *really* big deal."

It was this willingness to learn from different sources from the early times of the sport that helped GSP become a well-rounded athlete. Many fighters are content to specialize in one area of strength. Examples are UFC light-heavyweight Chuck Liddell falling in love with his knockout power, and utilizing excellent takedown defense and scrambling ability to keep the fight standing; or submission specialist Demian Maia, who often appeared helpless on the feet (at least before meeting Nate Marquardt and becoming more motivated), but took his fights to the ground like Ben Stiller took to making unfunny comedies.

When Fabiano moved on from the Brazil Top Team-affiliate school, Fabio Hollanda took his position. Hollanda instructed Georges until money became an issue sometime around 2008—some sources suggest Fabio wanted a percentage of GSP's purses. St-Pierre was only too happy to move on to other top class trainers such as Bruno Fernandes, who presented St-Pierre with his black belt in October 2008.[4]

There are many trainers who, at one time or another, were assigned credit for GSP's success as a fighter—Firas Zahabi, Greg Jackson, John Danaher, Phil Nurse, Howard Grant, even boxing legend Freddie Roach. There was one man who came along at a critical point early in

St-Pierre's career and truly helped guide him toward his first championship: Victor Vargotsky.

The Soviet Union's occupation of Afghanistan created one of the bloodiest and most dangerous combat zones in the history of modern warfare. Initial success by the Soviets in capturing major centers was eventually met with guerilla warfare waged by the US-backed mujahideen.

Ukrainian Vargotsky served in Afghanistan during the '80s in the special forces—a difficult job due to insurgents, the lack of support and conditions that resembled hell on earth. It was Vargotsky, a former kickboxing champion, who taught St-Pierre the most critical skills in his development as a fighter.

"I did a lot of full-contact stuff, kickboxing, in the military," said Vargotsky of his history.

Victor had done his mandatory service in the military at the age of 18, serving for two years, and then re-enlisting with a five-year contract for the special forces. He was in a sniper unit used for special operations that made short sorties into Afghanistan.

"We were never stationed there—just in and out, let's say five days to two weeks. I was down there [in Afghanistan] altogether roughly 20-25 weeks."

Vargotsky's viewpoint from the ground differs from the anti-Soviet viewpoints disseminated through Western media during the Cold War. He points out that Afghanistan wasn't occupied, since a pact existed between the Soviets and the ruling government of Afghanistan. The Soviet forces could not run rampant—they would be court-martialed for any illegal acts against civilians.

"Guys stuck in the middle of that stuff don't know who to shoot, what to shoot—it was terrible, and mostly young guys down there," says Vargotsky of the conditions in Afghanistan.

"You're stuck in the middle of that conflict between different tribes. You just have to make decision[s] as it goes. If they shooting at you, you shoot back. If they not shooting at you, you just stay like a friend.

And that's it," Vargotsky says of the lack of true ideology or other tags applied by observers or media present among the warring factions.

After his service, Vargotsky was involved in amateur boxing; if you couldn't make the cut for the Olympic trials, you had "no future," according to the cut-and-dried trainer. He began operating a boxing and kickboxing school in Kiev. Years later, as his kickboxing career faded, he immigrated to Montreal, Quebec. In the local scene, he recalls sparring more than 100 rounds with the Hilton brothers, Alex and Davey Jr.

"They were beating [the] crap out of me," said Vargotsky. "That's how I learned real professional boxing."

Vargotsky also dropped a unanimous decision to future World Boxing Council (WBC) super-middleweight champion Eric Lucas when Vargotsky was called up on one day's notice in 1992.

Then-Tristar gym owner Alexandre Choko remembers planting the seed for Georges to link up with Vargotsky after St-Pierre had challenged UFC welterweight champion Matt Hughes at UFC 50 in October 2004.

St-Pierre had been 7-0 in MMA before the Matt Hughes bout; outside the octagon, he claimed to have begun a degree in kinesiology from l'Université du Québec à Montreal.[5] With the match occurring on October 22, 2004, St-Pierre likely only attended university for several weeks maximum before dropping out, although this is impossible to verify without St-Pierre authorizing the release of his information, which is protected under privacy laws in Canada.

At UFC 50, Georges entered the ring in awe of champion Matt Hughes. He put on an excellent effort, but was not ready to surpass his idol. After out-striking Hughes on the feet and managing a takedown, Georges made a mistake and got caught by an armbar with just one second left in the first round. It was a bitter loss that opened the door to two realities—first, that St-Pierre was on par with the best welterweight in the UFC; and second, all Georges needed to take the championship from Hughes now was a mental edge.

Victor Vargotsky became the natural choice, with St-Pierre linking up with him and reaping tremendous rewards. All fighters experience breaking points where they step away from victory because they allow themselves to relax or relent in their efforts. Vargotsky never allowed this—he would bite his trainees in the ass and refuse to let go until he got the result that he wanted from them.

Allison Lampert, of the *Montreal Gazette*, recorded a snapshot of the visceral coaching methods of Vargotsky. "Georges, stab it in! Punch up like you're stabbing someone in the intestines!" Lampert wrote in a 2006 profile of St-Pierre.[6]

Gradually, the idea that he had to step forward and *take* the title became more and more entrenched in St-Pierre's mindset. Georges would become successful because he began to believe in himself in a new way.

"If it wasn't for the way Victor broke Georges down after the [first] Matt Hughes fight, and built him back the way that he did, he would never have become Georges St-Pierre the way people know him today," said Choko of the GSP who soon autopiloted to dominance. "Georges is still surfing the wave that Victor created for him."

The reasons Georges needed to be broken down and remade were twofold. First was the obvious gap in confidence between American Matt Hughes and himself. Hughes was a cocky farm boy and former collegiate wrestler. Georges initially viewed Matt with hero worship, not quite understanding that he meant nothing in the eyes of Hughes. Georges had to overcome his own sense of humility to win. The second reason St-Pierre had to be broken down was to give him a chance to learn about his physical tools in a new way that would give him the edge. Instilling near-perfect muscle memory while maintaining conditioning, power, strength and weight control is a perpetual work in progress, one made all the harder by the ego of athletes. That St-Pierre was coming off a loss helped him change (fixing something that *was* broken) for the better.

The darker question of whether Vargotsky used too much force to get results from his charges remained. Were Victor's methods ever mean or abusive?

Alexandre Choko gave the example of working on push-kicks with Victor. "At some point, he doesn't like the way I'm doing them, he gets pissed off, so he starts showing me—but he forgets that he has his running shoes on. In literally a minute, my arms are bleeding, because you either block them with your arms, or you get the kicks in the stomach."

As excessive as they seemed, Victor's methods and psychological approach were designed to prepare his fighters for when the real test came. A fight is an all-out war—not a simple contest for points or positioning. You perform or you die, without any gray area in between.

When St-Pierre was considering quitting after the first round after an accidental eye poke in his first fight against BJ Penn, Victor Vargotsky was instrumental in not only getting St-Pierre back into the fight, but in lighting a fire under his ass to actually fight BJ Penn back.

"He fights BJ Penn, Georges has Victor in his corner, goes back to his corner, he was just poked in the eye and probably had a broken nose—and, he's almost limping," said Choko of the UFC 58 bout. "Victor tells him the magic that he tells him, he goes back in there, fucking slams BJ Penn left and right, wins the fight."

The typical measure of a coach comes down to how many champions they build from the ground up. It's an unreliable way to gauge ability, partly because great athletes who can be molded into championship material are incredibly rare. Enzo Calzaghe, father and trainer of undefeated boxer Joe Calzaghe, also produced WBO cruiserweight titlist Enzo Maccarinelli and WBA light-welterweight titlist Gavin Rees at the Newbridge boxing club in Wales. Given the drinking culture of lads in Britain, neither Maccarinelli nor Rees was destined for much acclaim or greatness, and both fighters were identified as being of mediocre talent. It's the mark of a great trainer that Enzo Calzaghe was able to get the most out of Maccarinelli and Rees, along with the legendary achievements of Enzo's son, Joe Calzaghe.

There are very few stars in kickboxing and a myriad of made-up titles, making true top talent hard to identify. So how would a guy like Victor Vargotsky amass any respect? It's pretty easy when you consider that one of his other major protégés was former kickboxer-turned-boxing-superstar WBC heavyweight champion Vitali Klitschko, who joined Vargotsky's gym as a teenager in 1986.

"[Victor Vargotsky] used to call me 'Big Baby,' " Vitali said to Alexandre Choko on the subject of his former kickboxing trainer. "[Vargotsky] was right. I was a big baby then. I was very gifted, and I was always behaving like a big baby."

Vargotsky recalled the 15-year-old Vitali Klitschko panicking and fretting over small details during the young kickboxer's early days in the game. The mental side is crucial to success, so Vargotsky always reminded Vitali and his other fighters that they fought with their hearts, but that they could win by using their minds.

The physical techniques employed by Vargotsky are standard for boxing, kickboxing and MMA: roadwork, running, hills, cross-country. But Victor was always there adding motivation by challenging his fighters while they trained, ensuring that the work got done with the proper intensity.

Vargotsky also drew on his combat experience to alleviate mental tension in his fighters.

Said Vargotsky, "I used to say, 'If I get in trouble somewhere in the field, what's going to happen?' They say, 'You may get killed.' I say, 'If I get killed, I may get lucky. I will like that, but if they catch me, that's a different story.' "

The ring is a competition fought with rules, officials, doctors on standby and known quantities. The fighters under Vargotsky's tutelage understand the dialogue with their trainer: there's a big difference between a situation that could deteriorate into torture and limitless suffering, and a sporting contest.

With Vargotsky, Vitali Klitschko won the International Sport Karate Association super-heavyweight kickboxing title, but had to move on from Vargotsky's gym when he turned 18 and had to perform mandatory military service. There was no kickboxing in the military— just boxing—so that's where Vitali transferred his skills.

Vitali has made his mark as the premier heavyweight boxer in the world. His current trainer, German Fritz Sdunek, gets full credit for sharpening Vitali's game—Sdunek certainly deserves it. However, Victor Vargotsky's role should not be relegated to a little-known footnote in history.

Other developments ensured that St-Pierre would have an edge in his MMA fights. For instance, Georges was such a proficient boxer that he had six amateur bouts (five in 2003; the last one occurring on April 22, 2004). Georges won five of his bouts, with the sixth being an exhibition that had no decision rendered. He endured life-and-death sparring sessions at Club De Boxe Champions in Montreal with professionals like Paul Clavette (currently 15-3-1 as a professional boxer).

Alexandre Choko related the story of a boxing sparring session from late 2006 between St-Pierre and a decorated amateur and professional boxer that illustrated how Georges's perseverance could overcome superior skill—even across disciplines:

"Victor Vargotsky is more coaching his boxer, because he can't believe he's doing so bad. And I'm coaching Georges, and I'm encouraging him to continue to do well because he's getting the better of the guy. And [Georges] is in shock—he's in total shock, because after every round, he goes in the corner of the ring (the conversation took place in French), 'Alex, am I doing ok?' "

Choko was clear in his praise, telling St-Pierre, "Keep on going man, this is perfect. If you can get the better of this guy, you'll beat anybody in MMA."

The opposing boxer was Nicholson Poulard (currently 19-3 as a pro), brother of former WBC light-heavyweight champion Jean Pascal. After the session, Poulard needed consolation from Choko over his dismal result. Choko told it like it was—St-Pierre got the better of Poulard because St-Pierre was the one who wanted to be a true champion.

Of course, the Tristar sessions were tame compared to the philosophy at another boxing club GSP cross-trained at—Club De Boxe Champions, under the tutelage of trainer Jean-Pierre Deneault—where the goal of fighters was to beat the brakes off their sparring partners. If you survived, you were a better boxer (or so they rationalized). Some made it through, but as with any sink-or-swim approach, many more quit.

An interesting character feature that surfaced during St-Pierre's amateur boxing career was his unwillingness to challenge strong (but beatable) opposition.

"Georges wouldn't take fights he knew he was going to lose," said Choko, who once tried to set St-Pierre up on a boxing card he was promoting against a local banger named Yan Stafford.

Stafford was afraid of Georges, but on the other hand, Georges was not overly eager to chase Stafford down. St-Pierre and his boxing coach Jean-Pierre Deneault made the decision not to face Stafford.

Incentive was lacking for St-Pierre to challenge himself. At an amateur bout, there were no financial rewards that St-Pierre could be offered to entice him into the match; nor was Georges attempting to qualify for the Olympics.

"They have no hook," said Choko. "When you fight amateur [boxing], you fight for your own glory—you don't make money, you don't have a contract, but it's really just for you."

It was smart for Georges not to risk his livelihood as an MMA fighter for the sake of tougher boxing matches. His momentum could have suffered from lingering injuries or declining confidence were he to have the misfortune of losing or getting hurt. At the same time, there was the feeling that there was something more that Georges could have accomplished as a fighter—beating high-level amateurs could have brought even more confidence to his MMA career.

As it was, St-Pierre had a highly sophisticated foundation in all the related disciplines of MMA, thanks to his jiu-jitsu instruction, boxing training with professionals and wrestling with high-level wrestlers at the Montreal Wrestling Club. Vargotsky was the glue that held all the easily-frayed threads together, allowing St-Pierre to focus on the job of taking the UFC title.

As highly as St-Pierre was to rise, he was just a misstep or two away from falling, to become an object of scorn and humiliation again. Bigger wins would mean bigger money, opportunities and parties—

dulling the razor-sharp edge, the hungry lion becoming an inattentive gazelle. Georges would lose his hunger and forget about the danger lurking around him.

3

St. Isidore, Quebec

Georges St-Pierre grew up in Saint Isidore, a suburb of Montreal located on the south shore of the Saint Lawrence River, consisting of about 2,489 inhabitants as of 2006. While Saint Isidore is a mere 30 kilometers (18.6 miles) from the center of Montreal, for Georges St-Pierre it might as well have been an entire galaxy away.

Born on May 19, 1981, to Roland and Paulyne St-Pierre, the young St-Pierre spent his early days working on farms in the pastoral isolation of his hometown.

"It was a pretty quiet place where I grew up. It's a place in the country. It's very calm," said St-Pierre.

When pressed for the most poignant memory he held from his childhood, he recalled holiday hijinks played by his father:

"When it were Christmastime, I remember we always go at the midnight church. And after we went and came back, my dad told us, 'Oh, Santa Claus pass by the house. He left the gift underneath the tree.' So he said, 'Instead of going right back to the house, we're going to go to the street, you know, like make a circle like go for a little ride just to see, you can see him on the top of the house, and like, catch him, catch him, catch him on his ride.' And all that time we were so hurried to, to take our gifts we were tellings my dad, 'No, let's go back to the house right now!' We don't want to do the rides. But my dad he keep doing the ride, 'Oh we're going to see just in case you will see Santa Claus.' So we were all pissed at him, all me and my sister and saying, 'Come on! Let's go back to the house!' It's funny."

The story paints Roland in a positive light—taking his family to midnight mass, leaving gifts under the tree, and trying to provide St-Pierre and his two younger sisters with the fantasy of Santa Claus. Yet there was pain and sadness just beneath the surface.

As St-Pierre told Isa Tousignant of Hour.ca in a 2006 interview, "At home life was pretty hard too. I had a difficult childhood, and I'm not saying that that's why I do ultimate fighting, but it helped shape my character."[7]

What problem at home was causing St-Pierre so much difficulty? According to many sources, Roland suffered from severe alcoholism. Children of alcoholic parents can exhibit a number of characteristics, including perfectionism, difficulty having fun, seeking approval and attention, showing extreme loyalty even when undeserved and taking themselves very seriously.[8]

James Jones, author of *From Here to Eternity*, explained his theory behind Robert E. Lee Prewitt, a skilled boxer who was the protagonist of his novel: "What made Prewitt an artist, in my interpretation, was that his old man used to beat up his old lady, as well as himself; and that his old man, like so many human male animals, didn't give a damn about him one way or the other. He was always competing, in a sense, with this image of his father that he was always trying to please."[9]

In *The Striking Truth*, a documentary that features St-Pierre, his father seems on-edge. In one scene, Georges is thoughtfully signing posters for his father, while his dad berates him ("My father is freaking out, for no reason"), fearful that St-Pierre will somehow mess the posters up—posters that were easily obtained and endorsed by St-Pierre. In another thread from the movie, St-Pierre paid all his parents' debts (including the mortgage on their house), but the gesture appeared to threaten Roland, either because it questioned his ability to provide for his family or because it demonstrated Georges surpassing his father in terms of earning power.[10]

There was, nevertheless, love in the household, shared between St-Pierre and his parents. According to Choko, "He loves his mother—*loves* his mother. I think he loves his father, too."

The martial arts became what Choko termed an *échappatoire*. In English, the term means an escape—a sanctuary from the turmoil-filled world of St-Pierre's home.

A black belt in Kyokushin Karate himself, Roland began teaching St-Pierre at age seven. After that introduction, he took formal lessons at age nine and began competing in tournaments. The stimulation of karate pushed St-Pierre to a point where he wasn't weighed down with his family issues—at least as long as he was training or competing.

"I grew up with a lot of anger. In my school it was bad, and in my house it was bad," explained St-Pierre to *Maclean's* magazine in 2010, saying, "I needed a place I could go where I was not in conflict. Karate was a place where I could forget everything and be at peace with myself, and take out my aggression."[11]

As a family friend, Choko tried to get Roland to get his addictions treated—offering his personal "witch doctor" to cure Roland's chain-smoking, even offering to pick him up and drive him to appointments—but the desire to change has to come from within. No matter what support Roland was provided with, he simply fell back into his patterns of substance abuse. In a perverse way, Roland became an example of out-of-control and undisciplined behavior that motivated Georges to become a better person.

Later in his career, St-Pierre would employ Muay Thai champion Jean-Charles Skarbowsky as a trainer. When Skarbowsky made an appearance on *The Ultimate Fighter*, St-Pierre was vocal in pointing out something unique about the French trainer's routine:

"Jean-Charles, he live in Thailand for a very long time, so Thailand is a very different mentality—they smoke, they drink—and they fight every day."[12]

Georges's statement was a bit of a stretch. Usually only trainers and recreational fighters smoked cigarettes or drank alcohol on a regular basis; the active professionals were kept at arm's length from such distractions, as they had fights two to three times each month.

Was Georges trying to draw a parallel between his father, the karate black belt, alcoholic and chain-smoker, and Jean-Charles Skarbowsky, who had even shown up drunk on the set of *The Ultimate Fighter*?

The severe bullying at school that St-Pierre endured still haunts him to this day. In grade three, an older student slammed his head into a table because he would not hand over five dollars. High arches that made him walk on his toes also helped make him a target. Although his condition was eventually corrected by orthotics, the psychic scars remained.

"I had an acne problem. I was just not dressing very well. I was not very popular with girls," recalled St-Pierre of his social awkwardness.

When he was 10, a group of 13-year-olds—held back three years due to behavioral problems—systematically harmed St-Pierre. A tendency to repeatedly lick his lips gave him a red, chapped outline around his mouth that made him stand out like a circus clown. Older kids stole his money and clothes, taking pleasure from St-Pierre's suffering, as if he was a captive spider having its legs torn off one by one.[13]

Eventually, St-Pierre decided that he had had enough. Georges relished telling the story about how he took back his dignity:

"One day when school finished, I was with my friend, we got out of school, my friend was a nerd, you know? Not a fighter, you know? We get out of the school to take the bus and there was three guys lined up against the wall, like 3-4 years older than us and I pass by to go get the bus. I hear (makes spitting sound three times) and then I keep walking with my friend and then I say, 'Hey Mathieu, I think they spit on us.' 'No, no, no, no!' He knows that I am crazy so he says, 'No no, no. They haven't! They haven't!' And I'm like, 'Turn around. Yeah, look at this, they spit on us. Let's go back and ask them what is their problem.' And it was like, 'No, you're crazy. We're going to get our ass kicked. Wah! I'm not going.' And I said to him, 'OK. I'm going to let you go back to the bus. I'm going to go back for my honor. Back to these guy. So like that, I'm gonna have respect. You know I'm gonna get beat up by you, but I'm gonna have some respect.' He try to stop me and then I push him, let him go back in the bus. I go back, I walk back to the guys, I close my fists, in my pocket, I pretend like I was just going back in school, like I forgot something, then when I got close to the guy I sucker punched him. Then the two other guys jump on me. And it was a brawl. And I end up getting my ass whooped. You know, it was stupid story but I have a big—I am very proud person and even though I knew that it was not the right thing to do, by doing so they were leaving me alone afterwards because I was not an easy target."

By the time St-Pierre was 14 or 15 years old, the older kids at school knew to leave him alone.[14] At the same time, Georges claimed his record in street fights was dismal, but outside of some stories about working as a bouncer, Georges never shared much information about this early time period in his life.

No matter how quiet or innocent he appeared, there was always calculating ambition inside of St-Pierre. It wasn't by accident that he linked up with some of the bad boys in MMA—they were people who could move him ahead and do favors for him when he was unknown in the industry. One small—but critical—fact gleaned by *Montreal Gazette* reporter Allison Lampert regarding GSP's vision for himself was prescient of the greatness St-Pierre envisioned in his future.

"His mother told me that when he was a kid, he used to play with a Hulk Hogan-type figurine," Lampert revealed. "When he was older, he had told her, 'I want to have a doll like that of me.' "

In April 2011, in the lead-up to UFC 129, CityNews reporter Kathryn Humphreys showed off the latest edition of a Round 5 GSP action figure at a Toronto press conference.

Asked if he liked it, St-Pierre recalled playing with similar WWF figurines, like Hulk Hogan and Randy "Macho Man" Savage, in his youth.

"Now it is me that is on it, that's pretty crazy," said GSP to the audience.

There was nothing unusual, however, about someone as driven and ambitious as St-Pierre realizing his childhood dream—crazy as it would have seemed to others at the time.

4

ENTER THE PROMOTER

"I pretty much risked it all," Patry says of his decision to sell everything he owned to strike out into the business of promoting fights.

The young Quebecois had all the trappings of a comfortable life—a salaried job with Teleglobe, a condo, a car, company stock. But Patry claims that he chose to quit his job, sell all his possessions and enter the fight game, instead of coasting through an ordinary life. The glitz, glamour and excitement of being involved as a player in MMA drove Patry more than any rational or logical concerns. He would raise an entire stable of UFC fighters out of his MMA promotion, initially called the UCC (short form for "Universal Combat Challenge;" later Patry started a promotion called "TKO," which purchased the assets of the UCC). Eventually, Patry would lose virtually everything, becoming a nonentity within the sphere of MMA, avoiding the various individuals and groups that he owed money to. In the early going, however, Patry's role in the development of budding fighters is integral to the story of Canadian MMA.

Starting out at a small promotion on the Kahnawake Indian Reserve, Patry was wise to the fact that the early cards weren't drawing because they lacked local stars from the Quebec region that home audiences could root for.

Patry was proactive in visiting martial arts schools and boxing gyms in order to find local talent. There are many people who are proficient or talented at something, but who lack the confidence or inner drive to strike out and take things to the next level. Patry was the voice of affirmation that many unpolished local fighters could fight professionally—and perhaps rise even further.

It was Patry who discovered a 17-year-old David Loiseau at a jiujitsu tournament in Laval, Quebec. Patry saw something in Loiseau where others might have been dismissive, negative or indifferent. Unable to sign him until he turned 18, Stephane kept in touch, with Loiseau making his professional MMA debut on the first UCC show in 2000.

With Patry's help, Loiseau would eventually scale the heights to a title shot against UFC middleweight champion Rich Franklin on March 4, 2006. In the wake of Loiseau's defeat to Franklin via five-round decision, Loiseau chose to finally part ways with Patry.

As an unknown amateur MMA fighter, St-Pierre had to rely on Patry in order to start his career. UCC fighters Kristof Midoux and Stephan Potvin recommended St-Pierre to Patry, telling the promoter that they had someone who was good that they were training with who was going to be an awesome fighter. Midoux and Potvin clamored to put St-Pierre in an amateur show in Laval, on the north shore of Montreal, that Patry was promoting.

"He looked very good," said Patry of Georges's performance on the amateur card, which brought his amateur record to 5-0.

There was no sense in wasting time—St-Pierre secured his first professional fight on the UCC 7 card, slated to be held on January 25, 2002. Georges faced Ivan Menjivar (4-0 in the UCC), an opponent Patry wanted to veto owing to Menjivar's greater experience over St-Pierre. Instead, Stephane wanted Dirk Waardenburg (then 1-3) to face

St-Pierre, but Georges's team felt that Dirk was too heavy an opponent. While these concerns from the promoter and Georges's team may seem trivial in hindsight, for any debuting fighter, the slightest disadvantage could lead to a loss—an ugly way to start a career.

St-Pierre weighed in at 169 pounds; Menjivar weighed in two pounds over the welterweight limit at 172 pounds and was fined 20 percent of his purse. In the fight, Menjivar kept pressing St-Pierre, eventually scoring a takedown and even getting Georges's back. Menjivar was raining down blows from top position when the referee inexplicably stood the pair up. Georges secured his own takedown, and landed some blows before Menjivar scrambled back up. After another successful takedown, Georges scrambled up and took Menjivar down; he began to rain down punches from top position in Menjivar's guard, with the referee stopping the contest at 4:50 of the first round. It was a controversial end, as Menjivar really hadn't sustained much damage, and according to St-Pierre's post-fight speech, Menjivar kept telling the referee "OK, OK, OK"—meaning that he was fine, and wanted the fight to continue. The referee interpreted Menjivar's words as an answer to the question of whether he wanted him to stop the fight, and thus the tainted stoppage. Georges also said that he considered the fight to be a draw, something that would be forgotten (for good reason—the win was official in the books) as St-Pierre's career moved forward.[15]

St-Pierre's next fight was against 4-2 Justin Bruckmann for the UCC welterweight title at UCC 10 to be held on June 15, 2002. The UCC title might have been a self-appointed title, but the organization's belt would carry weight as a big motivator for St-Pierre. Still, St-Pierre was not confident, and required reassurance from Patry.

"He was freaked out about Bruckmann, he was scared of Bruckmann," recalled Patry. "I pretty much sat down with him a couple of times and told him how I thought he could beat Bruckmann, how I believed in him, and the reason why I gave him that early title shot after only one pro fight."

With zero sleep before the Bruckmann fight, Georges picked up the telephone and called Patry. It was a vulnerable moment for

Georges, as the anxiety that precedes a fight can swallow a fighter's soul. St-Pierre sold his soul, making the deal at the crossroads with the Devil: Stephane claims Georges asked him to handle his affairs on that phone call, cementing the business relationship, as in addition to being his promoter, Patry became St-Pierre's manager. It was the type of co-dependent relationship that would prove hard for St-Pierre to break away from later on.

In the fight the next day, St-Pierre submitted Bruckmann in the first round. Two more wins followed, against Travis Galbraith at UCC 11 and Thomas Denny at UCC 12. As good as St-Pierre was looking on the local circuit, Patry's organization was small-time. Only booking his fighters in bigger organizations, like the UFC, could bring in more money. For this, Patry would get his commission as a manager, but he also deserves credit for building up a slew of UFC fighters nearly from scratch.

"Georges St-Pierre, myself, David Loiseau, Jonathan Goulet, Patrick Côté—he made all of us stars, and able to fight at the next level," says Canadian MMA fighter Mark Hominick of the effect UCC and TKO had on developing talent.

Patry made mistakes, with different parties being taken advantage of and stomped on along the way—standard operating procedure for the mix of superficial and sociopathic personalities that are drawn to the entertainment industry. Ultimately, Patry believed in St-Pierre and shopped him to the UFC, an organization that used Patry as a feeder of live bodies.

David Loiseau had earned his place in the UFC by beating UFC-caliber opponent Tony Frykland. Georges was expected to pass a similar litmus test.

"They wanted Georges to beat a UFC guy. Pete Spratt was scheduled to fight in the UFC six months from my show. I called him and offered the fight against Georges," said Patry.

The quick-witted Patry knew that if Georges were to beat Spratt, St-Pierre would be the one headed to the UFC, not Spratt. At TKO 14, held in Victoriaville, Quebec on November 29, 2003, St-Pierre notched a first-round submission victory over Spratt, thus ensuring the forward momentum of his career.

There had also been a brief window of opportunity for St-Pierre to forgo the traditional route of competing in the North American promotions and instead venture to Japan to fight for PRIDE Fighting Championships, then the largest and best-paying MMA organization in the world.

"I tried to get PRIDE to sign Georges St-Pierre," said former PRIDE employee Jerry Millen. "I went to a TKO event in Montreal—I saw Georges fight, and saw this young good-looking kid like Jean-Claude Van Damme fighting back then—you know, spinning kicks, crazy shit—it was real raw-looking in the fight. I was like 'Wow, this kid's going to be a star.'"

During this time, in 2003, Millen was a producer at PRIDE's US office, but could not go backstage to talk to St-Pierre, as it would have been overstepping his boundaries. Millen's main job responsibilities were producing the US pay-per-view (PPV) feed for PRIDE, a venture that brought in a small amount of profit for PRIDE's parent company, Dream Stage Entertainment (DSE).

"I just remember it was Montreal, it was cold as hell in the wintertime, because the slush was frozen," recalled Millen.

Jerry Millen went back to his superiors in Los Angeles. Hideki Yamamoto and Yukino Kanda (supposedly a pair of pharmacists from Nagoya, the same Japanese city PRIDE president Nobuyuki Sakakibara was from), operated DSE's American office. Millen told them to check Georges St-Pierre out, telling them that St-Pierre was a "really tough fighter" and adding, "He's good looking, too." Their response was muted, telling Millen, "Just send him some of our materials."

PRIDE's American representatives, Hideki and Kanda, had little experience related to either MMA or entertainment. Part of Hideki and Kanda's duties included handing out payments of fight purses to PRIDE fighters post-fight—payments made in cash that could circumvent taxes. This method of payment ended when the authorities from the Japanese tax office finally clued in and brought some scrutiny to PRIDE, giving a talk to all the fighters and managers in 2004.

Although Georges was blowing guys away in the smaller North American shows, he was but a faceless, nameless blip, not even on the radar of DSE executives. There was no 170-pound class in PRIDE at that time, and as a foreigner, could St-Pierre forge a connection with the Japanese audience?

According to the book *PRIDE Secret Files*, a PRIDE insider rationalized the failure to acquire St-Pierre by saying "GSP is a fighter suited to the cage. He would have lost in the ring."[16]

"He could have been in PRIDE, but Hideki blew that one," said a rueful Millen.

The UFC had been owned by the Semaphore Entertainment Group (SEG) when it was acquired for two million dollars in January 2001 by Station Casinos executives Frank Fertitta III and his brother Lorenzo Fertitta. Their father, Frank Fertitta, Jr., helped run a Las Vegas casino during the '70s that was connected to the Kansas City mafia; Frank Fertitta, Jr. was also the right-hand man of notorious casino skimmer Carl Thomas. In 1979, the FBI swooped in and arrested dozens of people, including Carl Thomas, who was sentenced to 15 years in prison.[17] Fertitta, Jr., however, was not charged with skimming money from the Fremont casino, where he held the position of hotel president. After Fertitta, Jr. stepped down as chairman of Station Casinos in 1993, his son Frank Fertitta III took over the position.[18] Carl Thomas died in Oregon on November 4, 1993, in a single-car accident when his truck swerved and rolled over.[19]

Contrary to a myth disseminated by UFC parent company Zuffa and other tainted media sources, at the time of the sale SEG—not Zuffa—actively sought sanctioning for MMA (getting the UFC sanctioned in the state of New Jersey) and had implemented most of the rules that are currently used today.[20] Lorenzo became CEO and chairman of Zuffa, with his brother and himself each holding 45 percent of the company shares. Dana White, a friend of the Fertittas from high school, was appointed president and given 10 percent of the company.

A lot has been written about Dana White since his rise to prominence as the front man for the current largest organization in MMA—much of it mythologized, exaggerated or otherwise misrepresented. For all his bragging about being a "Southie," White grew up in the depressing mill town of Ware, Massachusetts.

"My dad was an alcoholic, and was never around," White told interviewer Graham Bensinger. "When he did show up, you didn't want him around, you know what I mean?"[21]

White was raised mainly by his narcissistic mother, June. There's no greater evidence of this than the book, *Dana White: King of MMA*, that June self-published in July 2011, which sought to capitalize on Dana's newfound success while slandering and denigrating him for his understandable desire to put some distance between his mother and himself.[22]

The upshot of such an upbringing was not pretty. Rather than disavow the negative traits of his parents, White came to embody and further propagate qualities such as egotism, entitlement, greed, backstabbing, attention-seeking and addiction through every means available to him as president of the UFC. Targets were ample and eager: reporters, ring card girls, sponsors, Twitter followers, and—the easiest prey of them all—fighters, most of whom depended on White to such a degree that he had almost complete leverage over them.

Negotiations with the then-fledgling UFC in 2004 were similar to those with the modern-day organization: whether Zuffa, the parent company of the UFC, was losing or banking money at the time, there was no room for negotiation, especially with an unknown prospect like Georges St-Pierre.

"At that time, it was such a big thing to get into the UFC for the athletes that there wasn't really any money negotiations," said Patry. "The money negotiation started after their first contract, which was usually a three-fight deal. And everybody was getting the same money for their first fight, which was three-and-three."

The "three-and-three" specified by Patry meant $3000 to fight, and in the event of a win, a $3000 bonus. Six thousand dollars wasn't a tremendous amount of money, with a manager taking a 15- to-30 percent cut, coaches and cornermen to pay, living expenses, the cost of missing work in order to train and paying for all the medicals required by athletic commissions.

With the boom of MMA that occurred in 2005, many fighters were—and still are—upset at the low purses offered to even the very best UFC fighters. The idea that Lorenzo Fertitta would spend $1.1 million to buy Muhammad Ali's gloves at a fundraiser for brain research[23] while denying the UFC stable financial parity proportional to the profit Zuffa reaps from the very same fighters, sits about as well with the fighters as the story from World War II German tank commander Otto Carius, who describes how, after a fierce day of fighting, the battalion's men were parched and desperate for water; however, his battalion commander had ordered himself a bath prepared with their coffee water. [24]

The market value of UFC fighters was always low, as few competitors stuck around, and Zuffa was not keen on giving up any more ground than it had to in order to retain talent. For Zuffa, it was a wise strategy that allowed stronger control and contractual servitude over the fighters.

After winning two fights in the UFC against Karo Parisyan and Jay Hieron, St-Pierre lost in a title bid to dethrone UFC welterweight champion Matt Hughes. Going 2-1 with an impressive showing against Hughes granted him only minimal leverage in the next round of contract negotiations.

"There was a bit of a negotiation, but it wasn't really our negotiation," said Patry.

Career advancement would require superior performance on the part of St-Pierre. On November 18, 2006, St-Pierre tipped the scales in his favor by defeating Matt Hughes at UFC 65 to win the UFC welterweight championship. In the fight, Hughes was unable to take St-Pierre down. A superman punch followed by a left hook dropped Hughes near the end of the first round, nearly ending the fight there. The second round saw St-Pierre land a head kick that knocked Hughes down to the mat, where St-Pierre pounced on him with a barrage of vicious punches and elbows, prompting a stoppage at 1:25.

The UFC quickly rewarded Georges with various bonuses, including a Humvee sport utility vehicle.[25] Due to the impressive title win, Patry claimed, St-Pierre was the first UFC fighter after Chuck Liddell to sign a 1.5-million dollar contract.

With the championship belt came the realization of a long-held dream—and many invites to functions and outings where Georges gorged himself at the trough of excess. Enjoying himself was important—it was part of why he had worked so hard for so many years.

"Georges was very young, and after he won the title, he partied a lot, didn't train as much, drank a lot, partied a lot, drank a lot, partied a lot," said Patry.

As he was spiraling out of control, both Patry and trainer Victor Vargotsky tried to rein St-Pierre in. As much as Stephane Patry underwent scrutiny and criticism for his management style, he was a friend to Georges, as well as other fighters.

"He always had my back, because he would always say that I was his favorite fighter," said MMA fighter Mark Hominick of his personal relationship with Patry. "We did have a good relationship outside of the promoting side. I did see a side to him that other people didn't see—a friendship side. But I know that in the game, he's not respected too much among the fighters just because a lot of guys felt they got gypped [by] him [over] different payments."

The nature of Patry's relationship with Georges changed, with Patry becoming more authoritative in an attempt to restore order. Patry took Georges's lack of dedication to his craft as an affront, and the dynamics of their once-easy-going relationship shifted before St-Pierre's first defense of his belt against Matt Serra.

It wasn't only Patry who noticed that St-Pierre had lost the "Eye of the Tiger."

"I was having arguments with Georges, trying to make him understand every night he was partying, he was taking months—killing months—of his career in the long run," said Alexandre Choko.

There have been many fighters heralded as future greats, famed for putting on fantastic performances, but who otherwise fell short in the history books due to drug or alcohol addiction. Boxer Kelly Pavlik had undeniable talent, winning the middleweight championship, but he fell by the wayside due to alcohol abuse. Oscar "The Golden Boy" De La Hoya had similar excesses, albeit on the downside of his already-legendary career.

Patry knew that the underlying reason for Georges entering a dangerous situation without understanding the possible repercussions—whistling past the graveyard, as it were—was owing to his unheralded opponent in 9-4 Matt Serra.

"For him, if he would have fought someone else, he would have trained more," says Patry, "but it was only Matt Serra, so he didn't have to."

As much as 5'6" Long Island resident Matt Serra insisted, "Everybody's gonna owe me a big apology" after the St-Pierre fight, Serra just wasn't the kind of opponent that could be taken too seriously. Many things went against Matt Serra in public opinion: he had won the title shot competing on the fourth season of *The Ultimate Fighter*; he had spent the best days of his career at lightweight, and he had lost to weaker opposition than St-Pierre.

In the lead-up to the GSP fight, Serra told an interviewer at T-Nation.com a story about getting in a street fight when he was 26: "Guy cuts you off, big guy gets out, you get out. You try to tell the guy it's not in his best interest, but he doesn't believe you because you're up to his bellybutton."

While the motorist ended up with stitches and launched a lawsuit against Serra, the lesson was clear: professional fighting was a much more viable outlet than street fighting.[26] In MMA, Serra was free to act out his Napoleon complex without any legal complications.

St-Pierre's first UFC title defense against Matt Serra had been twice postponed, until it was scheduled for April 7, 2007, at UFC 69, hosted in Houston, Texas. Going into the fight, there was a persistent worry shared between Patry and Vargotsky that a win over Serra could negatively impact St-Pierre's future performances worse than a loss could, as it would give credence to a philosophy of no requirement to prepare properly or thoroughly.

"If it's too easy and he didn't train, then we're going to have an even bigger problem on our shoulders," said Patry. "The warm-up was going very well—he was sharp, he was slick, he was strong—we were like, 'He's going to win the fight!' "

Patry pointed out the small detail that sets St-Pierre apart from other less-nuanced fighters—his high degree of sensitivity to small details.

"The inspector from the commission walked into the dressing room, and he said the thing he should never have said," explained Patry. "He said, 'St-Pierre, are you ready, it's your turn.' When [the inspector] said, 'St-Pierre, are you ready?', we all freaked out inside and we looked at Georges, and we could tell that the question triggered an answer in his mind: '*Fuck, I'm not ready, I didn't train for the fight.*' I swear to God—if the inspector walks in that room, and doesn't say to Georges 'Are you ready?' Georges wins that fight."

The rest of the fight played out like a waking nightmare for Georges, as he was clipped by a Serra forearm and was stopped via strikes in the first round. This loss snapped St-Pierre back to reality—but he could not yet accept responsibility for his actions that led to the loss.

"To see what was happening after the fight where Georges was blaming [the loss] on other people," said Patry, "I didn't feel good about that."

No one was more upset about the way Serra had routed St-Pierre than his own trainer, Victor Vargotsky. Weeks of pent-up frustration at seeing Georges shortchange himself by simply going through the motions boiled up inside of Vargotsky, and he gave it to St-Pierre straight.

The impact of Vargotsky's sage words—along with the implication that St-Pierre had handed his title to Serra on a platter—had the unintended effect of making Georges feel even worse about losing. Victor Vargotsky was soon fired from St-Pierre's camp and remains bitter to this day about starting the wave that so many others would take credit for later on.

"Who?" asks Vargotsky at the mention of Georges's name, as if St-Pierre never existed.

While Matt Serra's Rocky-esque upset of St-Pierre had stunned the MMA world, Serra was locked into his current UFC contract and just wasn't able to capitalize on the performance in the way that other athletes could by leveraging a massive win into a huge payday. James "Buster" Douglas, for example, who had won the upset of the century in boxing by handing an undefeated Mike Tyson his first loss on February 11, 1990, went on to earn $24.6 million in his first title defense against Evander Holyfield. An unprepared Tyson claimed he'd spent his time in Japan "fucking Japanese girls like it was eating grapes," before the Douglas fight, but critics saw the loss as delicious proof that Tyson was mediocre.

Georges was not the kind of person to make the same mistake twice. At the St-Pierre vs. Serra rematch held at UFC 83 on April 19, 2008, in Montreal, St-Pierre implemented his new risk-free style against Serra and won via second-round stoppage.

Serra would go on to drop a controversial decision to Matt Hughes, knock out a washed-up Frank Trigg, and lose a decision to fan-favorite Chris Lytle. Serra earned just $75,000 against Hughes and $210,000 against Trigg; good money, but certainly not enough after taxes, manager's commission and other expenses to retire on. Luckily, Serra still had his two jiu-jitsu schools in East Meadow and Huntington, New York, that he currently runs with the help of his brother, Nick.

In many ways, getting that taste of glory was as dangerous as doing your first line of cocaine. You wanted more to recapture that amazing feeling, "I am the best. The best in the world." Still, Serra sometimes suspected that he hadn't faced the real GSP, and it diminished the value of the win.

The Matt Serra loss had big consequences for Stephane Patry. He was hit by a vicious one-two combo, where he lost his hold managing many UFC fighters, then watched his MMA promotion (now called TKO) go under water. The foundation of Patry's fledgling MMA empire had always been built on sand; it was just a matter of time before the cracks in the façade of stability gave way to collapse. There were also seedy undercurrents to running a promotion in Quebec, a hotbed of outlaw biker gangs, traditional mafia groups, and upstart ethnic gangs—not the kind of people a promoter wanted as financial backers.

A profile story of Patry for *Financial Post Business* magazine that ran in May 2007 noted something fishy—the telephone number for TKO's South Shore office was neither listed in the telephone book nor was it on TKO's elaborate website.[27] Why didn't Patry want the contact information for his company to be freely available to prospective business contacts, sponsors, potential fighters and promotions?

Fighter Mark Hominick mentioned who some of the usual suspects involved in the Quebec MMA scene were:

"A lot of businesses and clubs, a lot of promotions—anything to do with a lot of cash—the bikers or organized crime are going to be involved. Especially since Quebec is so heavily influenced by the Hell's Angels."

In October 2008, Patry issued a press release stating he was resigning as president of TKO to move on to other ventures.

"To be quite honest with you," reflected Patry, pausing to choose his words carefully about why he left TKO, "I was quite tired with a lot of things that were going on."

TKO 35, held on October 3, 2008, would end up being the very last TKO event. Patry might have been a typical promoter, promising more than he delivered, taking more than he gave and stepping on toes all along the way, but for all his faults, Patry had helped with the development of grassroots talent that the UFC would benefit greatly from well into the future.

The real downfall of Stephane Patry as Georges St-Pierre's manager came, not through St-Pierre being assertive and taking charge of his career, but through the machinations of the UFC.

"[The UFC] had expressed a desire to get Patry out of the picture, Georges had expressed a desire to change managers—to go with a winner instead of a snake," said Alexandre Choko.

What could have happened next needs to be remembered as one of the biggest 'What if?' moments of GSP's tragically mismanaged career. As it was for Iris from *Taxi Driver* getting into Travis Bickle's taxi, only to be re-acquired by her pimp later, cutting loose of a toxic relationship can be difficult.

Georges began speaking with Alexandre Choko about a change, asking Choko to help find a manager who spoke French. Choko could not find anyone suitable, but offered to take up the position himself. Georges was elated; he had been so insecure, doubting Alexandre Choko would want to become his manager, that he had not even asked him outright.

As it stood, St-Pierre had often sought advice from Choko on what to say during interviews or during in-ring speeches. Thus the process of laying down a new future for St-Pierre began, as Patry did not have a valid management contract to hold over St-Pierre. Georges could walk away and still maintain his presence in the UFC on improved terms.

"I went to the UFC. They were willing to renegotiate the contract that Patry had just secured for Georges, because there were things that needed to be changed," said Choko.

Choko reminded St-Pierre not to sign any new management contracts with Patry—but it was too late. Patry had already got wind of Choko's interference in speaking to St-Pierre's then-girlfriend in the VIP section about changing St-Pierre's management—a conversation that an acquaintance of Choko had eavesdropped on and reported back to Patry.

St-Pierre is similar to former heavyweight boxing champion Lennox Lewis, as neither champion had a trophy girlfriend, wife or mistress who was prominently presented front-and-center to the public during their respective careers. Some fans speculated that Lennox Lewis was, in fact, a closet homosexual; the same rumors made the rounds regarding St-Pierre throughout his career. Two years after retiring from boxing, Lewis married former beauty queen Violet Chang on July 15, 2005.

Georges himself said that his first girlfriend was a "beautiful and smart" girl from the Republic of Congo—most likely the same girl in the VIP section whom Choko was talking to.

"She's still one of my good friends," St-Pierre stated when asked of his first girlfriend in 2008; "I went out with her for like four years."

Quizzed about what attracted him to her, he was too much of a gentleman to mention physical attributes.

"Her attitude, I like it," said Georges. "She's somebody who respects herself. That's very important."

Montreal Gazette reporter Allison Lampert recalls meeting a girl named "Solange" while on assignment at the St-Pierre family home in March 2006, on the night of the first BJ Penn fight. Described as a "curvy" woman, she sported green contact lenses and identified herself as Georges's current girlfriend.

The attraction of women toward prominent athletes meant that St-Pierre had an endless number of conquests to choose from and no reason to attach himself to a long-term relationship.

St-Pierre's Muay Thai trainer, Phil Nurse, teased St-Pierre by telling him about a woman who kept calling him to ask for his number. "Should I give her your number?" asked Nurse. " 'You know the type of woman I like,' " St-Pierre replied.[28] The conversation alluded to how it was rumored that Georges preferred black women.

After Patry had heard about Choko's plans for a regime change in St-Pierre's camp, Patry cornered St-Pierre and managed to get him to sign a contract valid with the Quebec Athletic Commission (RACJ).

"He threatened me to this, to that, to lawsuits," Choko said of the excuses St-Pierre gave for re-upping with Patry. "I said, 'You're acting like a stupid prostitute who signed new papers,' " said Choko to GSP. " 'I had everything, I had the commissioner for you to be free of your pimp, and you went back.' I said, 'There is nothing that I can do for you anymore.' "

In short, the intervention—one that would undoubtedly have brought GSP to a higher level of financial security and international visibility and even given him some control over his destiny—was stopped cold. As much as Patry might have staved off the first round of attacks on his hold over St-Pierre, the next wave would push him back into the sea.

5

POT MEETS KETTLE

"When I was heavyweight champion of the world, I believed I ruled the world. I had homes all over the country; I had luxurious apartments all over the country; I had the most exquisite cars. But I loved leeches, I wanted them to suck my blood. I just wanted them to suck my blood. All of my blood—I wanted them to suck my blood, and then sell my blood, and then I buy my blood back and allowed them to suck it again. And that was my downfall."

—*Mike Tyson*

Tyson (2008)

Ascribing dishonest motivation to others in order to hide one's own deceit is a classic technique employed in the fight game (and politics, boardrooms, high-school cheerleading teams, you name it).

One of the most graphic examples of this phenomenon was UFC president Dana White's friendly/fatherly advice directed at then newly-minted light-heavyweight champion Jon Jones through his favorite tool, the MMA media.

"The dirtiest, nastiest, scuzziest, scummiest, most disgusting human beings on the face of the Earth will start to cling on to this guy and become barnacles and get in his ear and try to pull him in different directions," White stated to the press in May 2011.[29]

Jones had worked his way into a good position, winning a Junior College wrestling title and earning a scholarship to Iowa State. After the unplanned pregnancy of his girlfriend, Jones was unable to accept the scholarship and moved into his girlfriend's mother's basement in upstate New York. He was unable to find regular work, except for a gig bouncing at a local bar. A transition to MMA seemed like a step up.

"All we had down there were two mattresses. It was this nasty, dark basement. I'd come home from training and load up these YouTube clips of UFC fighters and watch them for hours—study their moves. And then I'd stand up and practice what I had just seen. I'd kick a spot on the wall over and over until I got it right," Jones told *Men's Journal*.[30]

According to Ryan Ciotoli, the self-styled owner, operator and trainer of Bombsquad MMA in Cortland, New York, Jones always showed potential from his earliest wrestling days.

"I watched him in high school," said Ciotoli, who had been recruiting for Ithaca College as an assistant coach. "I actually saw him wrestle as a sophomore and junior, and I could tell he was pretty gifted as a wrestler. He just had a unique style—something that most wrestlers don't have is that relaxed disposition."

Jones spent a semester at Morrisville State College in New York, working with their wrestling team, but never competing. Ciotoli obtained Jones's phone number from a mutual friend and contacted him in fall 2007.

"I told him he could be good and make money doing MMA," said Ciotoli. "If he trained with us and let me manage him, I would do my best to get him to that place."

Jones, who had limited options at that point—even being denied a job as a janitor in a local factory—saw a way out for himself.

"I started training with Team Bombsquad out of Courtland," explained Jones, "I had no money, and was pretty much bumming a ride 45 minutes or otherwise ended up training at the Bombsquad training facility, knowing I wouldn't have a ride back and forth, and it just sort of worked out."

After six months of training with Bombsquad, Jones had his first MMA fight on April 12, 2008, winning via first round TKO. Jones had racked up a 6-0 record in smaller shows when the UFC came calling. Unlike other weight divisions, bigger fighters—especially guys like Jones, who had finished all six of his opponents with five stoppages and one submission—were harder to come by. The UFC signed Jones for a four-fight deal in 2008[31], with his first fight just two weeks out as a late replacement facing Andre Gusmao.[32]

In the UFC, Jones made it to 3-0 against higher-level competition like Andre Gusmao, Stephan Bonnar and Jake O'Brien. Jon Jones also relied on his natural physical talent to overcome the underdevelopment of his skills that Team Bombsquad couldn't correct.

"I've gotten this far with not good coaching at all," said Jones in 2009, speaking of Team Bombsquad. "No disrespect to the guys who are working with me, these guys weren't the best coaches and they knew it and I knew it."

Despite his position as one of the top draws in the sport, Georges St-Pierre took the time to help Jones with his technique when he was assigned the same dressing room to the then 9-0 Jones at UFC 100 where St-Pierre was slated to face Brazilian Thiago Alves.

"[St-Pierre and his trainer Firas Zahabi] basically told me flat that, 'man you got so much potential but you're doing this wrong, you're doing that wrong,' and I respected their honesty," said Jones, who took the constructive criticism to heart. "It made me fall in love with them right away because they had no reason to care about what I was doing."

This led to Jones putting in training sessions at the Tristar gym in Montreal and eventually joining Greg Jackson's MMA team in Albuquerque, New Mexico.

Jones would have an acrimonious split from Ciotoli made official in January 2011.

"*After months of trying to 'officially' separate myself from team Bombsquad, I can finally say that as of today I have NO association with Bombsquad or ryan ciotoli*," Jones posted via Twitter to signify his separation from Ciotoli.[33]

While Ciotoli wouldn't disclose any financial reasons behind Jones's leaving, he did point out the limitations of the Bombsquad gym at that point.

"We were basically training out of a barn at the back of my house," said Ciotoli, "We didn't have any trainers like we do now."

By 2012, Jones was 11-1 in the UFC (17-1 overall) with his sole loss a controversial disqualification to Matt Hamill due to "12-to-6" elbow strikes.

In the UFC, Jon Jones was exploited, in a sense, by those closest to him. For instance, Jones's participation as a fighter in the UFC video game *Undisputed* netted him a hefty paycheck of $5000. Since the typical UFC contract to buy his video game rights extended forever, no matter how much leverage Jones garnered in the industry, he would never receive a royalty per game sold, nor could he participate if another manufacturer making a competing MMA game, such as EA Sports, offered him a contract to license his likeness for their video game.

There were other tricks, like the UFC buying Jon Jones a 2012 Bentley Continental GT as a gift. Were Jones to receive the same cut of pay-per-view revenue that boxers who drew similar numbers of buys made, he could easily have bought the $190,000 car. Pro athletes have always been given similar bonuses of cars, because the flashy objects could distract and dazzle them, corrupt them to the rush of high-end spending, and thus further indenture them to their respective sports.

By overtly ascribing nefarious qualities to outsiders—many of whom did have malicious schemes that preyed on the rich and famous, such as Diego Sanchez being conned out of $175,000[34] or Chuck Liddell losing $1.5 million in a bad land deal[35]—Dana White effectively distracted people from much bigger issues in the legitimate contracts that Jon Jones had signed and agreed to that would handicap both Jones's long-term earning potential and his ability to maintain some say in how his career was run.

The case of Georges St-Pierre's management was a sordid affair where the wrong type of people repeatedly asserted themselves over his career. On the surface, the general public often operated under flawed assumptions when it came to understanding St-Pierre. For example, initially, a rumor circulated that he came from a wealthy background, perhaps owing to his classy character. Later on, the value of his sponsorships with Gatorade and Under Armour would be overestimated in public opinion, papering over the actual details of the financial compensation he was receiving from the massive pay-per-view numbers that he brought in for Zuffa.

Serra's spectacular first-round TKO finish of GSP was the final hammer blow to disintegrate St-Pierre from his first manager, Stephane Patry. However, St-Pierre would simply find himself moving laterally on a conveyor belt from one manager to the next with respect to his new representation.

It wasn't enough to spur GSP into concrete action that Patry was allegedly forging St-Pierre's signature to collect sponsorship checks, or that he allegedly traded Georges's comped airline tickets for earlier or later flights to pocket extra money. Nor was the neglect from Patry being preoccupied with promoting TKO and managing several other fighters enough to get Georges to leave. Georges was dissatisfied, irate, even angry at his mistreatment, but the move to "save" him had to come from outside his own locus of control. Patry had tapped into something in Georges's subconscious that gave him a foothold no matter how exploitative the relationship became.

"[Patry's] the type of guy that got the 20 [percent], then was probably charging Georges another ten for this and that, but at the same time, he was also pocketing money directly for his shows, making the sponsor believe it would go to Georges—but it would go to him," said Choko on Patry's financial arrangement with St-Pierre.

After St-Pierre renewed a valid management contract with Stephane Patry, there was still a possibility of challenging the legality of the relationship. After all, Patry had been St-Pierre's promoter for UCC and TKO; now he would act as St-Pierre's manager—it was a clear conflict of interest between roles. All Georges had to do was call the Quebec athletic commissioner, Mario Latraverse.

"If Georges wants out of his contract," Latraverse had told Choko, "tell Georges to come and see me."

Both Choko and UFC vice-president of regulatory affairs Marc Ratner passed on the message to St-Pierre.

"Georges said, 'Yeah, I'll call Mario Latraverse,'" related Choko.

Weeks dragged by, but Quebec commissioner Latraverse never got a call from St-Pierre. Choko was powerless, and Georges seemed unable to help himself.

Without any warning, there was a new player in the equation who'd had no previous contact with St-Pierre: Shari Spencer, the then-girlfriend of holistic therapist Steve Friend. Steve Friend provided regular treatments to Dana White, as well as numerous high-profile MMA fighters, including Matt Hughes and Georges St-Pierre. In terms of previous workplace experience, Spencer claimed to have previously been the CFO for "public and private companies"; she had also worked from 1988 to 1995 as a director at "Accounts Recovery International Inc," a debt-collection company. Up to this point, Spencer's only direct business experience with mixed martial arts had consisted of looking at some T-shirt contracts for Randy Couture.

According to Spencer's version of events, Friend made the introductions between herself and St-Pierre.

"He saw there was a potential deal they were trying to reach with Georges and asked me to take a look at it," claimed Spencer. "It started with a T-shirt licensing deal, and then it moved into all this business management, and eventually, into the fight management role."

The way St-Pierre explained the situation to Alexandre Choko suggested that someone more powerful was pushing forward the arranged marriage between St-Pierre and Spencer.

"I remember Georges coming to my office at Tristar. 'Remember my doctor? His girlfriend is going to become my manager,' " St-Pierre told Choko, who felt relief that Patry would be disposed of. "I said, 'Great, how are you going to pull that off?' and Georges said, 'The UFC has it all under control. It's all arranged.' "

"My understanding," said Choko, "was that the UFC had made an enormous effort to get rid of Patry and propose someone that they could—I don't want to say 'control,' but that they could gear in the right direction."

The changing of the guard between Patry and Spencer occurred in July 2007, about a month before the first Josh Koscheck fight.

"One day, Georges said, 'I have this girl that can help us with sponsorships,' and I had nothing to say about it," said Patry.

Patry was no dummy—he knew Shari Spencer's intentions were far more than limiting herself to obtaining sponsorships for St-Pierre.

A sponsor dropped St-Pierre; Patry was blamed, and Spencer used the opportunity to weaken the already tenuous relationship between him and St-Pierre.

"Georges told me, 'I don't want you to be my manager anymore,'" said Patry.

There were, however, still legal obligations tying St-Pierre and Patry together, if only on paper.

"I had a contract with Georges till 2011," said Patry.

When St-Pierre signed to have Shari Spencer represent him, she would get 20 percent of his income. At the same time, if Patry held a valid contract, then Georges would have to pay an additional 20 percent to Stephane Patry for the duration of their contract. Even though these kinds of legal issues were inevitable due to St-Pierre's method and timing when changing managers, it was none of the UFC's responsibility to sort out.

"[The UFC] didn't care," speculated Choko. "As long as Georges was doing what they wanted him to do, if the guy has to pay 40 percent of his purse—twenty to Patry and twenty to Shari—it's none of their business. They probably couldn't care less. They had their show, and they made their money, right?"

For the UFC, Georges St-Pierre had one purpose—fighting in their shows to generate revenue for Zuffa. In this regard, Zuffa was no different from any company in wanting employees to show up and work, period.

Now out in the cold, Patry launched his own lawsuit against St-Pierre in order to recoup the management fees he may have been legally able to collect. Although the lawsuit dragged on in court, after a couple years there was eventually a settlement reached between Patry and St-Pierre's lawyers.

"Everything was taken care of outside of court," said Patry.

After the settlement, the differences between Patry and St-Pierre were reconciled to the point where they were on speaking terms again. Shades of Stockholm Syndrome, perhaps?

Shari Spencer's new management of Georges St-Pierre was a self-proclaimed success—at least from the viewpoint of Spencer. During Spencer's tenure as Georges's manager, Georges never lost a fight, was now represented by powerhouse Creative Artists Agency (CAA) and had signed sponsorship deals with Under Armour and Gatorade Canada (Gatorade Canada was a different and marginal company compared to the US entity that sponsored sports luminaries such as Michael Jordan and Sydney Crosby).

Meanwhile, Shari was reaping huge rewards for her role in representing St-Pierre.

"I believe it's 20 percent plus all expenses to run her office, to go places, to stay [in] places," suggested Choko. "She is probably pulling down $600,000 a year net."

Choko's 2010 estimate was based on St-Pierre clearing $3 million per fight; in 2011, Georges told Agence France-Presse that he made $4 to $5 million per fight.[36] In public opinion, those might have sounded like huge numbers ("for one night of fighting!"), but relative to the revenue boxers earned for drawing similar pay-per-view numbers, St-Pierre was being grossly underpaid.

This was made obvious in 2007 when Randy Couture claimed to have received only $500,000 per fight, and in response, the Fertitta brothers disclosed a contract that showed Couture received a salary that, escalated with pay-per-view buys, totaled $936,000 per fight and topped out at about $3 for each pay-per-view buy. If we average the numbers GSP drew for UFC 94, UFC 111 and UFC 124, we get 830,000 buys. At an average price of $50 per buy, that comes out to $41.5 million in net revenue, of which about half goes to cable and satellite distributors. Going by these estimates, St-Pierre's $4 to $5 million salary represented about 20 percent of the pay-per-view revenue Zuffa received for his fights.

To compare St-Pierre's salary, boxing superstar Manny Pacquiao was guaranteed $6 million plus a percentage of pay-per-view receipts and other revenue that would swell his earnings to about $26 million for his June 9, 2012, fight against Timothy Bradley.[37] The Pacquiao-Bradley fight was estimated to have sold between 900,000 and one million pay-per-view buys, but in boxing and MMA, there are additional revenue streams that count for a lot.[38] Foreign sales of broadcast rights, closed-circuit revenue, site revenue and sponsorships are such lucrative areas that Floyd Mayweather Jr., who promotes his own fights and got a cut from each of those areas, reaped a paycheck close to $40 million for his September 17, 2011, fight with Victor Ortiz.[39]

The only way that St-Pierre could get a bigger piece of the pie would have been for him to challenge Zuffa; failing that, St-Pierre was only getting pennies on every dollar he brought in for the company. Spencer could have taken St-Pierre to competing promotions like Affliction or Strikeforce—a move that would have granted St-Pierre numerous concessions from a new promoter eager to break into the pay-per-view business—but why upset the UFC?

Georges St-Pierre's public image was hurt by Spencer's attempts to mold him into an even more non-threatening and empty person who could therefore be available to have any corporate identity branded onto his flanks. If you have no beliefs, people can project their own thoughts, feelings and dreams onto you—the same marketing shtick used to promote boy bands. Shari Spencer was always vocal and direct about keeping St-Pierre's public image "clean"—a philosophy that was almost religious in its attempt to present St-Pierre as a saintly figure.

Georges claimed to have had zero knowledge of the situation between former opponent Jon Fitch and the UFC that arose when Fitch hesitated to sign over his video game likeness rights *in perpetuity* to THQ, a company licensed to produce *UFC: Undisputed*. Fitch was fired from the UFC on November 20, 2008 (just three months after losing to GSP), but was quickly reinstated within 24 hours when he capitulated to Zuffa's demands.

"I didn't even know that. I don't follow those things. Nobody has told me that—you're the first one," St-Pierre said in 2009 when quizzed about the Jon Fitch-THQ situation.

Zuffa had tried to get all its fighters—including high profile stars like BJ Penn—to sign their video game likeness rights to Zuffa, so Georges knew about the contract. There was little or no compensation being offered, which was offensive to the fighters giving up something in exchange for nothing. It's hard to believe that St-Pierre wasn't aware of Fitch's plight; he just chose the safe route of pleading the Fifth to avoid complications with Zuffa. This might have helped St-Pierre avoid butting heads with Dana White and the Fertittas in the short term, but in the long run, the bargaining power of all MMA fighters—including GSP—was weakened.

"We're getting a lot more opportunities these days," Spencer told *Maclean's* magazine in September 2010 of sponsorship and endorsement opportunities. "Frankly, we're almost maxed out."

It was, of course, a slanted perspective on reality—there is no limit to the amount of high-level sponsorship that an athlete can undertake (although there are limits on the amount of PR duties an athlete can take on, as burned-out Formula 1 driver Lewis Hamilton noted in July 2011, when he claimed the duties for sponsors were overwhelming him[40]). "The Spencer Firm" was failing to bring St-Pierre to the next level of mainstream appeal, and no amount of flowery doublespeak could hide that reality.

Even Shari's appearance and mannerisms left a lot to be desired, something that even the most oblivious onlooker would pick up on.

"She looks like someone who was found on the street—not even decent clothes on her, and she's probably doing the best she can," said Alexandre Choko.

On the professional front, cracks appeared in the façade as early as mid-2009, when Spencer began to both listen in on and record interviews that Georges conducted with journalists via telephone. When this writer was on site at the Tristar gym in Montreal to speak with Georges for a pre-arranged magazine feature, St-Pierre nervously averted his eyes and gave the writer Spencer's telephone number. A telephone interview was scheduled for later that evening, where Spencer listened in while recording the proceedings.

The disconnect between Spencer and market realities was captured thoroughly with a September 2010 *New York Times* piece by Alex Williams where Georges was thrown into a mix of New York party scenes, hoping to tap into the hysterical public reaction to celebrities. In the piece, Spencer came across as an overbearing, neurotic mother pushing her unwitting firstborn into beauty pageants. The shock of the night was St-Pierre denigrating his celebrity status by attending a party for the designers Viktor & Rolf at Saks Fifth Avenue:

> **It didn't help that the party turned out to be open to the public. There were no handlers to escort him and no celebrities to be photographed beside. Instead, Mr. St-Pierre, in his crisp D&G jeans and black patent leather basketball sneakers, stood frozen near the corner behind the Gucci suits, looking like a bully version of a store mannequin.[41]**

Bringing GSP to a *public* party (with a writer for the *NY Times* in tow to survey the scene!) was an act of total incompetence on the level of Tyson's corner not having an enswell (also called an eye-iron, used to reduce swelling of facial cuts) in the Buster Douglas fight. And even though St-Pierre was associated with the celebrity culture, his heart was far removed from vacant poseurs and trendy types.

Despite his success, St-Pierre did not abandon the friends he had made on his way to the top. One of St-Pierre's closest friends is ex-con Eric O'Keefe.

"In the '80s, I was involved in a crime in the United States," said O'Keefe. "The crime that I was accused of was drug importation… conspiracy to distribute 'X amount' of cocaine."

After getting caught, O'Keefe was sentenced to 154 months in federal prison in the United States. He served eight years in maximum security prisons, and upon parole, utilized his background in amateur boxing to gain entry into MMA as a trainer.

A licensing incident between St-Pierre's friend and training partner David Loiseau and the Quebec Athletic Commission—the *Régie des alcools, des courses et des jeux*, or RACJ—had temporarily suspended Loiseau from competing at UFC 113 in Montreal. Loiseau had been part owner of XMMA, a small Montreal-based promotion that the RACJ alleged had ties to the Hell's Angels.[42] Similarly, the RACJ refused to renew O'Keefe's license to corner fighters before UFC 113, supposedly for having ties to organized crime.

"At my gym, one of my partners was a Hell's Angel." O'Keefe acknowledged. "But his business, whatever he did—he didn't bring it to the gym and I didn't get involved in whatever he was doing."[43]

The Sherbrooke gym, called Force Xtreme, was a place where certain types of people congregated—but it was also an environment where troubled kids could redefine themselves.

O'Keefe recalls his first meeting with Georges, a friendship that started around 2006:

"He was very funny, very green. He comes from the outskirts of Montreal. Not very streetwise."

"He was sitting at my table for dinner in a restaurant, he was raving about the food—and it was an okay restaurant—you could see that he hasn't gone out much."

As far as enjoying the massive sense of entitlement that comes with championship status, St-Pierre dismissed such trappings.

"Georges, even to this day, is the most down-to-earth guy I know. He'll stand in line for a cab when he could just order a limo," says O'Keefe. "He doesn't want to hang out with the stars. When he goes to Vegas, he's got all these people wanting to hang out with him—Mandy Moore, and all these artists—he just wants to be with his friends."

There were other reasons why Georges steered clear of other celebrities—St-Pierre often didn't know the people he was being introduced to. With the bar for what qualifies someone as a public figure having been lowered dramatically with the advent of Paris Hilton- and Kim Kardashian-types, who could blame GSP for not knowing (or caring) about supposed stars?

This did not mean that Georges was oblivious to the privileges of his fame. If anything, he was well aware of how he could use his name to his advantage.

Said Georges in 2009, "The thing that is nice is that sometimes you have a ticket, a cop's ticket. And the police let you go because 'I'm Georges St-Pierre.' (Cop's voice) 'Hey, good fight. Keep us proud!' and stuff like that."

There were a few cries for support regarding St-Pierre's friends David Loiseau and Eric O'Keefe's licensing issues, but there was no condemnation from the few MMA fans who were even aware of the issues that Loiseau and O'Keefe were bad seeds. In the mind of Spencer, however, Georges's association with such people tainted the "pure" and "clean" image she had been cultivating as part of her "plan." A visit to Canada's capital of Ottawa was organized for St-Pierre to meet with the Members of Parliament on May 4, 2010, just four days before the UFC 113 event in Montreal.

According to a blog posted by Karina Roman on CBC.ca, "Heritage Minister James Moore…told me that he has extended an invitation to

GSP several times before but only now [St-Pierre] has a 'coincidence of schedules.' "[44]

The obvious PR ploy was disguised as St-Pierre doggedly pursuing yet another one of the UFC's strategic objectives—legalization of the sport within Ontario, which had been a priority of UFC president Dana White's since 2008. The timing of St-Pierre's sudden interest in humoring an MP who had been inviting him over to play (or to be the shiny new toy to be shown off) for years was suspect.

As far as Spencer's interpersonal skills went, she was a collection of passive-aggressive behaviors. Spencer had a reputation among insiders as being condescending, pushy and unreliable. She often spoke for Georges, concentrating on her own grandiose sense of self-importance, rather than catering to St-Pierre's needs as a person and as a fighter.

"Everybody wants to be so important, that it sometimes sucks for the guy in the ring fighting," said Choko of the attitude of narcissism and entitlement cultivated amongst some of St-Pierre's management.

On January 20, 2011, a boilerplate press release went out announcing the split between St-Pierre and Spencer: "They felt they had a different vision for the future of Georges's career and it was best to remain close personally but dissolve their business relationship."[45]

Spencer's only other client, then-UFC lightweight champion Frankie Edgar, quickly followed suit and walked out on "The Spencer Firm" just a few days later.[46] As with St-Pierre, the biggest benefit for Frankie Edgar being with Spencer was that one of Frankie's previous managers had been dishonest in financial matters. The bar in MMA management was set so low that anyone else could only be an improvement, and yet in the end, Spencer had fallen short.

Georges could say little about the breakdown between Spencer and himself.

"We had a different vision of the future," St-Pierre said of the split, his hands tied by possible legal action on Spencer's part.

Patry, back in the game promoting MMA under his "Instinct" banner in 2012, had his own explanation for St-Pierre's actions.

"The problem with Georges—I believe he will always be the same—is that he does listen to too many people," says Patry. "I guess it's part of his personality where he wants to be nice to everybody."

"He did listen to the wrong people on a few occasions. The best example is what happened between him and Shari, what Shari did to him."

Patry wouldn't elaborate on what Shari had done exactly—but his take on their relationship was telling:

"My personal opinion of her is not very good…she's the one who put in Georges's head that I wasn't a good guy for him, or a good manager for him. But the thing that she didn't realize is that she did break a business relationship, but she also broke a friendship, which is something that I will always be angry at her for. Not only did she do that, but she only did that for her own personal benefit, and she ended up screwing him."

Was Patry really that unaware of how his own actions had hurt St-Pierre, or was this statement a deliberate attempt to assign blame elsewhere? It's human nature to gloss over one's own mistakes and criticize the missteps of others, but the fight game seemed to take devious human tendencies to the next level of selfishness.

6

ATHLETE OF THE YEAR

"I'm going to have a different look. I'm going to look like a totally different guy, and people will understand when they see that fight."

—Georges St-Pierre, on his rematch with Matt Serra

Sherdog.com, January 16, 2008

All of the changes in St-Pierre's camp after his knockout loss to Matt Serra bore fruit in the win column with seven title defenses achieved against Jon Fitch, BJ Penn, Thiago Alves, Dan Hardy, Josh Koscheck, Jake Shields and Carlos Condit. It was a worthy résumé made even more impressive by the fact that St-Pierre had won 33 consecutive rounds since losing the first round to Josh Koscheck in their first non-title encounter in 2007. Jake Shields snapped GSP's streak of winning consecutive rounds at UFC 129 when Shields won the fourth and fifth rounds against St-Pierre on two of the judges' scorecards.[47]

"I rely on control, and I think it's the most methodical way to fight," said St-Pierre in the press conference leading up to UFC 129.

"It's the best way to not get injured and [to] have a long career and implement your game plan."[48]

Even as St-Pierre had appeared so dominant in these victories, his new post-Serra style of avoiding damage and controlling the fight was alienating audiences. His last fight that ended inside the distance occurred in 2009 when BJ Penn refused to come out of his corner for the final round.

"It's like Mike Tyson [in his prime] not trying to go for the knockout," said Alexandre Choko.

There was fierce defense of St-Pierre's new style from his teammates, coaches and supporters within the media.

"He doesn't deserve the criticism," said teammate Kenny Florian. "He's not fighting chumps. It would be one thing if he was fighting guys coming up in the game, new guys, guys who aren't well-rounded—he's fighting the best guys in the world."

"Georges is fighting the best guys in the world," said Greg Jackson-coached middleweight Brian Stann, "sometimes guys he's fought twice now. That's very difficult. Rematches are tough; guys are continually trying to figure him out, and guys are figuring out new ways to nullify some of Georges's attacks."[49]

The argument was made that his opponents were in peak condition, entering the ring with a different mindset than any previous fights.

"They're very tough," said St-Pierre. "When they go to fight for a title, they are ready to die."

It's true that most of St-Pierre's opponents were the best of the best. Englishman Dan Hardy, whom St-Pierre beat via decision at UFC 111 on March 27, 2010, was a notable exception to this rule. Hardy had been submitted in three losses prior to meeting Georges, and was finished via knockout and guillotine choke after his loss to St-Pierre. St-Pierre had Dan Hardy in an armbar, but failed to complete the technique correctly, allowing Hardy to escape. The fault for not finishing a B-level fighter like Dan Hardy clearly lay with St-Pierre.

Georges also deflected blame for his inability to finish fights onto other parties, such as fight officials.

"It's not really me who is safe. I tried to finish my last fight [against Josh Koscheck]," said St-Pierre. "If it was not for the doctor, most of the [other] doctor[s] would have stopped the fight. I broke the eye socket [in] two different places of my opponent."

The argument could be made that St-Pierre was escaping damage by choosing a safe style of fighting. At the same time, if he had notched quick knockouts or submissions, St-Pierre would be fighting fewer rounds, and absorbing less offense from opponents. For instance, striking with Jake Shields—a mediocre striker—became nearly fatal for St-Pierre's win streak when an eye poke from Shields caused internal bleeding in Georges's left eye. Shields won two rounds on the judges' scorecards, not enough for the win, but a close call, nonetheless.

Steve Lott, assistant manager for Mike Tyson, had a unique explanation for why Mike Tyson underperformed after leaving manager Bill Cayton and trainer Kevin Rooney. In Lott's view, it came down to emotional interference:

> **Mike Tyson would return to the corner and sit down and dwell on his life. You can't see this in his face but that is exactly what happens to athletes when there is no activity. Like a soccer player on the sidelines waiting to be put into the game. He thinks briefly about his wife and kids. His mother and father. The payments due on his house. And even the possibility of his wife discovering he has a mistress on the side. A lot goes through an athlete's mind when they are still. Like a fighter in the corner. And in Mike's case he knows he did a terrible thing leaving Cayton and Rooney. He knows that Don [King] is stealing tens of millions of dollars from his fights. He knows that the scum Don has placed around him has slowly influenced Mike to return to a street thug mentality. Throw in the ear biting and the three years in jail for the rape and you get an idea of what goes through his mind. When he gets up for round two he is mentally and emotionally shot. The emotional well? It's dry.[50]**

A similar theory that the mental side of an athlete influenced their performance was touted by author Timothy Gallwey in his ground-breaking book *The Inner Game of Tennis*, first published in 1974. Gallwey's concepts, which included ideas about silencing self-doubt, not being overtly judgmental and trusting one's capabilities, had an impact on a broad spectrum of performance-based initiatives outside of tennis.

St-Pierre was never convicted of rape, nor did he serve time in prison, but he was certainly aware that the UFC was taking the lion's share of the profits generated through his fights, as well as a cut from any sponsors that St-Pierre represented in the octagon. He had felt anger toward Stephane Patry, for a variety of reasons. There would certainly have been bitterness toward Shari Spencer for her machinations within St-Pierre's camp. Georges might not have fallen into the same traps of celebrity that elevated some narcissistic types into the headlines of TMZ, but the effect of constant media scrutiny, along with the unending PR duties of photos, signings and appearances would also have taken a toll on his psyche.

One of the changes St-Pierre made after the Serra loss was the addition of Brian Cain, a sports psychologist, to his team. Cain was later supplemented with Peter Bender; St-Pierre's camp confirmed that he still worked with Brian Cain at time of writing.[51]

The use of this training tool delighted BJ Penn, who latched onto it as a weakness in the conference call prior to UFC 94:

"Does that help you out, Georges?" taunted Penn. "You got psychological problems or what?"

No matter how many "experts" St-Pierre hired to massage his mental outlook, there was no going back to his pre-Serra blitzkrieg style. The pressure only increased with the explosion in popularity of MMA, as well as the organizational politics that hung over him as a UFC fighter. The more whitewashed St-Pierre's identity became, the more he distanced himself from the changes that could have improved his public image and made him feel better about himself.

Georges, by all accounts, is most definitely the sensitive type. He knew that he could nail the Rogers Sportsnet "Canadian Athlete of the Year" three years running from 2008 to 2010—but he was equally aware that while he was nominated for the ESPY "Best Fighter" award thrice (2008, 2010, 2011), he could never best the likes of Floyd Mayweather Jr. or Manny Pacquiao. More to the point, due to the pro-wrestling model favored by the UFC, it was beneficial for the brass at Zuffa that there were no surpassing stars who could break away and undercut the organization. Georges always carried this knowledge close to his heart, well aware that Zuffa acted like Cronus, devouring his children out of fear of being overthrown.

Georges's achievements would always come down to who he was compared to. Next to the exciting stoppages and submissions earned by Anderson Silva, Fedor Emelianenko and BJ Penn, St-Pierre just wasn't dazzling during his post-Serra career. Yet if any welterweight opponent could beat Georges, even via decision, it would have been the upset of the year (unless it was the same year Anderson Silva got beaten).

Think about the myriad of also-rans: tough guys in Tapout shirts getting run out of jiu-jitsu classes after being repeatedly submitted into humiliation. Uninitiated kids claiming they are going to fight MMA, and be in the UFC, with no real sense of how deep or dark the ocean between their dreams and reality is. Georges could trounce lesser-tier competition without breaking a sweat, but he only measured himself against the elites of the MMA universe.

It was all relative—and perhaps St-Pierre's sensitivity was his own undoing in understanding exactly how great he was while still being aware of the untold achievements that could lie ahead.

"He wants to leave a legacy," Georges's former manager Shari Spencer had arrogantly proclaimed back in 2007. "He wants to be the most dominant fighter the UFC and MMA has ever seen, and he intends to accomplish that by dominating the 170-pound weight class, moving up to the 185 weight class and then eventually the light-heavyweight class."[52]

As of 2012, Georges continued to be evasive on the idea of a super-fight with UFC middleweight champion Anderson Silva. There was no shame in holding the belt at 170 pounds for as long as possible; after all, many UFC champions would be lucky to make a single defense of their belt, let alone to have the longevity that Georges enjoyed. But Georges's legacy would suffer, as it had always been clear he had more potential than he demonstrated, even in winning.

7

ENDGAME FOR GSP

"I want to retire being the best pound-for-pound fighter that ever lived. It's very hard to say how to judge it, but when I think myself that I'm the best it will be the time to do something else in my life."

—*Georges St-Pierre*

The Globe and Mail, November 6, 2011

In chess, "Endgame" refers to when there are but a few pieces left on the board. How better to describe the position of St-Pierre, who was the UFC welterweight king, yet had simultaneously been played like an expendable pawn by so many different people in MMA?

Georges himself knew that the prospect of ending his career, on no matter how high a note (beating Anderson Silva?), would remove the thing that gave his life purpose and direction. The end of victories on the grand stage would cause the inner voice of doubt to creep back and slowly take hold over him. Why wasn't he good enough? Would he ever be good enough? Therefore, St-Pierre insisted he would continue to train after he left the sport, taking care of his body and continuing, perhaps, to compete in other sports. Could St-Pierre accomplish one of his long-held dreams and make the Canadian Olympic wrestling team in his late 30s? Georges has competed in very few official wrestling matches, although a few years into his UFC career, he did participate in the Quebec Olympic Wrestling provincial championships and did well. As far as Brazilian Jiu-Jitsu went, Georges was good for a mid-level black, but there were still elite jiu-jitsu practitioners who could tap him with ease. Even though he'd been slated to compete in the prestigious Abu Dhabi submission championships after the Thiago Alves fight, he pulled out due to groin injury; St-Pierre never rescheduled to make an appearance as a competitor at a future Abu Dhabi event.

Coaching was another possibility for St-Pierre to pursue. He had already taken French MMA fighter Francis Carmont under his wing, utilizing him as a training partner at the Tristar gym, getting Carmont signed to the UFC and cornering him at UFC 137.

"I make all my training count with Georges. He gave me a lot of advice for training," said Carmont prior to UFC 137.[53]

St-Pierre had also been a regular on the seminar circuit, where fans pay the equivalent of monthly gym dues—or more—for a one-day class with a UFC fighter. His rise to the top had made giving such seminars an inefficient way to earn money, but when St-Pierre damaged his anterior cruciate ligament (ACL) and was laid up for a year between 2011 and 2012, he used his free time to give seminars.

With St-Pierre, you could never say never and write him off. He had attempted forays into movies, made millions, owned a house in Montreal and had captured the hearts of fans all over the world. Yet the thing he prized the most—his status as a dominant champion—had been slipping in and out of his grasp since he'd first won the title from Matt Hughes in 2006.

Georges has always idolized Belgian action star Jean-Claude Van Damme. As high as Van Damme had risen, there came a point in the late '90s when his movies flopped and Van Damme's star power waned.

These days, JCVD can star in low-budget films shot on foreign sets with incompetent and delusional directors or producers; he can still make the odd return in specific vehicles like *The Expendables 2,* but he will never return to his former glory. A star who mistakenly believes his situation will be otherwise is in danger of becoming a hideous real-life variant of *Sunset Boulevard's* Norma Desmond.

MMA fans laugh at Ken Shamrock's embarrassing descent from the top; they reel in horror as Kazushi Sakuraba talks about "dying in the ring"—made all the worse with Japanese MMA promotion DREAM not having paid him in two years (according to MMA agent Shu Hirata on Mauro Ranallo's radio show[54]). Brazilian legend Royce Gracie getting smashed by Matt Hughes at UFC 60 on May 27, 2006 surprised few insiders, with Zuffa later backhanding Royce for daring to impose financial demands to appear on Zuffa's first Rio de Janeiro event in 2011. Trying to plot a nice, stable and secure line from the peaks of victory as if life were a piece of graph paper to be charted was nearly impossible for any athlete—let alone for MMA fighters, who worked under far more constraints than most other athletes.

In the Zuffa-produced *Primetime* television series leading up to the second BJ Penn fight, Georges said, "I don't believe there is pleasure in life. I believe there is only a relief of pain," perhaps channeling his interpretation of Nietzsche's theories.

After several years in the UFC, GSP sported lines around his eyes like those etched into pieces of driftwood that have traveled thousands of miles to various coastlines and endured the pounding of a million different waves along the way. He was tired of the fight game, the putrid lifestyle, the training, the dishonesty, and yet he still carried the same baggage from his difficult upbringing to every gym and octagon he performed in, pain amplified by the cutthroat business practices of the UFC and the relentless fans trying to get his attention.

Truly, this was going to be part of the real Endgame for GSP. Not a supernatural being flying high above the coils of non-celebrity mortals, but an exile from the place he loved—and where he was loved—the most. Those expansive feelings of greatness were sometimes replaced by sadness and longing.

Georges repeatedly spoke about wanting to leave a legacy as someone who made a difference in the sport. He was not really having much of a social or political impact when it came to mixed martial arts.

Far from bringing changes to MMA or dynamically shifting power into the hands of fighters, St-Pierre has done the most to entrench Zuffa's stranglehold over the industry. While boxing superstars like Oscar De La Hoya and Floyd Mayweather Jr. changed their sport forever when they promoted their own fights, St-Pierre simply toed the line for Zuffa. Georges rarely did anything notable or revolutionary outside the octagon.

St-Pierre will leave a legacy as a great fighter; perhaps not as the greatest MMA fighter of all time, but definitely the greatest welterweight that the sport has ever seen. Maybe that's more than enough success for someone who was written off his whole life: demonstrating what his real potential—his true self—was.

SECTION II: USA

BJ PENN

8

THE PRODIGY

Before the polarizing antics of American Chael Sonnen, who was famous for insulting Anderson Silva relentlessly to goad him into a rematch, BJ Penn was one of the original bad boys in MMA—although he had to compete with other egotistical showmen like Tito Ortiz and Phil Baroni for the crown. BJ was a super-talented "prodigy" who rampaged over the best competition while eschewing regular training and yet was constantly on the brink of rededicating himself. The acclaim and mass appeal that have so often eluded other comparable fighters came in a straightforward manner to Penn—almost like his no-nonsense verbal and physical style itself.

Mysticism in martial arts often comes from people's fascination with Bruce Lee and other action movie stars—the guys who cut down bigger, tougher and stronger opponents as if they were in there with truant kindergarteners. With BJ, that was the appeal: his lackadaisical attitude made him appear even more talented as he performed effortlessly what many others couldn't achieve no matter how hard they worked. Yet there was always the promise that if BJ was more disciplined, he could achieve more as a fighter.

BJ would frequently jump up the weight classes to face the best of the best in welterweights, Matt Hughes, Georges St-Pierre, Jon Fitch, Nick Diaz, and in light-heavyweight, Lyoto Machida (at a bout fought at the heavyweight limit).

BJ traced his unflinching desire to challenge the best—at any weight—from his early days of fighting on the street.

Says BJ, "If someone pisses you off, you're never going to ask him 'how much does he weigh?' "

In Brazilian Jiu-Jitsu, which BJ had a background in, weight was a similar non-issue. All jiu-jitsu and submission wrestling tournaments had an "open weight" class, where the heavier fighters sometimes got tossed around by the smaller guys.

"That's why martial arts were created: so the small man could fight the big man and do well," BJ said to this writer.

Even with the prospect of facing a bigger man, so hot was the competitive fire within BJ, so confident was he in his abilities that he fully believed he could grasp victory no matter what advantage his opponent held.

Evaluating Penn's career by glancing at his record doesn't give a true picture. The context of who he fought and when he faced them matters much more than comparing his wins or losses to other fighters. BJ was an example of magic and it was an insult to compare him to other fighters.

9

HILO BEGINNINGS

BJ Penn talked about "never having more than five dollars in [his] pocket" when growing up in Hilo, on the Island of Hawaii, a picturesque settlement covering 58.4 square miles, with a population of approximately 43,263 people as of a 2010 census. [55] The Penn family lives in a very nice house purchased at a good price when the local economy was depressed. The Penns had a lot of money, yet they never bought into the arrogant flash of smug socialites. No fancy cars were parked in their driveway, and BJ wasn't some pampered brat outfitted in Banana Republic apparel and being told he was superior to others.

BJ's parents, Jay Dee Penn and Lorraine Shin, are described by family friend Tom Callos as two individuals who personify the blue-collar values necessary to make the American Dream a reality:

"They were just hard-working. His mom, and still today—especially to this day—can work five guys under the table. I went with her to the UFC convention selling T-shirts; I could not hang. The woman knows how to work, she's just unbelievable. His dad's work ethic, sensibility—he's like the Cartwright patriarch in *Bonanza*. All sensibility, all hard work; he's got his political agenda—he's a character, I love him."

All of the kids in the Penn family had to work from an early age. Thanks to the grounded natures of Jay Dee and Lorraine, the family was very close.

BJ Penn had problems, but he wasn't a seriously troubled kid. As with many normal and healthy teenagers, boring school classes were supplanted by hanging with friends, partying and smoking marijuana. In a move that embarrasses Penn to this day, he was busted for getting high with several of his classmates in high school; Jay Dee promptly pulled his son out of St. Joe's and began home schooling him.[56]

After BJ begged his dad to buy him boxing gloves for his birthday, an older friend initiated him into semi-organized fighting while at the Penn family home.

"I remember putting on the gloves and kind of moving around with him; he just beat the crap out of me," said BJ. "I remember I was so scared and flinching—and I didn't want to get hit—I just kept moving away, and covering up and stuff."[57]

While the first session had gone poorly, the next day BJ rationalized that there hadn't been that much pain or fear involved. He wanted more "porch boxing," and, thankfully, it was the one activity BJ had interest in that his father supported.

Interestingly, Penn wasn't the best out of the group of guys he boxed with, recalling himself as being "tough," but not the toughest. The worst injuries sustained were the odd broken nose or black eye, and BJ laughed off questions about his safety practices.

"Never mouthguards, never any of that kind of stuff," he explained of those boxing sessions, with a hint of incredulousness. "Technique? All I knew was the overhand right...overhand right was the key to success for me."

At the time, BJ was staring at a dead-end, with no real ambitions for the future. He was lucky to have had the support of his family, in particular his father, Jay Dee, who had a special intuition when it came to nudging BJ along.

Tom Callos was a fourth-degree Taekwondo black belt under Ernie Reyes Senior, tasked with running two of the largest schools in the US, located in Reno, Nevada. As with any job, his class schedule, along with the administrative side of the job began to grind him down. He needed an out—he needed a change. After turning his schools over to senior students, he decided to become a writer and looked into the prestigious writers' workshop at the University of Iowa, as well as a John Grisham-funded school in Oxford, Mississippi. Due to luck, accident or misfortune, an associate of a business contact from Hawaii was having heart surgery and required someone to cover their martial arts school while they were gone. There just happened to be a writers group in Kona run by a Pulitzer Prize-winning writer.

"While I was in Hawaii, I compared—one side, Hawaii; the other side, Iowa. There was no comparison," said Callos of the fateful decision to move to Hawaii.

Accident and misfortune required yet another change when a woman in Callos's community was killed in a car accident in Waimea. Callos's concern for the safety of his then-girlfriend prompted a move to Hilo so his girlfriend wouldn't have to commute.

Callos was still a martial artist at heart, which required rededication to his training. Ernie Reyes Senior had made a course correction and pointed his guys toward Gracie Jiu-Jitsu as part of their learning beyond Taekwondo. As limited as his BJJ knowledge was, Callos knew that he could sharpen his skills while in Hilo if he could find someone to train with him.

Said Callos, "I had a year and a half of rolling, very rudimentary, a real grind—T-shirt ripping, neck cranking—where everyone was at that time because it was such a new thing, and there was very few qualified teachers around."

BJJ black belt Relson Gracie was located in Honolulu, but hopping on a plane to train was impractical for Callos. He decided to post some flyers seeking local training partners in order to hone his skills. It took less than an hour for Callos to get a response from Jay Dee, BJ's father.

Said Callos, "One of his boys—I don't know which one—had pulled the flyer down at the gym and brought it home in the time between me posting it and coming home and them calling me. I plug in the phone, and 30 seconds later, it rings, and it's Jay Dee Penn, and he says his boys are interested in this."

It took some goading from Jay Dee to get BJ to actually show up at Callos's school. Part of this was owing to BJ's belief that striking was serious fighting. In boxing, the challenge between fighters is much more evident than in a grappling session. Action movies often incorporate wrestling moves, but the bulk of the scenes are composed of flashy strikes. BJ himself was a massive boxing fan during an era of great fighters.

"Evander Holyfield was my man when he went to war with Riddick Bowe a few times, and Riddick kicked his butt, and he came back and had some mean wars with him," recalled BJ.

Boxers like Julio César Chávez, Evander Holyfield and Mike Tyson left a much stronger impression on BJ than fighters in any other styles of martial arts. But Jay Dee understood the value of jiu-jitsu from his own experience as a former practitioner of judo, having earned a black belt in the grappling art that was similar to Brazilian Jiu-Jitsu.

The self-assured BJ simply didn't believe Tom Callos had anything to teach him. But Callos and Jay Dee persisted, with Jay Dee goading BJ to just go once. BJ finally gave in, and decided to go once, and then he would be free to quit.

Callos recalled that when BJ showed up with a few of his buddies, he explained how little he actually knew about BJJ. That didn't stop Callos from easily dominating BJ, leaving BJ in awe.

"He choked me, armlocked me," recalled BJ of their first session. "My mind just started going, 'Wow!'"

Almost immediately, Penn separated himself from Callos's other training partners by having the discipline to show up consistently. This is a hard task for the average Joe, as most people make excuses to avoid the sacrifices that come with hard work of any variety—let alone the high amount of exertion—and humility—that comes with BJJ training.

Six months into BJ's training, Jay Dee saw potential in his son that had Tom Callos rolling his eyes.

Said Callos, "[Jay Dee would] come to me and say, 'You know, my boy's going to be world champion.' Yeah right, like so many dads have come to me. And I said [in a hesitant voice], 'Yeah, I know.' "

While BJ's home situation wasn't dire, he received no real direction to speak of. He wasn't an inner-city miscreant forced to choose between prison, the grave or prizefighting. However, traditional career paths available through school were a poor fit for BJ, and the ruffians he was hanging out with wouldn't lead him anywhere better.

Penn was more talented than the average training partner, demonstrating flexibility and strength in addition to his regular discipline. He enjoyed the physical nature of the BJJ game, and sometimes utilized jiu-jitsu to dominate his own street fights. A slap-boxing session with Callos really challenged the Taekwondo instructor's perceptions of his own skill relative to BJ.

"I was tired, so one day I just said to BJ, 'Let's just spar it up a little bit,' " recalls Callos. "I was a top point fighter—I was good, I was fast—and he hit me about three or four times in the face before I could move."

The master then chased the student around the gym, seeking payback.

"I think I went back and punished him pretty good for as long as I possibly could," said Callos of the jiu-jitsu session that followed. "You go back to grappling, and you got that bittersweet taste in your mouth where *'This kid just slapped me around for a bit, so take one of these!'* "

On the way home after that session, the voices of negativity and self-doubt clouded Callos's mind in the age-old cycle of youth surpassing experience. *"I just got my clock cleaned by a 17- or 16-year-old. What's wrong with me? I must be getting old."*

At the time, no one knew how the dice were going to roll. Not BJ, not Jay Dee, not Tom Callos. BJ was green, untested and unproven. Only time would salve Callos's wounds from being beaten by a mere teenager—and that would take years.

10

EVOLUTION

The beauty of competition is achieving peaks of greatness.

The testing for Tom Callos's fifth-degree black belt was rigorous. Spanning five days, the Taekwondo instructor performed a 10-mile run; a 40-foot fire-walk; grappling; training with traditional weapons as well as handguns and rifles; traditional breaking; Brazilian Jiu-Jitsu; sparring; capoeira; Taiko drumming; boxing; as well as the traditional Taekwondo tests. For color, Callos also gave a filmed performance to 2000 spectators that involved 10 costume changes.

Upon passing the test, part of his journey was complete. He had the satisfaction of his reward. He also had a body shopworn by years of use and abuse. By his late thirties, Callos's hips were giving him serious problems and he had to cut back on his training.

Two years after his training with BJ, Callos ended up getting both his hips replaced. Callos infers that most of his injuries occurred from his extreme over-training between the ages of nine and 18 years. He would kick objects heavier than his body for thousands of repetitions, including a mattress tied to the wall for lack of water-filled heavy bags.

"In the '70s, nobody knew what proper training was," Callos reminisces of a largely ignorant fitness culture. "When I was trying to make the Olympic [Taekwondo] team, I was sometimes doing a thousand kicks a day."

The upshot of Callos's diminished drive was BJ being left without consistent training—as well as the mutual understanding that it was time for the student to surpass his master. Fortunately, Callos had just the solution that would enable BJ to continue to grow as a jiu-jitsu player—and beyond, should he desire it.

When Tom Callos's Taekwondo instructor, Ernie Reyes Sr., was having his fiftieth birthday party, Callos was invited to attend in California. Callos hatched the scheme to bring BJ because Ralph Gracie's BJJ school was just down the street. Jay Dee agreed to send BJ on his first-ever plane trip with Callos in order to meet Ralph Gracie at his Mountain View academy.

"BJ brought his girlfriend, and BJ and I didn't have a lot in common other than training. He was 17, and I was 37, so I was like a father or something," said Callos. "I think I have a son his age, so [to him it] was like going somewhere with his dad, so he took his girlfriend as a buffer."

BJ's arrogance was such that he actually believed he would tap black belt Ralph Gracie out, return to Hilo, and that would be the end of his jiu-jitsu diaries. BJ recalls telling an older woman sitting next to him on the flight that he believed he'd found what he was going to do for the rest of his life.

While the idea of BJ schooling Ralph was absolutely ridiculous, in his defense, he had been visiting different academies in Hawaii—including that of an ill-fated judo instructor whom BJ had easily tapped out, much to the chagrin of Callos, who had tried to teach BJ to respect the instructor wherever he trained.

The pair headed to Ralph's academy to work out. Penn recalled rolling with two of Ralph's then-blue belts, Kevin Graham and Dave Camarillo. They had been tasked with humbling BJ, yet BJ's guard held firm, as he had more experience and innate ability than Ralph's students realized. Ralph approached from the sidelines and dummied Penn, easily controlling him—an act that perhaps instilled something important in BJ that his losses in MMA would later confirm—the realization that BJ didn't know it all.

Ralph saw potential in BJ and told him to return to his school, because he could excel at jiu-jitsu. However, once BJ was back in his comfort zone of Hawaii, he withered from the same lack of direction that had afflicted his entire young life.

"At the time, I was just working odd jobs here and there," said BJ, "working for my parents' employment agency, just got out of high school, working landscaping."

Jay Dee warned BJ that if he didn't make the decision to return to school or do something meaningful, he'd send him back to California to train with Ralph Gracie. BJ didn't take his father seriously, and four months passed like nothing. Jay Dee held firm, and BJ was sent off.

BJ rented a small studio apartment near Ralph Gracie's school. The fact that Penn had no friends to party with meant that he was forced to dedicate himself to BJJ at a new level.

Said BJ, "I would just walk to the gym, and walk back every day."

BJ excelled at Ralph's, quickly earning his purple belt, winning many tournaments and even participating in an underground MMA bout in 1997 against a kickboxer, which he won via rear naked choke.[58]

There was still a question of the next step for BJ in integrating his passion for jiu-jitsu and some sort of career. Logically, professional MMA was an avenue that BJ could take—but there was trouble brewing between Ralph and BJ that would have to be addressed first.

Nova União was revered in Brazilian Jiu-Jitsu circles as being an incredibly hard team to join. Founded by BJJ black belts Wendell Alexander and Andre "Dede" Pederneiras, its main gym was located on the top floor of the Upper Sport Club in the Flamengo district of Rio de Janeiro, Brazil. When BJ Penn walked into that building in 2000, he described it as old—built around the 1960s—with a dark, steep staircase.

In later years, the Upper Sport Club was transformed into an all-the-bells-and-whistles athletic club, boasting top-notch facilities including weight rooms, fitness classes, a physiotherapy office and everything else you'd expect from a high-end gym. In the month of December, the sexy front-desk girls are outfitted with Santa hats that add festive flair to their look.

The spirit of the fight gym lives on the third floor, where a modest room holds a boxing ring and matted area. Even traditional martial arts classes are run at the Nova União club—but the cock-of-the-walk MMA fighters hold court at their own appointed time.

"My team trains hard more now than ever," said coach Andre Pederneiras, "because most of the guys come from poor families."

Rather than succumb to the lack of opportunity, crime, negative influences and general apathy toward the have-nots, the few who had escaped the *favelas* (the shantytown slums, usually located on the hill-sides of Rio de Janeiro) came to Nova União in order to build something better for themselves. The best example of the team's success was UFC featherweight champion Jose Aldo, a fighter who had broken through against the odds, going from unknown to being ranked among MMA's pound-for-pound best.

On a day in December 2010, this writer witnessed Jose Aldo training at Nova União. Aldo had been prohibited from sparring or doing any kind of training by doctors, due to pain in his C5 and C6 neck vertebrae sustained in the Mike Brown fight. After the Brown fight, Aldo had pushed himself through his next two fights even as he felt a tingling sensation down his arms[59] (a symptom of spinal injury), but was now forced to take the time to rehabilitate and recover. It was, however, impossible to keep him away from the gym, where he engaged in playful light sparring with his elite teammates, from Sengoku and Pancrase champion Marlon Sandro to UFC featherweight contender Diego Nunes.

With his unshaven face and fiery intensity, Nunes resembled a rein-carnated version of boxing legend Roberto Duran, snapping high kicks rather than body punches. In the training session, Nunes was taken down and had his back taken. He was upset at himself for this, with his teammates adding insult to injury by taking photos of him while he was being choked out for a laugh. After practice, Nunes sulked, his head down, pretending to be occupied with a damaged hand. Andre Pederneiras did his best to cheer Nunes up, but there was no consoling him.

"All the guys train hard, everyday," said Pederneiras of the intense session, "and nobody got an injury."

The first part of his statement was true; the second part was covering up for an incident that occurred with Marlon Sandro in sparring. It appeared that Sandro's knee was damaged; he dropped to the floor in pain before collecting himself and continuing to spar against fresh partners until the end of the training session. Two weeks later, he would drop a lopsided decision to Hatsu Hioki in Japan, losing his Sengoku featherweight title. Did the knee somehow play a part in Sandro's loss to Hioki? Injuries were common in all MMA fighters going into fights, so much so that they were considered a part of the game that had to be dealt with. Some critical fans speculated that Aldo had faked his injury in order to duck various contenders.

"Aldo go to the United States right now, and go to the doctor, and everybody see his injury and the scan," said a bewildered Pederneiras of the accusations. "It doesn't matter what people think."

Keeping Jose Aldo away from the gym had meant standing up to him, as Aldo loved to train every day, three times a day. Aldo's physician had no idea that Aldo was still in the gym instead of stretched out on the couch watching *Rede Globo*.

Something unique to Nova União was the presence of mostly smaller guys on the team. "Everyday, there's more guys that come to my school. Never the bigger guys, I never know why," said Pederneiras.

Although there were constantly many fighters from other gyms who wanted to jump ship to Nova União, Pederneiras had his own philosophy about how to manage his team.

"I prefer to make the guy in my school," said Pederneiras. "Come from the white belt to black belt and train whole life in my school."

His reasoning had to do with loyalty—difficult to coax out of many prima donna personalities in MMA. So prevalent was disloyalty that Carlson Gracie adopted the term *creonte,* from the name of a Brazilian soap opera star who constantly shifted allegiances, to describe teammates who left for competing schools.[60]

Penn could be labeled a creonte by Ralph Gracie, as BJ's repeated dalliances with Nova União in the late '90s infuriated Ralph.

"I trained BJ Penn, jiu-jitsu training," said Pederneiras of the frequent visits from Penn over the years, with many visits lasting for three to four months. Pederneiras seemed fond of BJ, describing him as a nice guy in the gym who was liked by all his training partners at Nova União.

As a US-based fighter, Penn wasn't bound by the condition that a Nova União member be exclusive to the team, headquartered in Rio de Janeiro.

BJ had fond memories of his first trip to Brazil, as he had never been outside of Hawaii and California before taking a trip down for a BJJ tournament, the *Brasileiro.*

"When I first flew over to Brazil, I had no idea what to expect," said Penn. "I remember [thinking] when I was sleeping, 'Oh man this flight's long.' I remember waking up and looking out the window and just seeing a bunch of boats; I was like, 'It's like a big world here too!' "

In 1999, Penn broke away from Ralph Gracie for good. Ralph never accepted BJ's reasons for training with Nova União.

"He's a traitor motherfucker," Ralph told a documentary crew following Renzo Gracie. "I opened my doors. Didn't hold back anything. I used to trust in him."[61]

Penn corroborated Ralph's version of events.

"Ralph's disappointed in me and stuff, you know what? I can see why," said Penn. "He would take the time to help me, he would always be trying to improve my game. It's not like I was just another guy training there and he doesn't care . . . he did put a lot of time into it."

After two years at Ralph's, BJ was tired and homesick. The split wasn't amicable by any means, but Penn now had a group of experienced black belts in Nova União to guide him forward. Furthermore, Nova União would cater to BJ's needs, rather than viewing him with the eyes of a jealous partner when he mingled with others.

Renato "Charuto" Verissimo, one of the top black belts under Pederneiras, had gone to Hawaii to train BJ on a more permanent basis.

In 2000, shortly after receiving his black belt from Pederneiras, BJ would take first place at the World Jiu-Jitsu championship in Rio. The first non-Brazilian to do so, BJ had demonstrated that the holy grail of BJJ could be claimed by anyone, regardless of lineage. The next comparable event was American Eddie Bravo's submission win via triangle choke over Royler Gracie at the 2003 Abu Dhabi World Submission Wrestling championships—another indicator that Americans could dominate elite Brazilians in competition.

Brazilian Jiu-Jitsu wasn't enough for BJ. He did some wrestling at West Valley junior college, competing on two occasions. BJ also approached former kickboxer Javier Mendez, who ran American Kickboxing Academy. "Crazy" Bob Cook was an MMA coach at AKA and student of former UFC middleweight champion Frank Shamrock. Together, Mendez and Cook began to furnish BJ with the tools he'd need to excel at MMA.

"Javier Mendez has done a lot for me over the years," said Penn. "He inspired me to do [MMA]; he'd always be like, 'Man, you can punch hard!' . . . 'You should fight in the UFC.' "

BJ made his MMA debut as a professional in the UFC rather than having fights in a smaller organization. This was not a big deal, as the UFC was far from the Behemoth it would become in later years.

"They were just struggling," said BJ of the UFC's financial difficulties. "I guess you would picture it no different as if someone you knew owned a local promotion."

"[MMA fighter] John Lewis basically pulled some strings, and gave me his spot," said BJ of how he got into the UFC, after Lewis had had his jaw broken by Jens Pulver in 15 seconds at UFC 28.

UFC matchmaker Joe Silva had heard the glowing endorsement of BJ from former UFC middleweight (200 pounds and under) champion Frank Shamrock. Silva believed in "The Prodigy," even though BJ had had no sanctioned MMA bouts, and bought into the hype wholeheartedly.

On May 4, 2001, at UFC 31, BJ stopped Joey Gilbert (then 1-1) in the first round, winning his first pro fight and earning $3000 ($1500 to fight; $1500 to win) in the process; Gilbert earned $2000, having failed to earn a $2000 win bonus. BJ did not have to lose any weight to make the 155-pound limit for this fight.

"I remember the first time I fought in the UFC, I never had to cut any weight. I remember 'I just won't eat the day of the weigh-ins,' " said Penn.

He followed his successful debut with first-round knockouts of Din Thomas (2:42) and Caol Uno (0:11); the amazing prowess of the "superkid" seemed to have no limits. Penn was then slated to meet UFC lightweight champion Jens Pulver at UFC 35.

Going into the fight, the consensus was that BJ would crush Jens Pulver.

"Everybody was saying I wasn't going to win," said Pulver. "I was going to get destroyed…I was going to get decimated. I wasn't going to make it a round."[62]

Jens Pulver proved his heart in defending his UFC lightweight title, winning a majority decision against the highly-touted Hawaiian. Pulver then vacated the UFC title, leaving the organization over a contract dispute (a nice way of saying the Fertittas wouldn't offer him what he perceived as a fair salary) in 2002.[63]

As for BJ, he later revealed in a 2012 interview with Sherdog.com that had he beaten Pulver, he would have retired, as he would have accomplished his twin goals of a World Jiu-Jitsu championship and a UFC championship.

"I was just trying to avenge the loss my whole life," said BJ of the Pulver loss, "still to today, that night, just trying to avenge that night."

It isn't really believable that BJ would have hung the gloves up. He'd had other losses in his past—in street fights, jiu-jitsu competition—and when a new lightweight came along that the world paid attention to, he could have been drawn out of pseudo-retirement in a millisecond.

Rather than rededicate himself to training at American Kickboxing Academy—a world-class facility that would continue to churn out champions and contenders well into the future—BJ left the team to do his own thing.

"I think he wanted to be a little more comfortable," said AKA teammate Frank Shamrock. "I'm not sure if he was ready for the big spotlight."

BJ Penn returned to Hilo, and sought out local trainers and fighters to cobble together a camp. He had his brothers, Nova União black belt Charuto Verissimo, a boxing trainer named Adrian Silva and MMA fighter Wesley "Cabbage" Correira, among others. AKA trainer Bob Cook would still corner BJ for his fights, but BJ's Hilo setup would always be a sticking point with pundits and fans who thought he should have maintained permanent residence at a more serious camp where he would have been challenged on a regular basis by other A-level fighters.

BJ bounced back with an easy win over 3-0 Paul Creighton, retiring Creighton from MMA competition permanently. The UFC's plan for the now-vacant lightweight belt was a four-man tournament between BJ Penn, Matt Serra, Caol Uno and Din Thomas to crown the new champion. Penn won a decision over Serra, and Uno beat Thomas (also via decision), with the winners—Penn and Uno—to fight at UFC 41.

BJ's trainer at AKA, Bob Cook, had told UFC president Dana White that one of his other charges, Sean Sherk, could beat BJ. After Dana White told Penn this, BJ responded by severing ties to Bob Cook and (further) retreating to Hawaii.

Former kickboxer and Hilo local Rudy Valentino became one of Penn's main stand-up coaches. Valentino had been a professional surfer and had experience in a number of martial arts styles. He hailed from the time when many traditional martial artists in kickboxing didn't even know to keep their hands up.[64]

At UFC 41, held on February 28, 2003, the fight between Uno and Penn was declared a split draw (48-47, 47-48, 48-48). The general consensus from viewers was that BJ won a close but clear decision over Uno. Even Zuffa CEO Lorenzo Fertitta thought BJ was the winner, telling him after the fight, "You're the champion." But despite all BJ's time, trouble and investment in his career, the 155-pound championship was dissolved, leaving Penn high and dry.

BJ's brother JD Penn had formed "Rumble on the Rock," a Hawaii-based promotion. ROTR turned out to be the perfect venue for BJ to fight in while the UFC dawdled over finding BJ a fight. Former Shooto 154-pound champion, Japanese fighter Takanori Gomi (then 14-1), was chosen to face Penn. The fight was even endorsed by UFC president Dana White, who attended the Honolulu show. In a way, the UFC's open acceptance of Penn fighting outside the UFC (as long as BJ fulfilled the rest of his UFC contract) would pave the way for a maelstrom later on.

At ROTR 4 held on October 10, 2003, BJ faced Takanori Gomi in the main event. The fight showcased BJ's dominance from the get-go: BJ took Gomi down to the canvas within seconds of the start, mounted him and took his back. The fierce toe-to-toe exchanges of the second round brought the kind of intensity BJ craved from the fight game. The third round saw BJ close the show with a rear naked choke.

Takanori Gomi would not retire from the fight game or wallow in the margins like so many other beaten fighters do. Rather, he went on to win the PRIDE lightweight (73 kilograms or 161 pounds) title in 2005.

As there was no title at lightweight in the UFC, Penn accepted a fight with UFC welterweight champion Matt Hughes. Hughes was 35-3 and riding a 13-fight win streak going into the Penn fight at UFC 46 on January 31, 2004—conventional wisdom dictated that there was no way Hughes would lose to someone who had never fought at 170 pounds before. BJ took no heed of this, submitting Hughes via rear naked choke in the first round.

A contract dispute with the UFC saw Penn move to other organizations like K-1 and ROTR where he notched wins against Duane Ludwig, Rodrigo Grace and Renzo Gracie. BJ's only loss during this time period was a close fight dropped to future UFC light-heavyweight champion Lyoto Machida at heavyweight (Penn weighed in at 191 pounds; Machida was 225 pounds).

"I knew [Lyoto] was real good, but a fight got put together because I think Lyoto was trying to come to K-1 to have me and I was already a world champion," said Penn.

When Lyoto was unwilling to cut weight, BJ responded that he didn't care, and accepted the match despite the handicap.

BJ returned to the UFC against Georges St-Pierre at "UFC 58: USA vs. Canada" in March 2006. The irony behind the UFC marketing the fight as Americans vs. Canadians was the fact that Georges St-Pierre believed that his French-speaking province of Quebec should separate from Canada. St-Pierre had a fleur-de-lis (a white lily that is an official symbol of Quebec) tattooed onto his right calf.[65] In the ensuing years, any mention of political beliefs or inclinations was airbrushed out of St-Pierre's vocabulary, but the tattoo of a fleur-de-lis remains a prominent symbol in the tapestry of the real Georges St-Pierre.

BJ Penn came incredibly close to stopping St-Pierre's momentous rise to the top in their fight at UFC 58—breaking Georges's nose and badly damaging his right eye in the first round. During the next two rounds, St-Pierre used takedowns to sway the judges into awarding him the fight via split decision.

With the win over BJ, St-Pierre earned a title shot against UFC welterweight champion Matt Hughes. When St-Pierre became injured and was unable to face Hughes, BJ Penn stepped in as a replacement and faced Hughes at UFC 63.

BJ looked to be on his way to a second victory over Hughes when an injury late in round two changed the course of the fight.

"I did end up breaking my rib," revealed BJ. "Hughes fought a great fight and he's the champ, he won the fight, my rib broke and that's what happened."

From there, the resurrection of the UFC lightweight division at UFC 58 (the last 155-pound fight in the UFC had occurred at UFC 49 in 2004) ushered in Penn's brief golden age. A stint coaching the fifth season of *The Ultimate Fighter* opposite Penn's old nemesis Jens Pulver was capped with a second round submission win over Pulver. In victory, Penn reached over and hugged a disconsolate Pulver. Their feud was over, but the desire to continue competing was alive and kicking inside of Penn.

The new UFC lightweight champion, Sean Sherk, had been stripped of his title by the UFC due to a positive steroid test after his first defense against Brazilian Hermes Franca. BJ fought for the now-vacated UFC lightweight title, winning with a second-round rear naked choke over a blood-covered Joe Stevenson on January 19, 2008, at UFC 80. The finish over Stevenson was the first ever win inside the distance in a UFC lightweight title bout. At UFC 84, Penn defended his belt with a stunning TKO over Sean Sherk in the third round, eliminating any doubt over who the undisputed lightweight champion was.

Beyond any shadow of a doubt, Penn had answered the critics and demonstrated where he belonged—at the top of an extremely talented heap of 155ers.

11

FIRE AND ICE

BJ was reigning as the UFC's lightweight champion when he chose to step up and face St-Pierre at UFC 94 on January 31, 2009. He could have coasted on easier defenses at his natural weight of 155 pounds, but going up seemed to be a good way to make history: if he won, he would be the first UFC champion to hold two belts at the same time.

Hearing Georges St-Pierre speak about the upcoming match revealed a calculating mental game. He knew that Penn liked to rattle his opponents and adamantly refused to show any weakness by responding to BJ's tactics. "I hear a lot of BJ Penn comments saying that he wants to kill me and stuff like that. It seems to me like BJ Penn is fight with his fear. Fight from his fear and from his anger. I fight from my heart."

In the *UFC Primetime* television show produced by UFC parent company Zuffa and aired on Spike TV to help promote the fight, Penn seemed to think it was his mission to antagonize St-Pierre. His talk, combined with the sensationalist editing of his statements made BJ seem like a lazy, dishonest, arrogant jerk.

The first episode of the three-part series contained a now infamous message for St-Pierre from BJ Penn: "Georges, I'm going to go to the

death. I'm going to try to kill you—and I'm not joking about this."
In the second installment of the series, Penn zeroed in on GSP's loss
to Serra as further proof that his opponent was mentally weak, Penn
saying, "If you tap from strikes, you're a little bitch." The final episode
had BJ targeting St-Pierre's head trainer, Firas Zahabi, with a low blow,
"Firas, after the fight, I want you to go to your bedroom, take your
shoes off, lie down on your bed…take about 20 to 30 minutes—and
go fuck yourself!"

Penn was a simmering cauldron of rage. While anger is often
linked to aggression and fighting, when it came to mixed martial arts,
other factors play pivotal roles in the final outcome: namely, the skill
set that a fighter can utilize and the maximization of those abilities
through proper preparation. Anger can't help you if you're too fatigued
to mount an offense with strikes or submission attempts. Since BJ had
legendary skills when it came to his striking and ground game, the first
and foremost question in everyone's mind was whether Penn would
show up conditioned so that he could execute his game plan later into
the fight.

"I've been training real hard. I've never trained so hard in my life,"
Penn claimed to this writer in a telephone conversation, just a few days
before the fight.

Sweating during intense conditioning drills and training sessions
is one thing. Making sure the recipe for a camp is perfect takes fine-
tuning by experienced coaches. Penn lacked that oversight, as he ran
his camp his own way.

Georges St-Pierre was preparing in Montreal with UFC title-holders and challengers as his sparring partners—guys who were instructed
to try to dent St-Pierre in sparring and not to hold anything back. Penn
had no stars or big names; it was thought that BJ surrounded himself
with too many "yes-men."

Penn himself confirmed that he had the stove on but hadn't dialed
up to the highest setting: "I've been working out with my coaches,
and not really big-name training partners. But a lot of good, great,
awesome guys."

Former Chute Boxe trainer Sergio Cunha had been working well with Penn for months in advance of the GSP fight. But Cunha's style, methods and experience were ignored in favor of a different approach in the final weeks of the camp.

"I think they did everything wrong," said Cunha. "We trained so hard six months; was going great. Two months before the fight, when we should just adjust and prepare our game plan and prepare our schedule, I meet with [BJ] and his brother to talk about make a nice camp. They just did everything different, and the way they did things doesn't work."

Penn had flown in brothers Joey and Jake Clark, a pair of standout wrestlers from Minnesota. The decision was made to use the Clark brothers to spar pure boxing, rather than utilizing them for sparring involving takedowns and other wrestling moves—this when St-Pierre was legendary for his superior wrestling ability.

"We had other good guys for striking. When it came time for those guys to come in the cage and do sparring, they had those guys take him down," recalled a bewildered Cunha. "It don't make sense: take the wrestler to strikes, and take the striker to wrestle."

Perhaps this was an exercise in building up BJ's confidence, but it was not the only problem with his training camp.

Conditioning was shit—shit! Crap conditioning, you know? Wasn't conditioning," said a visibly angered Cunha. "Was something stupid. Not plyometrics; not circuit; was bullshit, wasting time, I don't believe it."

BJ compared his upcoming match to a recent fight where Mark Coleman had nearly beaten Brazilian Maurício "Shogun" Rua at UFC 93, several weeks earlier.

"Let's just use a quote Mark Coleman said [to Maurício Rua] the other night, 'I respect you but I can beat you.' And there it is," said BJ.

Mark Coleman's statement had come after a third round stoppage loss to Shogun Rua. Shogun looked terrible, repeatedly getting tagged and taken down, gasping for air just minutes into the fight. It was noble that an aging Coleman had put up such a valiant effort, but this wasn't the model for Penn to emulate if he wanted to take out a danger-ous welterweight like St-Pierre.

***

For Penn and St-Pierre, the reality of their impending match at UFC 94 was both excitement and fear. As the hours before the fight counted down, they sweated over minor details, trying to push away negative thoughts and stress just so they could make it to the venue.

They had been told their opponent was strong, had great stand-up and formidable jiu-jitsu. They had each viewed highlight reels of the devastation wrought firsthand by those who stepped into the cage with the man they were about to do the same with. And most of all, they both had memories of their original encounter—a fight that Penn lost, but which also sent GSP to the hospital that night. Here it was coming around again—the chance for redemption as all eyes would be watching in one of the most anticipated pay-per-views since UFC heavyweight champion Randy Couture faced WWE sensation Brock Lesnar in November 2008.

If either fighter was anxious, they tried to work it off with move-ment during the fight introductions by Bruce Buffer. After BJ and GSP politely tapped gloves, referee Herb Dean separated the fighters to be-gin the contest.

"Let's do it!" the referee shouted, his words transforming the ten-sion into excitement as the action got underway.

From standing position, both fighters immediately clinched, ex-changing knee strikes as St-Pierre pushed Penn against the cage. Going for a single-leg takedown, Penn's balance made taking BJ to the mat very difficult. As they broke apart and returned to a stand-up battle in the center of the octagon, the commentators reflected on the transfor-mation of the sport.

"It's so crazy how far this sport has come since you and I [have] been involved in it, Mike," said Joe Rogan (famous for his roles on *NewsRadio* and *Fear Factor*) to his co-commentator, Mike Goldberg.

"Back in the old days, when we were in these little tiny arenas, and there was no one in the crowd, would you have ever imagined this?" asked Rogan, surveying the crowd of nearly 15,000 screaming fans.

St-Pierre threw a double jab, followed by a leg kick—all of which missed. The audience reaction could often be an accurate barometer of what was going on in the cage: North American viewers were becoming surprisingly adept in registering the slightest change in momentum, even gaining understanding of the ground game and cheering when a grounded fighter would re-establish his "guard." As the first stanza came to a close, it wasn't clear that either man had much of an edge. GSP had failed to take Penn down, with nothing significant being landed on the feet.

During the rest after the first round, St-Pierre's trainer and assistant helped plant the seeds of the controversy that was to follow the fight for weeks. As St-Pierre's coach Greg Jackson told him to calm his breathing, his Muay Thai trainer, Phil Nurse, applied Vaseline to Georges's face. Vaseline on the face is intended to prevent chafing of the skin that can lead to cuts—a fight stopped on cuts, after all, doesn't truly decide the better fighter. Right after his application to St-Pierre's face, Nurse rubbed the shoulders of the fighter, and then applied pressure to GSP's chest and back with each hand.

Round two saw Georges getting tagged with a left, and again he muscled Penn to the cage where he softened him up with close-range strikes before succeeding in taking BJ down. On the ground, Penn established rubber guard while St-Pierre did a little ground-and-pound. As Penn's legs slid down St-Pierre's back, Georges postured up and stood up—managing to go from half-guard to side control. If Penn could not manage to sweep or otherwise extricate himself from this position, he would lose this round to a steady attrition of strikes for which he could not answer with any offense of his own. With 1:56 left in the round, BJ managed to get back into guard, where St-Pierre was content to continue to rain down the strikes until he passed Penn's guard again with just under a minute remaining. Even as Penn used a "jailbreak" to regain guard, the punches kept coming. As the final horn sounded to end the round, St-Pierre walked back to his corner while Penn slowly rolled up from the ground.

After the fight—during a meeting with the Nevada State Athletic Commission—Penn would claim he had suffered a concussion during the second round. Whether or not this explains how the tide had swiftly turned in St-Pierre's favor, the next significant development in the now-building case against GSP, in what would later be dubbed "Grease-Gate," came as a red-jacketed official entered the octagon to caution St-Pierre's corner against rubbing his back; the official then grabbed a towel and tried to remove any lingering Vaseline that may have been smeared on GSP's body.

Georges would later credit his win to an attrition of BJ's shoulders that left Penn unable to utilize his boxing during the rest of the fight. It's a hallmark of St-Pierre's persona to point to a specific strategy devised beforehand as the reason he won—it made him feel as if he had outwitted rather than overpowered his opponent. St-Pierre enjoyed a 20-pound weight advantage that had helped him muscle around the smaller man, but this fact discredits the win; after all, BJ had beaten Matt Hughes at welterweight and taken a top-tier light-heavyweight in Lyoto Machida to a close decision loss in 2005.

The pattern for the rest of the fight saw Penn being taken down and pummeled on the ground. He absorbed a tremendous amount of punishment that would have had a lesser fighter quitting mentally. It was only his pride that allowed him to hang in there and focus merely on surviving.

In the fourth round, as St-Pierre dominated Penn with strikes on the ground, referee Herb Dean issued a stern warning, "BJ, you need to do something. You need to fight back." A stoppage could have followed, but the referee gave BJ the benefit of the doubt and chose to let him finish the round.

A look at Penn's body language at the break revealed only resignation. Penn's corner man, Jason Parillo, informed the doctor that they no longer wished to continue. Seconds later, a jubilant St-Pierre walked across the octagon to wish BJ well. Still disoriented from losing the fight, Penn was inconsolable and hardly acknowledged his opponent's gesture of goodwill.

The accolades came quickly—later that night, Georges was interviewed on ESPN.com's web show *MMA Live*, his UFC championship belt proudly displayed. A glowing Kenny Florian, the number one UFC contender to face Penn at lightweight and co-host of *MMA Live*, admired St-Pierre's skill in dispatching BJ. There was a sense of euphoria in the air for everyone who had supported Georges.

The outcome was crystal clear: St-Pierre had proved that he was the better man.

As much as the win should have been held up and cherished as the pinnacle moment of GSP's career, all hell was about to break loose: Penn's camp unleashed accusations that St-Pierre had cheated, throwing doubt over Georges's entire career. Four of Georges's former opponents—Matt Hughes, Matt Serra, Jason Miller and Sean Sherk—immediately chimed in to make (or repeat) statements that St-Pierre felt greasy or slippery in their fights against him.

Matt Hughes, who has an extensive MMA record, told this writer that Georges's skin felt normal in their first fight (won by Hughes), but that St-Pierre felt greasy in their second and third encounters (both won by St-Pierre).

Jason Miller's complaint against St-Pierre pre-dated the BJ Penn fight by a year, as he wrote about their UFC 52 bout for an article on cheating in MMA for the April 2008 issue of *FIGHT! Magazine*:

> **After a few more stiff elbows to my grillpiece, I felt the familiar slick I would get every day at kickboxing practice on my nose and eyes. My opponent, now up two rounds, was coated in Vaseline! Greasy bastard, I thought. I yelled to the ref, 'Hey! He is greased up!' But much like anyone else watching me get pounded, he didn't give a damn. This was followed by me taking another smash to the face. Yeah, ok for him, but I'm taking a beating over here and can't hold onto the bastard.[66]**

After his loss to St-Pierre at UFC 56, Sean Sherk was explicit in both praising Georges's wrestling ability, but also talking about how slippery St-Pierre was.

"He definitely had a great sprawl, there's no doubt about that," said Sherk in a post-fight interview. "He was—very, very slippery. He must have had some oil on him or something, but, I couldn't grab him for nothing."[67]

Jon Fitch said that all his opponents felt greasy, and that if greasing had occurred in his 2008 bout with St-Pierre, it wasn't decisive in Georges winning. This attitude may not have been palatable for BJ in his loss, but the lack of consequences levied by the Nevada State Athletic Commission was even more disappointing.

Now it wasn't merely a battle confined to the octagon, but a free-for-all, waged by public opinion, that would eventually change the way every fight in Nevada and other jurisdictions would be handled forever, as opponents would have their skin checked for grease before entering the octagon.

To this day, we don't know definitively whether St-Pierre had chiseled out an unfair advantage in many of his fights. Did Georges cheat due to some insecurity or fear of losing, or was Vaseline accidentally transferred from his face onto other portions of his body during the course of a fight?

St-Pierre, under more scrutiny than ever after the second BJ Penn fight, went on to perform well against opponents Thiago Alves, Dan Hardy, Josh Koscheck, Jake Shields and Carlos Condit, beating all via decision. The greasing scandal didn't seem to affect St-Pierre's ability as a dominant fighter.

For BJ, the second GSP fight was soul destroying. BJ had lost his confidence, and the loss to St-Pierre would haunt him forever.

12

MARV MARINOVICH

After the Georges St-Pierre fight, BJ's trainer Rudy Valentino stated that had Penn won against GSP, BJ would have retired.[68] It didn't take long for BJ's competitive fire to reignite. Realistically, BJ still had the 155-pound title to defend, was still a draw to the UFC and could still perform at the highest level.

Even the fight against Georges wasn't terrible—how many times had Penn avoided being taken down in the first round when he was fresh? Had Georges really been decisive on the feet? Was BJ ever in danger of being submitted? Could BJ have lasted for a decision loss had his corner not stopped the fight? How had the alleged greasing changed the dynamics of the fight?

The decision to make a change to BJ's Hilo-based training camp had been forced by circumstances. JD Penn began to audition for a new conditioning trainer after the loss, meeting the Marinovich brothers—Marv and Gary—in San Diego. Marv was a former NFL player who had extensive experience training athletes for improved performance.

Mired in controversy over the regimented upbringing that Marv forced his son Todd to endure en route to football glory, and that came to a head as Todd floundered in the NFL and suffered the ravages of drug addiction, Marv and Gary Marinovich were obsessive-compulsive when it came to training.

"The idea that you've got to win everything, never come in second. I maybe went too far with that," reflected Marv when speaking about his son Todd to *ESPN: The Magazine*'s Frank W. Ockenfels in 2010.[69]

At a San Diego tryout, Marv ran BJ through a quick workout and put him through some conditioning exercises. Marinovich's specialty was a reflex-based program in a pool consisting of hand-tapping and standing on one foot. Feeling off-balance and silly, BJ did not take to the program—at least, not at first. Back in Hawaii, two days later during a grappling session, BJ made two moves that he hadn't tried in years. Crediting the water workout, Penn told his brother JD to call the Marinovich brothers and hire them for the gig as his conditioning coaches.

The secret to breaking down Marv's unique methods lies within his own experiences as a football player. In his heyday, he was a weight-room fanatic, lifting huge weights for low repetitions. Plagued by injuries, he began to study Eastern Bloc training methods. Rather than focus on strength, Marinovich focused on developing speed and flexibility.

BJ became enamored with Marv, writing, "What Marv has taught me is so valuable, I don't even want to say it on the public message board," during a question and answer session on the BJPenn.com forums.[70]

The training that Marv put BJ through involved water workouts, rowing, sprints, weight exercises and other innovative methods. BJ believed that Marv's theories had helped him improve at takedowns and in being more explosive overall.

BJ also approached the "athlete vs. fighter" debate by explaining that his time still had to be devoted toward training in striking and grappling. All strength and conditioning coaches have to sell their systems to the athletes, as their workouts take away from sparring, hitting the bags and other fight-specific routines.

Wrote BJ, "When it comes to MMA, I am finally under the impression after 15 years of doing this stuff is that nothing can replace the real training (boxing, grappling, mma, sparring, bagwork) now the secret is using Marv's theories in those areas to make you better than everyone else."

One of BJ's favorite sports figures is Muhammad Ali. Penn points out how "The Greatest" never did any fancy workouts—just fighting and running. Other great pugilists like "Sugar" Ray Robinson or Mike Tyson were purported to have similar routines. Tyson always made sure that his training applied specifically to fighting in the three major areas of shadow-boxing, pad work and sparring (with a heavy preference for realistic sparring sessions that mimicked the conditions of fights themselves). Sport science can break down the pressure per square inch of strikes, and measure the VO2 maximum capacity of an athlete's lungs, but fighting is still fighting.

BJ related an often-repeated martial arts story that illustrated his point: "A student asked his karate instructor what workouts he can do to make himself better at karate while his teacher was gone. His student wanted to know what kind of cross training he could do…the master looked at him and said karate…the student was dumbfounded at first but then realized what the teacher was saying…the only way to get better at karate is by doing karate."

Is this the straight truth? Former football player Bob Sapp, whose only assets were size and strength, had a great run in K-1 and MMA—stopping legend Ernesto Hoost twice in kickboxing, and dominating Antônio Rodrigo Nogueira for one round before being submitted in the second round in just his third MMA fight in PRIDE. So strength and power can be great equalizers, especially in combat sports—even at the highest levels of MMA, where athletes can utilize strength in a variety of ways.

Championship bouts in the UFC consisted of five five-minute rounds, each round requiring anaerobic conditioning. Sprints are the ideal training for MMA—going all out in a limited amount of time. Yet old-school boxing trainers have always sworn by long-distance roadwork, which is aerobic in nature. BJ takes an interesting stance considering he had the advantage of proven scientific data in choosing to run long distances of three to five miles for conditioning.

Wrote BJ, "Running for a distance is the best way to build your aerobic capacity without breaking your body down too much…you only have so much energy in a day, week or year and you have to use it wisely."

This philosophy was one of many areas where Marv Marinovich would diverge from Penn's ideals. In preparation for BJ's first fight against contender Frankie Edgar, Marinovich had BJ doing a set of sprints that lasted 25 minutes, replicating the duration of a UFC title fight. When Penn hit a wall of exhaustion and Marv urged him to push on through, BJ remarked that had he not respected Marv so much, he might have quit were it another trainer making those demands on him.

In the camp before BJ's title defense against opponent Frankie Edgar, to be held in April 2010 at UFC 112, there seemed to be a series of rifts between Marinovich and BJ's other coaches. Boxing coach Jason Parillo always wanted BJ to devote his time to working his hands; wrestling coach Kenny Johnson always wanted BJ to work on wrestling—yet Marv was insistent on being the alpha male of the camp, the head coach, with BJ giving priority to Marinovich's workouts in the morning when he was freshest.

Marv and his brother opted to abandon Penn's ship a month prior to the Edgar fight. Penn presented the reason for the Marinovich's departing his camp as standard procedure as they'd done previously for his title defenses against Kenny Florian and Diego Sanchez—yet curiously, BJ mentions wanting Marv to stay for the entire camp this time around.

Accounts from many sources point to Marv Marinovich having a temperamental personality. His relentless perfectionism and utter conviction in the superiority of his own ideas weren't compatible with BJ's other trainers. Perhaps Marv felt some blowback over his methods, and that's why he left BJ's camp, this time permanently.

In July 2009, a video of BJ making a vertical jump out of a three-foot-deep pool went viral, logging 4.5 million views.[71] In the same way that Bruce Lee's films had a visceral impact, the explosive plyometric feat by Penn made people believe that BJ had improved.

If BJ had stuck with Marv after the first Frankie Edgar fight, Penn might have become a different fighter, with more longevity. But BJ returned to his comfortable patterns sans Marv Marinovich for his fights following UFC 112.

13

DIEGO SANCHEZ VS. BJ PENN

The winner of the inaugural season of *The Ultimate Fighter* at middleweight, Diego Sanchez had always seemed to have a hard road. No matter what opportunities were available, or what he achieved, his gains were always offset by his flaky personality and a lack of judgment. Prey to all kinds of schemers and grifters, Diego would probably have been exploited no matter what career he sought for himself—but the more low-key his career, perhaps the less he'd have been seen as an easy target.

Blood sport, like boxing, was in Diego's Mexican cultural background. He described his childhood as "rough and tumble," doing Kenpo Karate at age nine, then transitioning to wrestling where he won a state title for Del Norte high school in New Mexico.

His start at Greg Jackson's famed gym was aided at 19 by his mother. "My mom paid for a couple months...and within two months, I already won two [submission grappling] tournaments."

A job unloading trucks for UPS covered his fees for the next ten months, and from there, Diego forged an impressive undefeated record of 11-0 before heading into *The Ultimate Fighter* in 2004. Sanchez bested Kenny Florian to take the *TUF* title, and with it, a "six-figure" UFC contract that consisted of several fights over the course of three years, that if won, would escalate fighter pay and combine to make (or exceed) $100,000 in the final year of the contract. Many prospects who would sign with the UFC without a stint on *TUF* were often grateful, as they often earned more money than the *TUF* contract would have locked them down for.[72]

Continual struggles with addiction dampened what could have been an impressive run at the welterweight title for Diego. A 2009 article for Sherdog.com describes how he always found enough rope to hang himself, as he had taken to excessive amounts of drinking.

"It definitely slowed me down," Diego told Sherdog.com, rationalizing that he could have won the UFC championship had he moderated himself.

The other major incident that held Diego's career back was his well-publicized split from Greg Jackson's camp in August 2007. Diego privately told Greg Jackson that he had a kid out in California that he wanted to be closer to. This being around the time of GSP's resurrection from the Serra loss, Georges St-Pierre had chosen Greg Jackson as his official head trainer; Diego knew they were both fighting at the same weight class of 170 pounds—so who would be the top dog at Greg Jackson's gym?

"GSP could have gone to any camp he wanted," Diego told MMAmania.com. "He knew that place was my home, my dream. That took a little something out of my heart. He's training in the cage that I bled in, that I sweat in and cried in."[73]

After dropping a split-decision to AKA stalwart Jon Fitch on September 22, 2007, the title fight Diego had envisioned was out of reach. Diego rebounded with two wins at welterweight before making a decision Greg Jackson had urged him to make earlier in dropping down to 155 pounds.

After winning two fights at lightweight, Diego was rewarded with a title shot against lightweight champion BJ Penn at UFC 107 on December 12, 2009.

Diego's entrance won the gong show with his self-affirmation of pumping his arms and shouting "YES!" to no one in particular, a mental technique he claimed he had learned from self-help guru and motivational speaker Tony Robbins.

Neither Tony Robbins's instruction nor Diego being the originator of the "Yes!" cartwheel (a cartwheel performed while screaming "Yes!") proved decisive in the outcome of the bout. The fight itself was a one-sided affair where Sanchez was dropped and nearly finished in the first round. Penn made hitting Diego appear as easy as punching a heavy bag as Diego repeatedly tried for a single-leg takedown in utter vain. A kick landed in round five opened up a massive cut on Diego; the fight was stopped at 2:37 with Penn having won the first four rounds.[74] The win could be considered the high-water mark of BJ's career.

Facial trauma, bumps and bruises aside, the psychological after-math of the Penn fight was brutal for Diego, and he relapsed into his pattern of substance abuse and heavy drinking.

"I took the wrong path. I took the path of partying, and I was just drinking away my sorrows," Diego had told MMAWeekly.com in a candid interview.[75]

Alcohol abuse wasn't the only problem—a business associate Diego had trusted to handle his financial affairs embezzled $175,000, leaving Sanchez high and dry.[76]

For BJ, the accolades that came for dominating and stopping Diego Sanchez had a negative effect on his future performances. With decisive victory, Penn had validated his current methods and style of training, requiring no changes whatsoever for his next defense against Frankie Edgar at UFC 112 in Abu Dhabi. Had Diego hurt BJ, it could have lit a fire for Penn to rededicate himself.

Without a doubt, BJ's decision to stand and bang with Frankie Edgar at UFC 112 was influenced by his dominant win over Diego Sanchez. The adrenaline from out-striking Diego on the feet was just too pure a drug to pass up; it seems like BJ had wanted to recapture that feeling by keeping the fight with Edgar standing rather than trying a different strategy on the ground. The end result was a controversial decision loss to Edgar at UFC 112, one handed down by judges paid for by the UFC, as there was no athletic commission in Abu Dhabi where the fight was hosted.

The consistency that fans craved from BJ was too much for him to provide, but he would still fade in and out of greatness in his fights to come.

14

WHY I FIGHT
BOOK CONTROVERSY

BJ Penn's autobiography, entitled *Why I Fight*, co-authored with Dave Weintraub, was a hard slice of reality for any fan who carried the delusion that UFC fighters had the right to free speech. Penn had been extremely careful in editing the manuscript—constantly reading it, revising it, removing many details while clearing up others.

The image painted of the Fertitta brothers and Dana White was neither biased, nor overtly critical. The retelling of the essence of Penn's business interactions with the UFC told it's own truth:

> **In the beginning, you had the feeling these guys [Lorenzo Fertitta and Dana White] were on your side—at least until you started really negotiating and asking for things. I honestly believe they started with the intention of taking care of fighters, but in the long run it turned out to just be business for these guys. To them, every fighter is expendable.**[77]

Penn had no choice but to explain his reasons for leaving the UFC after capturing the title from Matt Hughes in January 2004. Although he was now the UFC welterweight champion—his first major title in MMA—Penn chose to fight under Japanese promotion K-1. In his view, it came down to a number of reasons, including the UFC's inability to find him opponents, the elimination of the UFC's lightweight division and—most importantly— the miserly pay offered by the UFC.

After Penn's impressive finish of Matt Hughes, he got an offer from Mak Takano, a representative of Japanese fight promotion K-1, for $187,500. An innocent conversation with UFC color commentator Joe Rogan at Las Vegas's McCarran Airport, where Penn mentioned in passing that he might go to K-1, was reported back to UFC president Dana White. Like a psychotic ex-girlfriend, White left expletive-filled messages on Penn's voicemail that collected during BJ's flight home. Penn gave the UFC credit in suggesting that his fights in K-1 might cost the UFC its reputation if Penn were to lose, thus diminishing the UFC brand—but there were more sinister reasons why Zuffa reacted the way it did.

The real explanation omitted by Penn's narrative was too painful to openly admit to—that the UFC viewed him as their "property," and by fielding competing offers, he was acting outside of the perceived nature of an object.

BJ's UFC contract for his title fight with Matt Hughes had paid out $25,000 to fight and $25,000 to win. Beating Hughes should have given Penn more leverage going into negotiations, but the highest Dana White was willing to go in terms of base pay was $30,000 per fight.

"The company always increased the payout by increments, not by big jumps," Penn noted.[78]

When you thought about it, what Zuffa was doing was just smart business when viewed from their end. Moving pay in small increments kept the talent in check, maximized profits and eased the way to get further concessions from fighters in the future. In 2009, Zuffa began taxing sponsors that fighters brought into the UFC octagon; 2011 saw this policy extended to sponsors of Zuffa fighters in Strikeforce. This policy created a barrier that was a hindrance to fighters, but allowed Zuffa to extract money on a sliding scale from the big name sponsors that UFC stars often brought in. If fighters didn't like Zuffa's practices, then they could find a new organization to work for.

In 2004, BJ wanted $50,000 (what Matt Hughes had been earning as champion), and would have settled for $40,000. K-1 was willing to splash out $187,500 per fight for Penn's services. When examining Penn's UFC contract, Penn's attorney discovered that not only was BJ free and clear of the contract, but also any matching period for salaries had also expired. Rather than pony up an offer of $50,000, the UFC chose to strip Penn of his welterweight title.

When Penn officially signed with K-1, Dana White's true face emerged:

" 'You're fucking done! You'll never fight in the UFC again! You're finished,' " screamed the irate UFC president over the telephone.

White threatened BJ with the same moves he'd carried out on other "enemies of Dana White" such as the threat of airbrushing BJ out of the UFC's official history (reminiscent of former UFC champion Frank Shamrock's treatment) or refusing to ever allow him to fight in the organization again (as had happened to former UFC fighter Matt Lindland).

Would the UFC really discard a marquee name because of a contract dispute, when they could much more easily make millions in pay-per-view revenue (as well as other streams) by utilizing said fighters on a regular basis? As the old maxim goes, you can shear a sheep many times, but skin it only once. In the end, many fighters who had contractual issues with the UFC, like Randy Couture and Tito Ortiz, were not expendable, due to their drawing power. Two years after BJ's first fight with Matt Hughes, BJ would be back fighting in the UFC.

As evident as Zuffa's nature was in controlling its fighters, the media and any hint of the internal workings of the organization, BJ was dismissive of the idea that there would be any blowback over the contents of his autobiography.

Said BJ in March 2010, a month prior to publication of his book, "I don't see any backlash. We did it how we did it. I don't think anything is going to come of it."

There were many sections of the book that were complimentary and positive about the Zuffa-owned version of the UFC. Penn took pains to point out how the Fertittas had invested their own money in marketing and related expenses above and beyond the $2 million they paid SEG for the UFC in January 2001.

Wrote Penn, "It was more like buying land with oil underneath as opposed to buying pumping oil wells. It took money to build and fix this thing, and one of the first things they spent money on was billboards and advertisements."[79]

The proverbial shit hit the fan when Dana White got wind of the book in the days before the official April 13 book launch. When Penn landed in NYC on April 13 (after losing his lightweight title to Frankie Edgar at UFC 112 in Abu Dhabi on April 10), he was bombarded with texts from Dana White.

"Why would you put out a book that is 90 percent not true?" asked Dana White of BJ Penn's lawyer, Gary Levitt.

In response to the pressure from Dana White, Penn retreated by tripping backwards over himself.

"He swore to me that he didn't write it or read it," said Dana White of Penn's private answer to him.[80]

Penn's co-writer, David Weintraub, suggested that Penn gave this particular statement, because Penn was hinting at the idea that there had been something inserted into the published book without BJ's knowledge—something that had offended Dana White. Penn couldn't fathom why the UFC president was making threats of a lawsuit or the mine-is-bigger threat from Dana: "I'm going to write a book, and my book is going to sell a lot more than your book."[81]

Both BJ Penn and his co-writer, David Weintraub, had read the manuscript that would be printed and bound into the final product. According to Weintraub, BJ's statement to Dana White about not having read his own autobiography was only accurate in the literal sense that BJ had not yet read page-by-page through the final product after it came off of the printing press. Penn had certainly known about the contents of his own book, with nothing having been inserted without his consent.

Before publication, BJ had joked to this writer about blaming David Weintraub for any issues with the book: "Any mistakes are Dave Weintraub's fault. Anything that makes me look bad, it's all Dave Weintraub."

Zuffa did, in fact, blame Weintraub. For his role in co-authoring BJ's book, David Weintraub was fired from his job as a producer at production company "Exit 9 Films" (Exit 9 produced material used as bonus features on UFC DVDs and webisodes on UFC.com; therefore, Zuffa had leverage to get Weintraub fired) and was dismissed from freelancing as a writer for *UFC Magazine*.[82]

"These were not my words," said Weintraub of the book on Sherdog.com's forums, "so to not have a job because of it really does hurt."[83]

Interestingly, the original manuscript was 440 pages. After careful deliberation, BJ had actually pared the story down to about 320 pages. Who knows what gems readers were denied? Obviously, something good was left out, because Penn spoke about possibly writing a sequel to *Why I Fight*—no doubt an unpleasant thought that must have driven shivers up the spines of certain people in the fight business.

15

THE END IS THE BEGINNING IS THE END

Nick Diaz was to BJ Penn what Larry Holmes was to Muhammad Ali—a former training partner who ended up dismantling him during the downside of his career. At UFC 137 on October 29, 2011, BJ looked good during the first round against Nick Diaz, securing a takedown and accumulating damage to Nick's right eye. Thereafter, he was beaten pillar-to-post for two rounds, losing a decision and announcing his retirement in the octagon.

"This is probably the last time you see me in here," Penn, whose left eye was closed and face visibly bruised, told UFC color commentator Joe Rogan. "I want to perform at the top level…I've got a daughter. I've got another daughter on the way. I don't want to go home looking like this."[84]

BJ had gone from a controversial loss to Frankie Edgar in Abu Dhabi to losing decisively to Edgar in a rematch at UFC 118. Penn then knocked out a faded Matt Hughes at UFC 123 and had a draw with natural welterweight Jon Fitch at UFC 127 before losing to Nick Diaz at UFC 137.

Sooner or later, every athlete's best days are behind him or her. When it came to Penn, who had trouble exercising discipline, it was inevitable that his time at the top would expire sooner than it needed to. It was sad that a man who had taken huge risks—fought in an exciting style against top opponents at any weight—was now seeing those decisions weigh against his future in the sport.

Like so many other fighters who announced retirement after a bad loss, BJ took time away from the sport and began to lick his wounds. During the months that he took off, an idea incubated within BJ's mind that often occurs to retired fighters—the belief that they had not yet achieved what they were truly capable of doing.

"I really do feel that I haven't reached my peak yet," said BJ. "That's got to eat at you eventually if you feel that there is a peak out there that you never hit."[85]

Eventually, overtures from the UFC and the persistence of fighters trying to make their name off of Penn's legacy ate away at BJ's resolve to retire. BJ Penn's first period of retirement ended after about eight months, when BJ officially announced Canadian Rory MacDonald (13-1) as his comeback opponent in June 2012.

Welterweight Rory MacDonald was a teammate of Georges St-Pierre at the Tristar gym where both MacDonald and St-Pierre were coached by Firas Zahabi.

"I definitely want to get redemption for UFC 94," said BJ of the crushing loss to St-Pierre.[86]

Would BJ finally have a transcendental moment in the fight with Rory that would wash away the painful memories of his fight with St-Pierre? Or was BJ Penn still visualizing himself battling the ghost of Jens Pulver from UFC 35? Maybe Rory MacDonald represented something else to BJ Penn—a reminder of the youthful ability and limitless potential that BJ himself had once epitomized.

Perhaps for a fleeting moment BJ would find something to thrill him within the fight itself. After that?

All bets on Penn were off.

SECTION III: BRAZIL

ANDERSON SILVA AND MAURÍCIO RUA

16

GUARDED SPIDER

The UFC 97 weigh-ins, held on April 17, 2009, a day before the night of the fights, began a little after 6:00 P.M. in Montreal's Bell Centre. It was the second time the UFC had ventured north into Canada, with middleweight champion Anderson Silva facing Brazilian challenger Thales Leites in the co-main event. Even though the evening's action consisted only of watching all of the card's fighters strip down to their shorts (or less, if they needed to lose the extra grams) to make weight, between four and five thousand fans had shown up to be a part of the mayhem. Rock music blaring, two beautiful ring card girls offsetting the homoeroticism of the nearly naked men, the atmosphere of the venue was positively electric.

Some onlookers watched in silent fascination and hope as Maurício "Shogun" Rua took to the scales. His face looked weary—perhaps affected by the discomfort and agitation of cutting 10-15 pounds of water in order to come in at the light-heavyweight limit—or maybe he was weighed down by the lingering doubt over whether he still had something left to give after two disappointing performances in losing to Forrest Griffin and looking terrible in a win against Mark Coleman.

Facing UFC poster-boy Chuck Liddell was no easy task; the majority of North American fans supported the entrenched Liddell over a Brazilian who had largely been absent from US radar.

Next up was Thales Leites, a lightly-regarded contender with elite jiu-jitsu, but little else to offer that could trouble Anderson, at least on paper. As Leites made weight, he struck a bodybuilding pose, pointing at his bicep to the approval of the crowd. When Anderson Silva came out of the backstage area, the cheers surged even louder. The crowd erased Leites from their short-term memory—after all, he was merely the pawn in this game, while Anderson Silva was the king.

Shogun weighing in before Anderson was a juxtaposition: just a few years earlier, Anderson Silva had been overshadowed by Shogun's status in Japan's PRIDE Fighting Championship. But now, Anderson was the star getting top billing in the more dominant organization. Shogun Rua, Anderson's former teammate from Chute Boxe and a former champion in PRIDE, was now regarded as a has-been.

Before the combatants ever set foot in the octagon, each fighter attempts to stack the deck in his favor. Training and physical preparation are one part. While strength, skills and conditioning might be the most important qualitative measures of a fighter's readiness, a psychological edge can also play a part in a fight's outcome.

After UFC color commentator Joe Rogan announced "182 for the champion," Anderson walked up to Leites to give the assembled press a photo op of the two in a pre-fight stare-down.

Anderson stepped forward with confidence, shook Leites's outstretched hand—and kept walking forward. Thales Leites backed up and even looked down as he feared toppling off the edge of the stage. The fight might as well have been over right then and there. Anderson had gained the mental edge by using Leites's fear to make the challenger second-guess himself. It was as beautiful a tactic as Robert DeNiro's character ambushing Sean Bean's character with a coffee cup in the post-Cold War thriller *Ronin*. There were no harsh words, insults or threats—Anderson had exposed a chink in Leites's amour, and would ruthlessly exploit the mental weakness he had tricked his opponent into revealing.

The stare-down was just as telling of their respective styles: Anderson's face betrayed zero emotion, whereas Leites smiled with nervous energy, his eyes repeatedly blinking. Anderson kept his hands by his side, while Leites had his guard up in a defensive posture. Even with his hands down, in any fight, much like his idol, boxer Roy Jones Jr., Anderson had the superior reflexes to elude punches—and even with his hands up, Leites exuded vulnerability. After the photos were taken and they hugged, one could sense a great deal of compassion within Anderson, despite what he was about to do to his opponent.

***

A live UFC event is a memorable experience. A sea of people wearing MMA-themed Tapout and Affliction brand clothing yells and howls, releasing angst and emotion. Saturday night at the Bell Centre, where a sell out crowd of 22,000 fans converged to celebrate their mutual passion and admiration for the spectacle of the fights, was a rare glimpse into the wild side of human behavior.

Unlike for boxing, where it was unfashionable to watch the undercards, the majority of the seats were full for the untelevised preliminary bouts. The arena was deafening, but it seemed to lack the extra bit of supernatural energy that had possessed the place when hometown hero Georges St-Pierre had graced the octagon against Matt Serra at UFC 83.

Proximity to the cage that high rollers, celebrities and media on press row sat in came with special benefits—those privileged few could actually *hear* the action, like the slapping sound when heavyweight contender Cheick Kongo's hammerfists repeatedly tagged Anoni Hardonk's body. It was like a mallet striking a slab of beef, an unpleasant sensation for Hardonk. At the moment when the referee stopped the Kongo-Hardonk contest midway through the second round, no doubt Hardonk was grateful that the punishment had ceased—but minutes later, he would come back to the realization that losing would cause his career to regress. Regret, disappointment and shame would seep into his mind as he thought about what he could have done differently.

After all the preliminarily bouts, it was time for the big names to take their positions as headliners. Shogun entered the octagon to the sounds of the techno song "Sail" by Armin Van Buuren—and the booing of the pro-Liddell crowd. The lilting melody seemed to mirror Shogun's hopes for a future at the top level while echoing the sadness over the setbacks caused by his poor performances and repeated knee surgeries.

During the introductions by Bruce Buffer, trainer Sergio Cunha gave last minute instructions to Shogun; in the opposite corner, coach John Hackleman did the same for Chuck Liddell. This would be the last corner advice given before the fight, but it was doubtful either guy could hear what they were being told.

"Fighting out of Curitiba, Brazil—Maurício 'SHOGUN' RUA!"

Shogun raised his arms in a gesture of confidence. The crowd hardly noticed he was there, some jeering, but most showing raw in-difference. After all, it was former UFC light-heavyweight champion Chuck Liddell who had been the face of the UFC for so many years, who had graced the cover of *ESPN: The Magazine* and who had been a fan favorite with his aggressive style of stand-up.

"In the red corner. This man is a kickboxer…"

It was ironic that they still highlighted the technique of the fighters and tried to pin it down to one single style. After all these years of MMA fighters cross-training in different disciplines, even the fact that Liddell had been a Division 1 collegiate wrestler didn't factor into the one-line moniker of "kickboxer" Bruce had just labeled him with.

"…presenting Chuck 'THE ICEMAN' Liddell!"

The match would not go past the first round. Two minutes into the bout, a left hook from Shogun found its mark against Liddell's jaw just as Liddell was throwing a counter left of his own. Call it skill, technique, timing or even luck, but Shogun's punch reached its target first. There was a hush from the crowd as they absorbed the disappointment of watching their hero fall—followed by cheering for Shogun. With the win, Rua had pulled back from the brink of obscurity.

After delays and a swing-bout used as filler (the quick knockout left too much TV time), Anderson Silva came prepared to show the audience why he was the model of perfection in the MMA octagon. As he warmed-up backstage, he appeared relaxed and confident, with just enough concentration to function without being overwhelmed by the nature of his business.

Leites made his biggest splash with a rock-star entrance to Guns N' Roses' "Welcome to the Jungle" while wearing sunglasses. From there onward, it was all downhill for the challenger.

As the fight got underway, Leites tasted Anderson Silva's power and chose to fight to survive rather than throwing caution to the wind. Had Leites chosen to be more aggressive in the stand-up or committed to a takedown, Anderson would have put his counter-punching to good use and stopped Leites cold. For their dollar, the audience was treated to a five-round snooze fest, a fact that was not lost on them as they chanted instead for Montreal local Georges St-Pierre—seated cageside—rather than acknowledging the battle in the octagon.

When it was over, Anderson Silva walked away with the judges' decision, but in the eyes of many, he had been a disappointment. During the post-fight press conference, when asked if he had been emotionally blocked, he rolled his eyes and ridiculed the journalist's question by pretending not to understand what was being asked of him.

His attitude was partially a reaction to criticism and partially his mask slipping to reveal his true character. After all, as close as he had been to his former Chute Boxe teammates Wanderlei "The Axe Murderer" Silva and Shogun Rua, he showed zero hesitation in attacking both. Prior to UFC 97, Wanderlei Silva had ignited a feud when he announced he was moving to Anderson's weight class. Anderson took the opportunity to remind the world that Wanderlei had done nothing years ago when the management at Chute Boxe blackballed Anderson from competing in Japan's PRIDE Fighting Championship. When it was announced in the weeks after Shogun's victory over Liddell that

Rua would face reigning UFC light-heavyweight champion Lyoto Machida, Anderson again criticized his former teammate Shogun Rua, for being undeserving of a title shot after only two wins. This was ironic, since Anderson himself had been granted his chance against then-UFC middleweight champion Rich Franklin after having only two straight wins, with only one of those fights in the UFC.

Scarcely noticed in the aftermath of UFC 97 was the fact that Anderson Silva had now pulled ahead of welterweight contender Jon Fitch into the lead for most consecutive victories in the UFC, with nine straight wins. With his next match scheduled to occur at the light-heavyweight limit, Silva would be risking his neck outside his natural weight class. It was a calculated risk that could see his win streak snapped, but he seemed to know enough about himself and his abilities that he was willing to lay it all on the line for a chance to answer the critics.

17

ANDERSON SILVA'S EARLY YEARS

In 2010, as America's status as an economic leader and international superpower declined, South America produced a notable success story in Brazil's fledgling economy, which expanded at its fastest rate in more than two decades.[87] Rather than posting losses or stagnating following the 2008 global recession, their GDP has steadily increased.

In the past, Brazil had an economy that relied heavily upon the export of raw materials, with fluctuating prices that offered little benefit to the exporting nation. The '80s saw the country struggling with enormous foreign debt (estimated at $54 billion in 1980) while needing to import increasingly pricey goods from abroad. The '80s—the era Anderson Silva grew up in—were referred to as "The Lost Decade" as inflation held steady at 100 percent, ramping up to 1000 percent in the mid-'80s, and peaking at an insane 6821 percent in April 1990. The 1986 Cruzado Plan, introduced by the government to eliminate inflation, had short-term success; however, adjustments weren't made at the right times, and inflation increased yet again. It wasn't until 1994, when the *Plano Real* went into effect, that Brazil first saw longstanding stability, as the new currency, the *real*, was tied to the US dollar.

Economic gains aside, the problems of Brazil persist into the modern era: corruption, crime and poverty are endemic. Some suggest that social inequality is the perfect breeding ground for fighters—this is not especially true, as neither India nor China, countries with extreme poverty, have produced any notable talent for professional boxing or MMA. It takes a culture of martial arts tradition and the right individuals to give careers forward momentum. The right people existed in Brazil, and Anderson Silva was fortunate to cross paths with them at the right time.

Anderson Silva was born in São Paulo on April 14, 1975, his road to glory hardly paved with gold. Coming from a family of little means, he had to make his way forward every step of the way. While privileged classes exist in all nations, the bitterness felt by some toward the elite of Brazil is proportional to the massive economic divide. Add racial discrimination of black Brazilians to the mix, and you have a rough understanding of Anderson Silva's background.

One then wonders how Anderson Silva interpreted his mother's decision to leave him and his older brother in the care of their aunt in Curitiba when he was just four years old. She had her reasons—no other viable options, and no way out. The subconscious mind interprets family discord in ways of its own. For instance, the children of divorced parents may blame themselves; incidents of mild neglect can leave lifelong scars on self-worth or self-confidence.

Despite this, Anderson Silva recalled an ideal childhood. "My childhood was super mellow, I had no problems," said Anderson in the documentary *Like Water*.[88]

Was this just window-dressing for the public? Only Anderson knows the truth.

With his uncle earning a meager policeman's salary to support five kids, Anderson simply wasn't afforded the opportunities available to others.

Later in his MMA career, Anderson spoke about how he had wanted to become a police officer like his uncle was, but perhaps that was just a fleeting thought in his childhood.

At the age of nine, young Anderson watched *Enter the Dragon*, the Bruce Lee vehicle that catapulted the martial arts master to stardom. The movie left an indelible impression on Anderson.

"When I saw Bruce Lee on the screen, I knew what I wanted to do with my life," said Anderson. "I wanted to be Bruce Lee."[89]

Anderson described himself as a hyperactive kid who needed some activity to calm himself down. Martial arts lessons were beyond Anderson's means. He would watch other students practicing Taekwondo under Master Kanji in Curitiba.

"I began Taekwondo out of nothing," said Anderson, "I had some friends who trained; I couldn't pay for the academy."[90]

Eventually, Anderson was allowed to participate in the classes, and this set the wheels in motion—but it was not enough to complete him as a mixed martial artist. While Brazilian Jiu-Jitsu was the playground of the advantaged castes, Anderson allowed his martial arts fantasy to blossom through his lessons in Taekwondo, and later, capoeira. It should be noted that neither discipline is considered ideal for budding MMA fighters, as the training methods lack realistic full-contact fighting. Ultimately, Anderson Silva would be renowned for his precise Muay Thai, a discipline he came into at the age of 16.

Fabio Seuchi Noguchi, a Muay Thai black belt under Nelio Naja (credited with bringing Muay Thai to Brazil), was Anderson Silva's first Muay Thai teacher. The interesting dynamic in martial arts circles was how conflict constantly led to students splitting off and forming rival teams—the same tried-and-true plot of the student turning evil on the master in Kung Fu flicks. Noguchi claims that Rudimar Fedrigo had an argument with Nelio Naja back in 1978 that led to Rudimar leaving Naja and forming the Chute Boxe gym in Curitiba.[91] Eventually, the rift healed, as Noguchi recalls Nelio Naja returning in 1986 to award a third Dan to Rudimar in a ceremony where Noguchi was awarded his own black belt. Eventually, Fabio Noguchi joined the Chute Boxe gym. After Rudimar Fedrigo made a failed bid to become elected to the city council in 1991, Noguchi claims, Rudimar was "emotionally distraught" and wanted to close the Chute Boxe gym. By the time Rudimar had stabilized and decided against closing Chute Boxe, Noguchi had already opened "The Noguchi Gym," splitting the master and student yet again.

It was in 1994 that Anderson first walked into the Noguchi Gym, hell-bent on doing more than just learning self-defense or getting by.

Says Noguchi of Anderson, "He saw fighting as more than just a refuge. He felt in his soul that it would be the boon he needed to carve out a better life for himself."

During the '90s in Brazil, when the top one percent of the population had more wealth than the bottom 50 percent[92], the good life was usually inherited rather than earned with sweat. Anderson found himself eking out a living between shifts at McDonald's, where he would work for five years, and working as a bicycle messenger—jobs that offered little chance for Anderson to advance beyond his class, let alone become a multimillionaire.[93] There were other negatives: in his autobiography, Anderson describes one incident at McDonald's where a patron refused to be served by him because he was black; Anderson's manager refused the customer service, and Anderson returned to work rather than taking the day off.[94]

The bright spot in Anderson's life was a girl named Dayane. They had met when he was 17 and she was 13. She became his high-school sweetheart, with Anderson moving in and supporting her after she became pregnant at 17. They broke up for a period of time, but eventually married. As they scraped by, guilt-wracked Anderson would make grandiose promises to Dayane.

Said Dayane, "He used to tell me, 'One day I will get you a nice house…One day you will have a nice car.' "

It was evident from the start that Anderson saw those around him as opposition to his own progress. Proficiency as a kickboxer requires regular sparring under conditions resembling a fight. To this end, Anderson sparred with Noguchi with the bravado and relentlessness that defines young men who have yet to encounter a soul-crushing knockout loss.

Noguchi describes knocking Anderson down, and Silva constantly dusting himself off and asking for more. "His persistence scared me at times, and I told him that he'd eventually hurt himself," said Noguchi.

Notable among Anderson's Muay Thai bouts were two fights with José "Pelé" Landi-Jons, a trailblazing fighter who embodied the core values of Chute Boxe's aggressive, take-no-prisoners style. Noguchi remembers the fights occurring when Anderson was 20 or 21, but the actual results are a matter of small controversy.

The first bout occurred when Anderson and Pelé both made it to the finals of the Curitiba "Thai Gym Tournament." According to Noguchi, Anderson was overawed by Pelé's status and lost the first fight via decision.

While Pelé officially beat Anderson in the second fight, Noguchi recalls a different outcome.

"I recall that I slapped [Anderson's] face twice, and that actually helped to up his tempo," said Noguchi. "He fought very well to earn the victory."

Pelé believed knocking Anderson down in the fourth round sealed his win, but the decision for Pelé had been unpopular and was met with boos by the large crowd.[95]

Anderson Silva's autobiography angered Pelé to the point where he created a video both to dispute several items in the book and to talk up his two Muay Thai bouts with Silva.

"The first time we fought, I got to confess you did good," says Pelé, "but every time I got you with my Muay Thai clinch, you would throw yourself to the ground, falling on your ass!"

Pelé claims that a throw is worth a 10-8 round under Muay Thai scoring. While sweeps and throws are scoring moves in Muay Thai bouts, they are not decisive in awarding a round like knockdowns are in boxing. Pelé's version of events is subjective and only a video tape of the bout would be an objective measure of what really had occurred.

"In the second fight, congratulations, you fought really well," said Pelé. "You threw some classic spinning back kicks, really nice moves."

Pelé again emphasized that his knockdown put him ahead on the cards, and that he was simply playing with Anderson in the final round.[96]

Whatever the truth, the outcome of these obscure Muay Thai bouts has little bearing on Anderson Silva's legacy as a fighter today. It is Silva's own understanding of his potential based on the fights that matters. Despite losing, Silva gained confidence in himself through facing a much more experienced and established name like Pelé.

At 22, Anderson made his MMA debut at the "Brazil Freestyle Circuit 1" tournament on June 25, 1997. He beat Raimundo Pinheiro via rear naked choke after just one minute and fifty-three seconds; then Silva defeated Fabrício Camões via stoppage after 25 minutes and 14 seconds of fighting. He won a purse of 400 *reais*, about $372 US.

Eventually, Anderson outgrew Noguchi's smaller team and moved on to Chute Boxe. Team size was not the only issue with Noguchi: Anderson described an incident where he was accused of stealing gym dues from Noguchi's gym; Anderson was found innocent, and Noguchi apologized. This incident could have been a justification for abandoning his former coach.

"Chute Boxe was the only place with power to bring you for another level; to put you to compete in other countries," said former Chute Boxe trainer Sergio Cunha. "Rudimar [Fedrigo, the owner of Chute Boxe,] was the only one who had the contacts if you are in Curitiba."

The split between Anderson and Noguchi was not amicable, a fact that was still etched into Noguchi's mind in 2010. "Sad to think that I used to hold him in my arms. It's like any son," said Noguchi, reminiscing on how Anderson would clam up whenever he ran into Noguchi after their split.

Most MMA historians point to patriarch Hélio Gracie as the most critical figure in Brazilian MMA history. After all, it was Hélio's challenge matches that proved the superiority of Brazilian Jiu-Jitsu in mixed-rules bouts. When it comes to the realities of the modern MMA game, where superior strength, explosive striking, and flexible game plans are required to be competitive, other figures need to be given credit.

Chute Boxe owner and founder, Rudimar Fedrigo, was critical to the evolution of MMA, both in Brazil and internationally. Rudimar's grandparents were Italian immigrants who settled in Rio Grande Do Sol, farming soybeans and raising cattle. When he was around 12 or 13 years old, Rudimar suffered a life-changing accident while riding his bicycle.

"A person opened a car door, I fell, and the car ran over my leg," said Rudimar.

For rehabilitation, Fedrigo chose Muay Thai, as doctors warned him that one leg would always be shorter than the other. Fedrigo's extra-curricular activity turned into a profitable venture when he established the Chute Boxe Academy at the tender age of 17. His obsession with all aspects of the MMA game came at a high cost, as the line delineating work from leisure is all but erased for those who run their own businesses outside the grind of working nine-to-five.

Said Rudimar, "Once I began the Academy, I thought about fights and the Academy all day. Sometimes I even held the punching mitts for my students in my dreams."[97]

The main things that differentiated Rudimar from any other close competitors were his relentless perfectionism in pushing his fighters and the high degree of skill of Chute Boxe's coaches. Many fighters are coached by instructors who know very few techniques and never deviate from set patterns. There are also far too many gyms where the fighters know the exact degree of difficulty that each sparring partner possesses; familiarity allows them to circumvent both hard training and the challenge of different styles of fighting.

This was not the case at Chute Boxe.

José "Pelé" Landi-Jons salivated while telling of one brutal sparring session with Wanderlei Silva: "Wanderlei knocked me out. As I fell forward, I managed to fire off a jab. Precisely as I fell, I lunged forward with my left arm and caught him right on the chin. Our bodies fell, chest to chest. The two of us were still standing, but knocked out."

The all-out mentality of Chute Boxe in the gym meant that its fighters were ready to rumble. Nothing can equal the emotional intensity and stress of a real fight, but Chute Boxe came as close as possible with their sparring.

"With Master Rudimar, we had no choice but to give it all we had," said Pelé of his epic war with Chuck Liddell. The bout between Pelé and Liddell was one where the towel should have been thrown in to save Pelé, but Rudimar made the executive decision to force Pelé to survive to the end of the time limit.

In 2009, when quizzed about Chute Boxe by Brasil Combate, Anderson described it as a "dead love," something that was once great, but now was committed to the past.[98]

With an entire contingent of Chute Boxe members cheering Anderson on, he fought Luiz Azeredo at Mecca: World Vale Tudo 1, on May 27, 2000. Although Anderson lost the judge's decision to Luiz Azeredo, Anderson had looked incredible on the feet and had shown definite potential.

Noguchi himself noted that the main benefit of Chute Boxe came through connections. "I knew that Rudimar had international contacts," said Noguchi.

The primary obstacle faced by fighters at all levels of the game lies in securing good fights. In office towers, workers lament having to get down to work, preferring to procrastinate through extended lunch and bathroom breaks, games of solitaire, or fluffing of miniscule tasks. In MMA, when a fighter has no work, he is facing obscurity. To a fighter, languishing unknown can seem worse than death.

For Anderson, the downside of signing with Chute Boxe was the transition from being a big fish in a smaller pond at the Noguchi Gym to being one of many sharks in the tank at Chute Boxe. Tension was constant, the pressure to succeed monumental, competition of more established teammates stiffer and storm clouds of mistrust over matters political and financial gathered on the horizon.

Thanks to his reach advantage and innate talent, Anderson gave everyone at Chute Boxe problems. Anderson excelled at Chute Boxe, in part, because of his different style and technique learned under Noguchi. He was always known as the most technical of all the Chute Boxe fighters.

"He came [to Chute Boxe] already being a fighter, and trained with them for only a couple of years," said former MMA fighter and analyst Bas Rutten. "He had a different style already. The Chute Boxe guys are known for coming forward. They're not known for throwing jabs and feeling out process. It's like one speed and they come full ahead and lots of power, great clinching, great knees in clinches—very wild. If you look at Wanderlei Silva, you ever see him throwing a double-jab or a right straight? You'll see it, but you don't see it a lot."

Chute Boxe fighter Nilson de Castro lamented Anderson's strong jab, saying in a 2002 interview that "[His jab] is annoying. It's still terrible! With those little 'mosquito' arms of his!"

After winning several domestic fights, Silva began making noise in Japan. He took victories over Hayato Sakurai and Tetsuji Kato in 2001, moving his MMA record to 7-1. His fight with Sakurai for the Shooto middleweight title was contested at 168 pounds (or 76 kilograms, as Japan's weight classes were based on the metric system). Sakurai got the takedown in the first round, but Anderson returned with a vengeance in the second, nearly submitting Sakurai with a rear naked choke. Sakurai again managed to take top position on the ground in the final frame, but he made an error in backing out of Anderson's guard and allowing Anderson to get back to his feet. Anderson managed a takedown and finished stronger on the feet to take the nod and deliver Sakurai his first loss.

Chute Boxe training partner Andre "Dida" Amado, a lightweight K-1 and MMA fighter, recalled the way Anderson consistently contributed to the team at Chute Boxe: "Anderson would be taping our hands and telling us what to do in a fight when we were young kids."

Of course, Anderson was still young in his career. He had to be there to corner his teammates because he was still a relative equal to them—he'd yet to really distinguish himself from the pack. Even at the height of Anderson's success as a UFC champion, he continued to coach prospects, performing many duties from taping fighters' hands in the gym to giving advice. However, later in his career, Anderson could be forceful and domineering as a coach, almost as if his charges were supposed to be extensions of himself. In *Like Water*, Anderson is seen cornering friend and teammate Damaso "Dan Dan" Pereira, but as Dan Dan loses his bout, Anderson is harsh and critical at the moment Dan Dan is most vulnerable in loss.

With six straight wins under his belt after the loss to Luiz Azeredo, Anderson was destined for bigger things. But his career in the limelight of PRIDE ended up being the undoing of his relationship with Rudimar and Chute Boxe.

18

THE CHUTE BOXE SPLIT

The Gracie clan claimed ownership in the formation and execution of Brazilian Jiu-Jitsu, with the family having a long-recorded history of issuing challenges to other martial artists in order to demonstrate the superiority of BJJ. The Gracie Challenge was the seed that grew into the first UFC when Rorian Gracie partnered with advertising executive Art Davie for the first event in 1993. Rorian helped mold the rules and format of the tournament, while his brother, Royce Gracie, was the BJJ representative in the event. As unsuspecting marks from competing styles were lured into the fold, Royce was the slick hustler armed with the submission skills to finish them off when they were at their weakest. Champion of three of the first four UFC tournaments, Royce stopped competing in the UFC after UFC 5 in 1995, likely to avoid the increasing competition and hang on to the mystique that he had built up through his wins. Five years later, meeting Japanese wrestling sensation Kazushi Sakuraba at the 2000 Pride Grand Prix finals, Royce saw the myth of his (and BJJ's) invincibility shattered, as Sakuraba forced Royce to quit after six 15-minute rounds of competition.

Kazushi Sakuraba was similar to Royce—a submission specialist who favored the ground attack. He was often overmatched in size and strength, but faced the absolute toughest and best fighters available out of a misguided sense of pride and a constant search for an adrenaline rush. Just as Royce had fallen to Sakuraba, Sakuraba fell to the next generation of MMA fighters when he was smashed three times (twice via TKO, once via KO) by Chute Boxe product Wanderlei "The Axe Murderer" Silva.

Wanderlei himself was representative of the new breed of well-rounded MMA fighters. Wanderlei had the BJJ knowledge to avoid being submitted, the takedown defense to mitigate attempts to get him to the mat, the size and strength to muscle others around and the aggressive ferocity to take the fight to his opponents, with a preference for brutalizing them with strikes.

As the major star of the Chute Boxe academy in Curitiba, Brazil, during the PRIDE era, Wanderlei was the predecessor and trailblazer to teammates Anderson Silva and Maurício Rua.

In 2010, to arrive at the main Chute Boxe academy from Curitiba's downtown area was simple—one just had to walk to a main street and take a bus or cab to the area known as Hauer. The neighborhood was described as upscale by a *National Geographic* writer who had visited the team in 2007, but that didn't mean Curitiba was devoid of danger—after all, Chute Boxe trainer Omar Dias had been shot dead leaving the gym at 1:00 A.M. on Tuesday morning, November 11, 2008.[99] Also suspect was how buildings in most areas of Curitiba—and the rest of Brazil—were outfitted with more concertina wire than a World War I battlefield.

The team had become more civilized as a result of time and business forces. By this time period, Chute Boxe no longer went balls to the walls in sparring since it hurt the gym's business by scaring off potential members.

The current main Chute Boxe gym is located at 1540 Rua Tenente Francisco Ferreira de Souza. The team logo is clearly visible on a sign that points to a large, gray building. A nice cobblestone courtyard leads to the entrance. The academy resembles a car dealership: it has huge windows, a large floor space and no dark basement or grimy underbelly, which most boxing gyms in the inner city have. Nor does it have the claustrophobic lack of space like urban gyms, where the only thing more brutal than MMA training was the rental prices per square foot of downtown real estate.

At one point, when Rudimar was furthering his political career early in the millennium, Rudimar closed his Chute Boxe academy, and trainer Rafael Cordeiro opened up his own downtown Chute Boxe location. Cordeiro's gym had everything going for it, from location to free parking.

"At the same time, a lot of coaches like myself, Zito, Noguchi, [Nilson de Castro] and Osmar Diaz [were] there," said Sergio Cunha. "We had our own [affiliate] Chute Boxes, but we meet together, everybody, in the morning. Make the main session at 10:00 A.M."

This group of coaches became the strength of Chute Boxe. Although Rafael Cordeiro would get most of the credit for Wanderlei Silva's and Shogun Rua's success, each individual fighter would put in sessions with specific coaches at the Chute Boxe affiliate gyms throughout Curitiba.

In recent years, the gym relocated to its current location in Hauer in a building owned outright by Rudimar Fedrigo. The gym in 2010 was far different from the glory years of Chute Boxe in the PRIDE era. Rudimar was rarely on site, because he pulled double duty as secretary of sport for the Curitiba government. The trainers and fighters who had ushered in Chute Boxe's glory years in the sport—Wanderlei Silva, Maurício Rua, Anderson Silva, Murilo Rua, Andre Amado, Rafael Cordeiro, Sergio Cunha, Cristiano Marcello—were all long gone.

"He needs his black belts," said Cunha of Rudimar's situation. "We was like a family. Now he's sad. He got money, he got everything he need. But he don't got his kids, like me, like Shogun, like Anderson, like Cordeiro. He's very sad because of this."

Nilson de Castro, a heavyset black man with '50s style glasses, was now the main trainer responsible for day-to-day operations. Nilson had an impenetrable aura wrapped in gentle warmth. A former MMA fighter (10-8-1), he had a vague resemblance to Anderson Silva in his appearance.

With a fighting event having occurred the previous night, many of the gym's pros were resting up. There was, however, one fighter who seemed to be preparing for an upcoming event, Ed "Monstro" Carlos. Monstro was a light-heavyweight who lived up to his nickname—you could read pain in his eyes.

Monstro jumped rope to warm up and then hit the pads with his trainer Luciano "Monge" Moreas.

"They call, and then they don't call anymore," said Nilson of the promoter for the card Monstro was supposed to fight on.

"Nemesis Fighting" had a card in the Dominican Republic on December 11, 2010, headlined by former UFC fighter Keith Jardine. There had been no communication from the promotion, leaving Monstro feeling angry and sad.

In truth, by not receiving a call back, he was dodging a bullet: When the event occurred, the promotion had been so disorganized, an official used his cell phone to time fights, rounding up to the nearest minute between his outgoing texts; there weren't enough MMA gloves to go around; the crowd consisted of between 20 and 100 people and the checks to the fighters had all bounced.[100] Still, at this moment, Monstro was not the happiest of customers that he had been left in the cold.

"I ready to fight anytime. Anytime!" Monstro said, matter-of-fact and tinged with rage.

It was an unsettling reminder of the daily struggles of MMA fighters. Even the best fighters in the world had difficulty obtaining marquee match-ups that would earn them prime dollars and audience respect; the lower-tier fighters had to deal with ruthless promoters, lack of recognition, and the general headache of having no leverage or ability to get someone of importance to invest in the unknown quantity that they represented to everyone involved in the industry.

Rudimar Fedrigo, the owner of Chute Boxe, had invested in all of his fighters simply by running the gym. MMA gyms are notorious money-pits, but thanks to the percentage Rudimar took from his fighters' purses, he got a big return on his investment. There remained, however, the question of transparency in Rudimar's dealings as a manager.

***

Two weeks before Anderson was to face Hayato Sakurai for the Shooto title in 2001, the UFC had floated an offer through an intermediary, Marcello "Tetel" Andrade: If Anderson was victorious against Sakurai, the UFC wanted Anderson's services.

"Joe Silva was interested and offered a title shot fight against Carlos Newton," said Tetel.

The match was to have occurred at UFC 34, held in November 2001. Rudimar signed a three-fight contract with the UFC, but declined to inform Anderson about it.

"Anderson was not even aware of this deal and signed contract," says Tetel. "Rudimar stated that he was entitled to legally represent Anderson."

When Anderson defeated Sakurai, and Japanese fight organization PRIDE announced that Anderson would fight Daijiro Matsui in their organization, the UFC was absolutely livid. Anderson Silva's management had been double-dipping, signing Anderson simultaneously to the UFC and PRIDE. Signing Anderson to a Japanese organization meant more money, and the lack of an athletic commission meant that the check would be written to Rudimar, with no disclosure of the purse amount.

"[UFC president] Dana White called me, very upset," said Tetel.

Rather than sit there and accept a screwing from both Rudimar and PRIDE, Dana White stood up for himself, and his organization.

"Dana sent a message to [PRIDE president] Sakakibara with the signed contract and said to him that if Anderson would fight in PRIDE, he would block the PRIDE pay-per-view in US, because Zuffa had a signed contract with exclusive rights to promote and broadcast Anderson's fights in the USA," said Tetel.

Japanese agent and PRIDE coordinator Koichi "Booker K" Kawasaki, who handled negotiations between Chute Boxe and PRIDE, had a take on why Brazilians sometimes didn't adhere to generally accepted practices:

"Understand about Brazilian people. They are not American, not Canadian, not Japanese. Most *Brasileiro* not go to high school, not go to University. Many peoples [have] just junior school. And many fighters come from a slum. Different culture."

According to Kawasaki and Tetel, the solution was to freeze Anderson out of the big leagues of MMA for one year.

"PRIDE president Sakakibara, and Zuffa, they had a meeting about Anderson Silva. So both don't use Anderson for one year," said Kawasaki.

It was believed that the UFC contract was part of why Anderson was upset with Rudimar and left Chute Boxe in late 2003; after all, Anderson easily dismantled Carlos Newton when they finally met at PRIDE 25 on March 16, 2003. The other major matter of importance comes back to the contract that Anderson had with Rudimar to represent him as a manager. It was a relationship where not all details are known, even to this day.

"The thing about that history," said trainer Sergio Cunha, "nobody know the real truth. The deal with the gym is that 30 percent of the purse goes to the gym. That was the agreement."

Whatever his reasoning, Anderson decided to split from the Chute Boxe family in November 2003. Although the Rua brothers contemplated leaving, they stayed on until 2007, then explaining in confidence about the high percentage that had to be paid into the gym as one of the reasons for their decision to move on.

Speaking just after the split in November 2003, Anderson was guarded, yet firm: "We really quit Chute Boxe. Assuério Silva, Rodrigo Vidal, Israel Gomes, Ed Carlos, Silvio 'Urutum' de Souza, Sávio, me and many others.[101]"

Rudimar then posted a request on Brazilian MMA news website Tatame.com asking for the fighters who had left to return their black belts. It was outrageous, as noted by Assuério Silva in an open letter:

"His request is out of the question, as never in the history of martial arts has anyone had to return their black belts due to leaving a team – once a black belt, always a black belt!!"

There were other major issues with the PRIDE contracts. Assuério Silva was adamant that none of the departing fighters had ever seen their respective contracts with PRIDE.[102] Part of this might have been owing to the criminal element of PRIDE, to whom paperwork was just a liability.

"PRIDE don't make a real contract," said Kawasaki. "It was just verbal contract. PRIDE many times, did not have contracts. No papers. Just verbal. Then, Anderson speak, 'Where is contract?' So fight money, everything, correct pay. So I got a copy of the receipt from the PRIDE; I give to Rudimar."

Up until 2005, payment to PRIDE fighters had been given in cash, so receipts were the only proof of Anderson's purses. There could have been more than one receipt for different amounts, so Anderson had no assurances of fair accounting.

Anderson recalled Rudimar trying to win him back to Chute Boxe by offering to show the receipts to him. Anderson didn't care anymore at this point. After all, if Rudimar had withheld information about the title shot against UFC champion Carlos Newton, forging a few documents (which PRIDE had done with other fighters, like Fedor Emelianenko) would have been child's play.

Although Rudimar insisted he had handled the contracts fairly, there was no way any fighters could account for the percentage taken off the top, given that there were Japanese agents who took their commission before Rudimar got his cut, and then passed off what was remaining to his fighters.

"We NEVER had access to those contracts," said Assuério Silva. "[We] NEVER knew anything about the negotiations or the value of our fight purses. That was the REAL reason why half of the team left."

Rudimar rationalized the loss of the departing fighters, but he knew that Anderson was unique among them. "We are just fine without them. The only one that I really feel bad about is Anderson Silva."[103]

Anderson was 11-2 at this point, with his most recent loss to Daiju Takase in PRIDE via triangle choke at a time when Silva was not as skilled on the ground as he would become with the Nogueira brothers as his coaches later on. He also claims to have had herniated a disc before the Takase fight. His PRIDE record at that point was 3-1, including wins over Alex Stiebling (TKO), Alexander Otsuka (decision), and Carlos Newton (KO). If there was one Chute Boxe fighter besides the Rua brothers or Wanderlei who could make noise in PRIDE, it was Anderson.

The irony of the situation was that had Rudimar been a better administrator of his coaches and the fighters, more great MMA champions could have been part of the team.

"2005 or 2006, even Nogueira brothers—a lot of guys from Rio de Janeiro—was thinking about move to live in Curitiba and train under Chute Boxe, because we was the biggest team," revealed Sergio Cunha, who was one of the first to leave Chute Boxe; Cunha went on to coach the Nogueira brothers in 2005.

After leaving Chute Boxe, Anderson Silva claimed he was blackballed from fighting in PRIDE due to Rudimar's dirty backroom dealings, using Wanderlei as a bargaining chip: "When I left Chute Boxe I was in a very difficult financial situation," Anderson told Tatame magazine. "Rudimar said [to PRIDE] if I fought in PRIDE, Wanderlei would leave the Japanese organization. As a result I was six months unemployed."[104]

Even if there was evidence that Rudimar threatened to remove Wanderlei from PRIDE, there were many other roadblocks and obstacles to any Brazilian fighter wishing to fight in Japan that would have stopped Anderson cold.

Two Japanese agents handled negotiations between all Brazilian fighters and Japanese fight promotions: Koichi "Booker K" Kawasaki, who had a stranglehold on Chute Boxe talent, and his former secretary, Motoko Uchida, who controlled most of Brazilian Top Team (Kawasaki points out that he managed BTT member Paulo Filho, so the generalization that Uchida managed BTT exclusively is incorrect). PRIDE made unofficial side-deals with Kawasaki and Uchida in order to control fighter pay; it's hard to imagine PRIDE working directly with a fighter and cutting the parasitic (but useful) middlemen out of the equation.

Kawasaki gave his own reasons for not representing Anderson independently of Chute Boxe.

"I work with Chute Boxe. My loyalty was Chute Boxe," said Kawasaki. "He was, in Portuguese, '*creonte*,' " said Kawasaki, using the word that described an opportunistic fighter who had left his team for another gym.

Anderson's questions regarding his payment from Chute Boxe were just the tip of the iceberg when it came to the question of fighter pay. Unless the teams and managers knew the value of DSE's contract with Fuji TV, the official gate receipts, and information about other related revenue streams against expenses, they had little idea what the true worth of their fighters was. $10,000 or $20,000 became the pay ceiling for many fighters appearing on a nationally-televised card. Racist DSE executives often joked about how far $10,000 would go in the underdeveloped countries where many PRIDE fighters came from.

"If you are only relying on what you are told by your Japanese rep and what you hear from other fighters about their fight money. Well, what else can you do?" said Miro Mijatovic, former manager of Fedor Emelianenko and Mirko "Cro Cop" Filipović.

Mijatovic explained the typical "bribe" deal floated to the agents who represented foreign (non-Japanese) fighters in PRIDE.

"DSE would offer a certain amount of money for a fight and it was up to the manager to negotiate the fighters fight money down," said Mijatovic. "DSE knew that fighters talk about money. It was in the interests of the Japanese side that fighters had shitty fight money so the rest of the money could be shared amongst the Japanese."

Bitterness remained for Anderson, even years after he had left Chute Boxe. In June 2012, when Anderson first published his autobiography, Rudimar Fedrigo was upset by various allegations made by Anderson.

"He questioned my qualifications, which is absurd," Rudimar told R7.com. "There is a part in which he says I am a bad person and in another he raises doubts about my gradings…Look, he missed the truth with all of that."

Rudimar took Anderson and his publisher to court, and succeeded in getting the book pulled from the shelves until revisions to the manuscript were made. [105]

After leaving Chute Boxe, Anderson went on to found Muay Thai Dream Team with Israel Gomes and Rodrigo Vidal.

"The name was kept for some time until it was changed to what it is currently, Killer Bees,"[106] Anderson said of the team's name change (a reference to Muhammad Ali, "Float like a butterfly/Sting like a bee").

Without international contacts, start-up capital or a reputation, Anderson's team was a paper tiger. Frozen out of the Japanese MMA scene, Anderson would spend six months unemployed, bitterly contemplating his retirement from a sport that had brutalized him with its favoritism, politics and dishonesty. There are moments in life when we feel the deck is so stacked against us that giving up on our dreams seems like a good option. Whether Anderson would have perpetually languished outside of MMA—working at McDonald's or some other low-level job—is hard to say, but we all have a breaking point.

Divine intervention in the form of twin brothers Antônio Rodrigo Nogueira and Antônio Rogério Nogueira changed MMA history as we know it. As members of Brazil Top Team (BTT), the Nogueira brothers were schooled under the Gracie's brand of jiu-jitsu reserved for la crème de la crème of Brazilian society.

"When I started out, [Brazilian] Jiu-Jitsu was really an elite thing in Brazil, and there was some prejudice toward poorer kids, so I had to learn things on my own," Silva told *FIGHT! Magazine.*[107]

The division between BTT and Chute Boxe was about class, culture and fighting style. The main fighters from each camp knew each other, with Anderson Silva making a good impression on heavyweight Rodrigo Nogueira early in Anderson's career.

"The first times that I saw his fight in the Brazil, I became a fan, because I'd never seen nobody fight like that," recalled Rodrigo. "I was like, 'That kid going to be world champ for sure.' "[108]

Rodrigo traveled to Curitiba to offer Anderson a chance to become his training partner. Rodrigo lent Anderson money and guaranteed Anderson several fights in exchange for Anderson's help as a training partner. It wasn't a purely altruistic offer—Anderson was versed in the Chute Boxe style and could offer valuable advice and training tips. It was inevitable that BTT fighters would encounter Chute Boxe fighters in MMA competition in the near future, so this was a wise investment by Rodrigo.

In return, Anderson gained entry into a variety of MMA markets and learned a more fluid style of BJJ. Although Anderson was a brown belt in Brazilian Jiu-Jitsu under the Chute Boxe system, a more highly refined BJJ game would improve Anderson's commitment to his strikes as he would be more comfortable if the fight went to the ground.

"If Minotauro didn't reach out to me, maybe I would have had to stop fighting because of it," said Anderson. "I consider [Rodrigo] and Rogério (Minotouro) my blood brothers. I owe them everything."

Would Anderson really have retired from MMA had the Nogueira brothers not stepped up to lend support? He would have been able to swallow his pride and crawl back to Chute Boxe, as others had done, or he could have become a domestic opponent in Brazil, living the life of a journeyman. It's certain that without someone powerful looking out for his interests, he would have remained rudderless in the MMA world.

The Nogueira brothers arranged a fight for Anderson against Waldir dos Anjos (2-8) at Conquista Fight 1 on New Year's Eve of 2003. Waldir's corner stopped the fight after the first five-minute round. With the win, Anderson had rebounded from the Takase loss.

His next fight was against American Jeremy Horn in Seoul, South Korea. Horn had amassed a prolific record of 70-12-5, including wins over Chuck Liddell, Chael Sonnen and Forrest Griffin. At the same time, Horn's success in beating elite MMA fighters never translated into recognition or greater rewards, as he never strung together the right series of wins while in a big promotion. He could still spoil Anderson Silva's party, however.

"That fight was worse than having to face two heavyweights at the same time in their home country," said Anderson.

The early going saw Jeremy Horn easily take Anderson to the mat, slamming him viciously on one particular takedown. After a stand-up near the end of the first round, Horn seemed lost on the feet, covering up and getting picked apart by Anderson. Unfortunately, Horn had torn his groin, making his right leg nearly useless. Anderson clearly dominated the rest of the fight, winning a decision.

Next was a stint in Britain's "Cage Rage" promotion. Anderson claims to have only paid a five percent commission on his Cage Rage purses to an intermediary named Alex who helped arrange the fights. The other benefit that Silva enjoyed through his arrangement with the promoter was direct payment of his purses. For Anderson, transparency was a welcome change from PRIDE's dirty dealings.

At Cage Rage 8, Anderson dissected now infamous British fighter Lee Murray (8-1-1) for a three-round decision to take the Cage Rage middleweight belt. Murray effectively retired from MMA after the loss. In June 2010, he was sentenced to ten years (a term later extended to 25 years) in prison for masterminding the Securitas depot robbery of £53,116,760 in February 2006.

With the former PRIDE heavyweight champion in his corner, Anderson finally had leverage to re-enter the Japanese organization. Antônio Rodrigo Nogueira had a contract clause inserted that stated PRIDE had to give Anderson another shot, or else they would lose Nogueira. PRIDE officials reportedly offered Nogueira "a few hundred grand" to drop the clause, but he was rigid in his belief that Anderson had earned a second chance.[109]

According to Anderson, he entered the fight with Ryo Chonan at PRIDE's 2004 NYE show with a broken ankle courtesy of training partner José "Pelé" Landi-Jons. Anderson was dominant at the start, securing the takedown, taking Chonan's back and locking him in a body triangle. Ryo escaped to take top position and attempted strikes on the ground until the pair was stood up and Anderson was given a yellow card (meaning a penalty of 10 percent of his purse would be deducted—a crafty way to inspire action or save a few bucks) for stalling. Throughout the fight, Chonan kept his eyes on Anderson, blocking the vicious high-kicks and delivering unchecked low kicks of his own. While watching Ryo take Anderson down and pound away from top position of Anderson's guard in the second round, commentator Bas Rutten hypothesized that Chonan was ahead on points. At 3:08 of the final round, Anderson was caught with a flying scissor heel hook and submitted. Had the fight gone to the judges, it's likely that the Japanese fighter would have been given the nod.

A post-fight video revealed that Chonan's arm was so hurt from Anderson's strikes, he complained about not even being able to drink his sake properly, Anderson was also banged up, his leg torn to ribbons by Chonan's kicks. In loss, Anderson was inconsolable—he did not know what other opportunities lay ahead after crapping out at the big show for the second time.

As for the significance of the PRIDE welterweight (183 pound) title, Anderson would have coveted a chance to take it. Years later, speaking of his unification bout between his UFC middleweight title and Dan Henderson's PRIDE welterweight title, Anderson was clearly bitter.

"To tell you the truth the Pride belt was mine, the opportunity to fight for it was just taken away from me, so it was just a matter of time until I would somehow fight for it," said Anderson.[110]

Like the other times when Anderson had approached the summit and slid back down, he did not give up easy. Anderson had to defend the Cage Rage title he had won from Lee Murray. At Cage Rage 11 on April 30, 2005, Anderson stopped Jorge Rivera (10-4) with knees and punches in the second round. After that bout, he knocked out Curtis Stout (10-6-1) in the first round at Cage Rage 14 on December 3, 2005.

"Rumble on the Rock 8," held on January 20, 2006, in Honolulu, Hawaii, was the opening round in a tournament involving a collection of eight of the best welterweights available during this era: Anderson Silva, Jake Shields, Carlos Condit, Frank Trigg, Yushin Okami, Dave Menne, Renato Verissimo and Ronald Jhun. Today, it's hard to imagine a scenario where Anderson Silva doesn't smash every name on that list, but Silva managed to get disqualified after knocking Okami out with an illegal upkick (a kick thrown from a fighter on their back) in the first round of their fight.

The sheer dominance Anderson had demonstrated on the feet made it hard to accept the loss.

"I do think he could have continued," said a still-bitter Silva to the *LA Times* in 2011. "But he had the rules in his favor."[111]

Jake Shields won a controversial decision over Okami at the next round held at ROTR 9. Shields then beat Carlos Condit (who lacked the defensive wrestling to stop the takedown) via three-round decision to take the ROTR welterweight crown.

Anderson returned to England, facing Tony Fryklund (11-5) at Cage Rage 16 on April 22, 2006. His preparation for the bout revealed the confidence laced with arrogance that would ultimately define Anderson as a great fighter. Silva had recently watched the martial arts action film *Ong Bak* and was inspired by a specific move utilized by the film's hero, Tony Jaa:

> **Instead of attacking with a side elbow or an over-the-top elbow, both of which are common in Muay Thai, Jaa stepped toward one of the villains and threw a lead reverse back elbow. I was so enamored with the move I went to my trainers and told them that I was going to use the strike in my next fight to knock out my opponent.**

Anderson recalls that his trainers were less than enthusiastic about the move, so he practiced it unofficially after each training session— making his wife stand on the couch holding a pillow, and throwing the elbow 100 times. When he went to warm up with the same move in the moments before the Fryklund fight, his trainers were critical yet again and urged Anderson to forget about that elbow strike. This only fired him up.

"I figured I had no other choice but to prove them wrong, so two minutes into my fight with Frykland, I stepped toward him, threw a lead reverse back elbow at his chin, and knocked him out," said a defiant Anderson.[112]

It was as perfect a fight as anyone could have had in MMA against a live underdog.

The doors to the UFC had opened before Anderson's fight with Fryklund, with an offer of a three-fight contract for $20,000 per fight on the table. Although the UFC had experienced an explosion in revenue due to the popularity of *The Ultimate Fighter* leading to high pay-per-view sales, their offer to Anderson was only marginally better than what Cage Rage paid for escalating risk against tougher opponents. As Anderson was earning $15,000 with Cage Rage, he had decided to face Fryklund on the basis of his verbal contract with Cage Rage. A Japanese contact had assured him that it would still be possible for him to return to PRIDE, an organization which Silva was attached to as he felt that it was the most prestigious promotion in the world. After his victory over Fryklund, there was no offer from PRIDE, so Anderson opted to sign with the UFC.

From Anderson Silva's perspective at the time, he was pursuing his second-best love in courting the UFC. There was no way for him to know that PRIDE was a sinking ship, and that within a year's time, the best and brightest PRIDE stars (save Fedor Emelianenko) would be at the UFC's beck and call. Anderson would also benefit from acclimatizing to the octagon, different rules, new owners and drug testing earlier than other PRIDE fighters, who would be forced to transition to the UFC later on.

In his debut UFC fight, Silva faced *TUF 1* alumnus Chris Leben (15-1) at Ultimate Fight Night 5 on June 28, 2006. Leben had performed various attention-seeking stunts during his time on the reality show, such as urinating on a cast member's bed, wrecking a door; he had also lost to show contestants Josh Koscheck and Kenny Florian in fights that were not counted towards his pro record.

At this point in time, Leben had won five straight bouts in the UFC, with his solid striking and granite jaw aiding him in his fights. With the confidence of a man who had never really lost in devastating fashion, Leben gave a memorable pre-fight interview:

> **When I get in there and I'm in his face, I'm pressing the action, I'm rough-necking him, throwing him around, punching him, he's punching me, I'm eating his shots and just blasting him back in the face, he's not going to be able to handle it; he's going to go 'What is this guy? This guy is a dump truck, he just keeps going, keeps moving forward!'**

It was, however, not to be—not as long as Anderson Silva lived and breathed, remembering all the injustices done to him in this life, eager to pay it forward to the man opposing him in the cage.

In the fight, Anderson utilized lateral movement and his jab against Leben. When Leben moved in to engage, Anderson had the right answer every time by either moving away or countering. After landing a head kick, Anderson followed up with straight punches that rocked Leben and sent him to the canvas. Anderson believed the fight was over then and there, so he hesitated before realizing Leben wasn't out cold, then decided to follow Leben to the ground, holding with one hand and punching with the other. Leben managed to make it to his feet—a move that exposed him to greater danger, as Anderson dropped him again with a perfect knee. Referee John McCarthy promptly stopped the bout just forty-nine seconds into round one.

Less than a minute in, and Anderson's UFC debut was over. What Anderson had always believed about himself was becoming obvious to others—Anderson Silva was someone special.

In 2006, Rich "Ace" Franklin was widely viewed to be unstoppable as the reigning UFC middleweight champion. A former math teacher, the Cincinnati, Ohio native had earned his nickname from his close resemblance to actor Jim Carrey, star of *Ace Ventura: Pet Detective*. In 2005, Franklin had beaten the now deceased Evan Tanner for the UFC middleweight title. His successful title defenses against Nate Quarry and David Loiseau gave further evidence of his dominance. With Franklin, the Zuffa brass had their dream fighter—good looking, English-speaking, American, Caucasian and talented. Under the right circumstances, Franklin could draw the same pay-per-view numbers as other major Zuffa stars as he continued his trajectory to the top.

Anderson had his own plan, and at UFC 64 on October 14, 2006, when Silva was matched with Franklin (then 22-1), it was finally "Anderson Silva time." Ed Soares, Anderson Silva's co-manager, was still nervous about the fight—even more nervous than Anderson was himself.

"Anderson kind of looked at me and winked," recalled Ed Soares as Silva was told to leave his dressing room for the octagon. "[Anderson] said, 'Relax, I'm going to go out there and knock this guy out quick for you.'"

All his suffering—the racism endured in Brazil, the string of shitty low-wage jobs, the gates to PRIDE locking him out, the petty disrespect he perceived from people around him—Anderson's righteous rage finally crystallized into an opportunity to take back what was rightfully his.

As the reigning UFC champion, Rich Franklin walked in last to AC/DC's "For Those About to Rock." The crowd's eruption at his entrance swagger was electric. In the cruel way the fight game worked, however, Franklin was like the prom queen peaking as a senior—his days at the very top would soon be behind him.

In the fight, Anderson Silva was his usual cautious self: moving laterally and being patient. Franklin had great striking, but Anderson had latched onto deficiencies in Franklin's technique in the clinch. Once there, Anderson broke Franklin's body down with knees. Franklin tried to counter Anderson in the clinch with knees of his own and dirty boxing, but he wasn't doing the same damage in return that Anderson was visiting on him. Franklin didn't attempt to crossface Anderson and escape the clinch. Eventually, Franklin resorted to using his hands to try and block Anderson's knees to the body. This was akin to a pugilist dropping their hands to stem the tide of vicious body shots ("Head, body, head!")—a temporary solution, playing right into Anderson's hands.

As Franklin backed down and out of the clinch, Anderson let his opponent step back and then rushed forward with a beautiful high kick to Franklin's face. After following up with another powerful kick, Anderson dropped Franklin with a knee to his head. Franklin was out of it, and the bout was over.

At 2:59 of the first round, Anderson Silva's reign atop the UFC's middleweight division had begun.

19

BUFFOONERY OR GENIUS?

Before UFC 97, held on April 18, 2009, in Montreal, Anderson had finished nine quality opponents in a row, eight of them in the UFC, five of them in title bouts. Anderson had even unified the PRIDE welterweight (183 pound) and UFC middleweight (185 pound) titles by submitting Dan Henderson at UFC 82.

On paper, he was the cat's meow, the finisher with no hesitation before going in for the kill. A closer look at some of his performances reveals chinks in his armor. Against *TUF* winner Travis Lutter, the crowd initially became bored and restless with Anderson's patient counter-punching, satiated only when Lutter took the fight to the ground. Five fights later, Silva's avoidance of mixing it up with heavy-handed Canadian Patrick Côté was the beginning of the sour relationship Anderson would endure with his critics, who included fans, media, and most importantly of all, the UFC brass. Anderson Silva notched a decision when Côté blew out his knee in the third round, but the damage was done, thanks to Silva's lack of aggression prior to Côté's injury.

There are many different theories as to why Anderson went the distance against Thales Leites and Demian Maia. Was Anderson in the pay of the mafia? Was he going easy on Brazilian comrades? Was it impossible to finish because his opponents had turtled up defensively? Was it his way of extending his middle finger to the Zuffa brass? Perhaps the "truth" is a composite of different theories and reasons, just as each brushstroke that creates a masterpiece is different, yet directed toward the same goal.

The irony was that even though Anderson's hand was raised at the end of both the Leites and Maia fights, his stock plummeted. Some fighters win respect in loss, but Anderson had lost respect in winning.

In the mafia-controlled boxing world of the '40s and '50s, boxer Sugar Ray Robinson was approached by gangsters in order to "carry" fights (extending a match for a certain number of rounds when he could have finished his opponents much earlier) in order to appease the criminal elements who profited from gambling rackets. When Sugar Ray was pressured by mobster Frankie Carbo to throw a fight against Jake LaMotta, Robinson held firm to his principles and refused to go along.[113]

Were there similar undercurrents in mixed martial arts? PRIDE had been closely linked to the yakuza (organized crime in Japan). There had been several fixed, or "worked," matches in PRIDE, including Mark Coleman allegedly dropping a fight to Nobuhiko Takada at PRIDE 5.[114] North American UFC bouts were overseen by an athletic commission, but this did not mean that fights were impervious to corruption.

If Anderson Silva were to carry a fight, there was always the potential of a loss via judges' decision. With a loss, Anderson could be denied millions in earning potential for future fights.

In 2012, Anderson gave an interview to Brazilian MMA news site Tatame.com, where he explicitly stated that he had carried Thales Leites.

"We went until the last round because he's a friend of mine and I respect him," said Anderson.[115]

In response to Anderson's comments, Leites vigorously denied any friendship with Anderson. But what about the question of carrying Maia and Leites because they were fellow Brazilians? Anderson Silva had certainly felt no need to carry fellow Brazilian Vitor Belfort at UFC 126 in Las Vegas, as Anderson knocked Belfort out in the first round.

UFC 112, held on April 10, 2010 in Abu Dhabi, was an extremely important show where Anderson was headlining against Demian Maia. Behind the scenes, a deal had been struck where the power base of the Zuffa ownership changed, making the event a critical showcase of what the UFC represented. In January 2010, a 10 percent stake of Zuffa was sold to Sheik Tahnoon of Abu Dhabi (Flash Entertainment); the Fertitta brothers' shares fell to 40.5 percent each, with Dana White now owning 9 percent of Zuffa.[116] After the sale, the Fertitta brothers were able to refinance the loans on the then-bankrupt Station Casinos and regain their majority shareholder status.

In the main event of UFC 112, Anderson clowned Maia, emulating a variety of fighters' stylistic trademarks to the derision of audiences and the horror of the Zuffa brass. It's the nature of great artists—and even mediocre ones—to be out-of-touch with their audiences at times and believe that their genius is finding a home, when onlookers are, in fact, bewildered. Michael Jackson's post-*Thriller* antics qualify here.

Said MMA coach Greg Jackson on Anderson's antics in the fight: "I actually really enjoyed the first part of the fight, with Anderson changing up his style, like he would do Machida, then he would kind of do the Diaz brothers' thing, then Muhammad Ali."[117]

The Maia performance represented Anderson's true intent. Just as he had thrilled the crowd by using an unorthodox elbow to knock Tony Fryklund out, here, Anderson was going for a heightened level of entertainment and artistry by showboating. Being unable to land the knockout shot, his actions backfired. He was the pretty girl who had applied too much make-up and made herself ugly.

A big reason that Anderson had not finished Leites and Maia was perhaps because the opportunity to do so wasn't there. Leites spent much of their fight retreating and butt-flopping to guard. By the end of the Maia fight, Anderson's energy level had diminished to the point where Maia made an argument to win one or two of the later rounds (official scores for Anderson were 50-45, 50-45 and 49-46). Even though Anderson was a masterful fighter, he could not simply guarantee a finish in every match, any more than he could guarantee the win (although at the height of his UFC career, he came pretty close on both counts).

The audience had grown restless and bored with Anderson; animosity against him multiplied exponentially. Waiting in the wings was a man who would exploit this, as well as Zuffa's favoritism toward sycophants, to the fullest degree.

American Chael Sonnen was an NCAA Division 1 wrestler for the University of Oregon who had risen as far as being an Olympic alternate in Greco-Roman wrestling in 2000. He was 25-10-1 at the time that he faced Anderson, with victories over Paulo Filho, Yushin Okami and Nate Marquardt.

When Sonnen's father, Patrick, was dying of colon cancer, Sonnen made a promise that haunted him throughout his MMA career. "I told him I was going to beat Tito Ortiz and win the championship," said Sonnen.

"That's the only promise I ever made him and never kept," he said in May 2010, during the lead-up to the Anderson Silva fight.[118]

Patrick died in 2002, and Sonnen was left with the psychological scars of an unfulfilled promise: self-loathing and regret that pre-dated his MMA career.[119]

"My dad—he was intense," recalled Sonnen in the UFC 117 countdown show, "There was only one goal—to be the best."

Sonnen recalls a high-school wrestling tournament in which he didn't place. The punishment handed down by Patrick was to fill a wheelbarrow with rocks and stones.

"I had to move it through the field, and load these rocks into a different pile. Once I got all the rocks moved, I just had to move all the rocks back."[120]

Patrick's constant criticism of his son's performances was not good for Sonnen's emotional development. Sonnen fell into a pattern of approval seeking—first from his father, then wrestling coaches and eventually, UFC president Dana White. Sonnen diagnosed himself with social anxiety, but the fractures in his fragile psyche went far deeper.

On August 7, 2010, Anderson fought Sonnen at UFC 117 in Oakland, California. Very few people anticipated the all-out war and dramatic reversal of fortune that would take place in the cage that night.

"This is a guy who is willing to take a beating to give a beating," said Dana White of Sonnen in a promo for the fight.

White's words would prove prescient of the way Sonnen took the fight straight to Anderson rather than freezing up or waiting to be picked off as so many others had done before him. In the first round, Sonnen hurt Anderson standing and took him down. Anderson Silva was susceptible to the takedown, as fifteen of his previous opponents who had managed to score at least one takedown on Silva had all proven.[121] Sonnen was ultra-effective in taking Anderson down at will and keeping him on the ground, dominating Anderson like no one had ever done before.

Anderson had his moments, cutting up Sonnen's face from the bottom with elbows and threatening Sonnen in the early part of the rounds where the fight began standing. Sonnen was still in control, making Anderson look like a novice and backing up every bit of his pre-fight trash talk.

Past the midway point in the fifth and final round, Sonnen was on his way to a clear-cut decision victory, as the judges scored the first four rounds 40–34, 40–35, and 40–36 for Sonnen. Anderson was enduring a quagmire of punishing blows while being unable to mount any offense from his back. Near the end of the fifth round, while Sonnen was in Anderson's guard delivering punishment, Sonnen made a fatal error in his posture. Anderson used the moment to catch Sonnen in a "Hail Mary" triangle choke. Sonnen had been finished three times via triangle choke before—against Forrest Griffin, Renato Sobral and Demian Maia. As referee Josh Rosenthal rushed in to stop the fight, Sonnen began protesting that he had not tapped. An instant replay quickly put that notion to rest and Anderson's arm was raised in victory.

Why did Sonnen lose—especially to a submission that he had been caught in before, therefore would have taken pains to learn to defend against? Sonnen knew how the fight was going, yet he had felt unworthy of the victory. Sonnen's body echoed the sentiment in the form of a mental lapse that allowed himself to be submitted. Blame his father Patrick for seeding doubt and lack of confidence in order to nudge his wrestling career along. Sonnen simply hadn't exorcised the bad mental coaching that had haunted his mindset throughout his career.

Sonnen made a name for himself in defeat by continuing with the pro-wrestling antics that had elevated him in public interest. He should have had his credibility destroyed by being caught with an elevated testosterone/epitestosterone (T/E) ratio of 16.9:1 from test results released just after the Anderson Silva fight.[122] In January 2011, Sonnen pleaded guilty to a money laundering charge related to mortgage fraud from his second job as a realtor, but the incident hardly scandalized Sonnen.[123] Rather, Sonnen's value as a fighter had shot through the roof—he could increase interest in the UFC product, and as such, he had to be protected in order to guarantee a lucrative return bout with Anderson Silva.

Anderson might have won the fight, but Sonnen had won the event.

20

THE X-GYM

The X-Gym was the gym that housed the Black House MMA (*Casa Preta*) facility in Recreio dos Bandeirantes, Rio de Janeiro. From Copacabana beach, getting there is a short taxi or bus trip west. The scenery en route to the gym is breathtaking: misty mountains to the left, exotic beachfronts to the right. In a 2010 visit, the facility itself appeared similar to any commercial fitness center, with the X-Gym located inside a strip mall full of the usual suspects in electronics, women's shoes and knick-knacks.

Recreio is an exclusive area for the rich. All of the gym clientele, save Anderson, his trainers and training partners, reflected this division in society. Even the front desk attendants and gym employees were a couple of degrees cooler than their counterparts in other areas of Rio. Gym members needed to walk one floor down for the main fitness facility of change rooms, studio floor space and the cafe; another floor down was an impressive array of weight machines and cardio equipment. At the very end of the sub-basement of the X-Gym lay the martial arts training area; it included a ring, octagon and generous mat space.

Although Black House is the name of the team, the entire camp was just a loose association of fighters loyal to their own teams, with the X-Gym being managed on the ground level by former Brazil Top Team member Rogério Camões. Anderson Silva officially belonged to the Nogueira Brothers' team, and paid 10 percent of his fight purse (according to Camões) to the X-Gym, with every coach and partner in his camp there to support Anderson.

Anderson Silva strolled into the X-Gym for training at high noon. Carrying a red, four-liter water jug and hauling his own gear, a casual onlooker never would have suspected just how much power and prestige Anderson commanded from MMA fans. Even when he flirted with bubbly female gym admirers at the end of the day's training session, Silva still came across as a grateful and free-spirited gym rat (albeit one whom women were much more attracted to than, say, anyone else at the gym).

After wrapping his own hands, the "Spider" warmed up by shadowboxing, then doing arm circles. On this day in December, his boxing training was with Luiz Dórea—the Nogueira brothers' striking coach. Dórea hailed from Champions Gym in Salvador, and was both loved and respected for tailoring his approach to the individual rather than trying to remake the fighter into his own image (a common flaw of many trainers). Silva threw quick one-two's while switching his stance to avoid the takedown. A couple of repetitions later, he mixed in a pivoting motion, along with a hook at the end of the sequence. When Dórea gave instruction, Anderson listened to him with complete focus and dedication.

When Anderson moved on for no-gi BJJ practice, then-number-one UFC heavyweight contender Junior dos Santos was also training that day. The current number- one middleweight, training alongside the then-number-two heavyweight, would be interesting to witness.

Anderson and JDS slapped high-fives, then crawled into position with their respective grappling partners, starting from the knees. It was obvious who the stars of the gym were—well-muscled, shining, TV-friendly, with flowing body language—dictating the tempo of the BJJ practice. BJJ stars were typically low-key by comparison, as they got next to zero exposure outside of some industry publications. The lesson began with Anderson and JDS taking turns being dominated like absolute beginners by an undersized black belt named Ramon Lemos. A third-degree BJJ black belt, Lemos had the knowledge and familiarity with jiu-jitsu to control Anderson and JDS with ease. Lemos was holding back from completely embarrassing his employers by submitting them, as sparring partners often pull their punches in boxing gyms.

Anderson was a great artist—always aware of the fragile nature of his own dominance, never willing to accept the title of the greatest fighter in the world.

"My friend BJ [Penn] is the best fighter in the world," said Silva to this writer.[124]

In another interview, Anderson had called Rodrigo Nogueira the best fighter in the world.[125] It was part false modesty, and part devaluing his own work in order to squeeze more juice from his ever-maturing talents.

With an upcoming fight against Brazilian rival Vitor Belfort, there was secrecy and paranoia surrounding Anderson Silva's training camp. The daily rhythms of the gym were hidden from the public, both to hype the fight as a clash of superhuman men, and to help the fighter believe in himself by avoiding unnecessary criticism or prejudgment.

After taking a three-hour break for lunch and to see his physician, Anderson's evening training session consisted of weight training supervised by his conditioning specialist, Rogério Camões. Being thrown around like a rag doll by Chael Sonnen had reinforced the necessity of strength and conditioning. Between the exhausting workouts, Anderson was still smiles and cheer, doing a dance with his hips while poking fun at teammate and Strikeforce fighter Rafael "Feijão"

Cavalcante for drinking champagne, because "it was a girl's drink," and enjoying the reactions from onlookers. Far from the overtaxed celebrity driven to tears searching for quiet time, Anderson lapped up all of the praise, accolades and smiles. And yet, it always seemed that a part of him was missing, obscured within the ruins of a world that the people watching knew nothing about.

***

UFC and PRIDE veteran Vitor Belfort had very briefly been a member of Black House back in 2006, but his lack of commitment and loyalty to any specific gym or team made him drift onward. Some considered Vitor to be an absolute head case—he was a man with obvious and undeniable talent, but his desire and will fluctuated according to the situation.

Anderson had a special grudge against Vitor Belfort, owing to class differences. The favoritism that Vitor had been granted his whole life contrasted starkly with the endless struggles that Anderson had endured.

"First thing, [Vitor] was never my friend," said Anderson, of Vitor's time at Black House, to Tatame.com. "Second, a fight is fight. I'm here to fight and whoever is better prepared will win and one of us will lose. I'd be upset if I had to face Rodrigo, Rogério, Feijão, Lyoto or even Wanderlei or Shogun, but Vitor? He's just another opponent like everyone else."[126]

A black belt under Carlson Gracie, Vitor Belfort notched impressive early showings in winning the UFC 12 heavyweight tournament and in stopping Wanderlei Silva in just forty-four seconds at UFC Brazil. Despite his success, right from his early fights, Vitor displayed mental weakness when he was put under pressure against dangerous opposition. He demonstrated this when he dropped a decision to Kazushi Sakuraba in PRIDE in his eighth fight due to repeatedly butt-flopping to guard. Vitor had later stated that he'd broken his hand in the Sakuraba fight, but as the larger fighter and a superior striker, he still could have fought Sakuraba in a more dignified way—win or lose.

Vitor's biggest win had been a TKO over Randy Couture due to a cut eyelid for the 205-pound UFC championship.

Vitor Belfort versus Anderson Silva was slated for UFC 126, on February 5, 2011, in Las Vegas. The pressure to succeed against Anderson Silva was tremendous, with Vitor riding a five-fight win streak going into his challenge for the UFC middleweight title. Anderson's reputation as a backstabber preceded him. Vitor addressed the issue in the media, speaking frankly about Anderson's two-faced nature.

"When you say silly things and you do silly things, it's because you're worried and you're trying to wear a mask," Vitor told the media the day before the weigh-ins.[127]

At the Friday weigh-ins, Anderson retaliated in a manner that demonstrated how Vitor's words had found their mark. After announcer Joe Rogan read Anderson's weight of "185 for the champion," a member of Anderson's entourage handed Anderson a white Phantom-of-the-Opera-type mask. Anderson put the mask on and got right in Vitor's face, then pushed the mask to the top of his head to reveal his "real" face. There was serious tension, anger and fear involved in this stare down; a weigh-in incident was a possibility, but these were rare in MMA, as UFC fighters were better controlled.

Vitor Belfort much more easily incited Anderson's wrath because Vitor had always been in possession of the free acceptance and privilege that Anderson was so keenly aware had eluded him throughout his life. Vitor had come from a wealthy family and was revered by the Brazilian press and public alike, whereas Anderson had come from poverty and obscurity. Married to Joana Prado, model, star of the popular Brazilian TV show *H* and *Playboy* centerfold, Vitor had the cachet necessary to make headlines. Vitor's life had been touched by extreme tragedy, as well: in January 2004, Vitor's sister Priscilla was kidnapped with no ransom demand made; years later, a woman would confess to taking part in Priscilla's murder. The upshot of this tragedy was wide public sympathy for Vitor, further entrenching him within the Brazilian people's hearts.

According to one story, when Anderson sparred against Vitor, Anderson sparked his better-regarded rival. That he was far superior in ability to Vitor, yet it was Vitor Belfort getting all the accolades did not sit well with Anderson.

There was also the psychological dimension of their interaction— Anderson lending a helping hand to a downtrodden hero in his time of need due to the lack of closure over his sister's disappearance. Yet dissonance between the two remained. In fact, to Anderson, it was an affront that Vitor was even challenging him in the first place.

The main event between Vitor and Anderson at UFC 126 was quick and decisive. There was no touch of gloves at the start of the opening round to signal good sportsmanship. The two strikers circled, feinting and awaiting the right moment to attack. At 3:25 of the opening frame, Anderson floored Vitor with a front kick and then followed him to the mat with punches to secure the stoppage win.

It had taken years, but the Anderson-Belfort match finally captured mainstream interest in Brazil and demonstrated something Anderson always knew about himself: that he was the superior fighter. In a bizarre twist to the proceedings, action movie star Steven Seagal, who had inspired many to take up the martial arts, was credited with the win. Manager Ed Soares translated for Anderson at the post-fight presser, "I was training at Black House with Steven Seagal, and he helped me a lot with that kick."

Of course, Anderson had always known how to throw a front kick. He simply suggested that Seagal had helped him get the most from it.

"I did that kick for a long time, and he actually helped me perfect it," said Anderson.[128]

Seagal was disliked in most MMA circles due to stories about him being a difficult person. Former PRIDE analyst Stephen Quadros told a story where he felt Seagal was trying to square up with him in order to kick him in the groin. Then again, it was a longstanding tradition within the fight game that celebrities would be comped tickets to sit ringside in order to add to the glamour of the spectacle. Anderson's camp enjoyed crediting Steven Seagal with the win, a tactful move that would garner Anderson more attention from the media.

The final footnote to the Vitor knockout was that it involved the use of a front kick, known as the "teep" in Muay Thai. When one throws a teep to the face, it shows that they have no respect for their opponent—at least in Thailand, as the feet are considered the dirtiest part of the body. As a Muay Thai specialist, Anderson knew this better than anyone. Some pointed this out, or criticized Anderson for breaking this unwritten rule. Why Anderson needed to show reverence to traditional Thai beliefs while fighting in the US in an MMA fight is not clear, but at the end of the day, the kick wasn't an illegal or unsportsmanlike tactic.

Despite the win, Anderson still carried animosity toward Vitor well into the future. During an episode of *The Ultimate Fighter: Brazil,* former Chute Boxe teammate Wanderlei Silva quizzed Anderson Silva for some advice on how to beat Vitor, the opposing team's coach, in their scheduled fight.

"I know his weakness, he can't step back. He's a coward," replied Anderson, unaware that his mic was still active.[129]

It was one thing to suggest that Vitor couldn't fight going backwards, or that Vitor was helpless against aggressive opponents. Vitor's weak mental disposition had been an open topic of discussion for years and years. It was, however, disrespectful of Anderson to label an ex-opponent a "coward." A man who steps in the cage with a fighter of Anderson's caliber is not a coward.

With the unintended slip, Anderson had revealed what lay beneath his façade.

21

BRIGHT LIGHTS, DARK SHADOWS

The final—and undisputable—assessment of Anderson's still-evolving career is that he is one of the greatest mixed martial artists of all time.

It's typical for all-time rankings to be biased in favor of an individual generation's greatest era. Old-timers believe that Muhammad Ali easily takes out fighters who came decades later, like Mike Tyson or Vitali Klitschko. Every generation is tied to the heroes from its time period, with open bias against the next group of fighters.

MMA promoters like Dana White tend to shift their opinions of the pound-for-pound rankings based on self-interest. At one point, White elevated UFC fighters Frankie Edgar and Jose Aldo when they required promotion to the public, while simultaneously demoting reigning UFC champions Anderson Silva and Georges St-Pierre, two of the greatest fighters in the history of the sport.

In the end, Anderson Silva's achievements speak for themselves: 33 wins, a record 16 straight wins in the UFC and a record ten title defenses. Three fights at light-heavyweight where he smashed James Irvin,

Forrest Griffin and Stephan Bonnar in one round. All of the above by utilizing explosive striking, fancy footwork and uncompromising skill.

The financial rewards of his achievements didn't translate as easily into large pay-per-view numbers for Anderson. Yet he still enjoyed far more leverage than revolving-door champions, and benefited from the rivalries with various challengers, such as Chael Sonnen. The Silva-Sonnen rematch at UFC 148, where Anderson stopped Sonnen in the second round, was estimated to have drawn about 925,000 pay-per-view buys.[130]

In terms of fight sponsorship, Anderson lucked out due to Brazilian soccer superstar Ronaldo Luis Nazario de Lima—considered one of the best players of all time—creating a sports-management marketing agency called "9ine" after his jersey number, and signing Anderson as his very first client in January 2011.[131] The relationship began to yield dividends almost immediately as Anderson got $100,000 from Brazilian men's grooming company Bozzano.[132] Burger King signed Anderson to advertise their brand in July 2011; shortly after, Ronaldo used his connections with his former soccer team, Corinthians Paulista (of which Anderson was already a fan), to engage Anderson in a multi-tiered marketing plan. Nike entered the fold in August, allowing Anderson to join an eclectic roster of fellow-MMAers sponsored by the shoe giant, from Yoshihiro Akiyama to Caol Uno.[133]

A Burger King commercial showed Anderson lip-synching to Minnie Riperton's "Lovin' You" in a mockery of his effeminate, high-pitched falsetto voice. The irony was that Anderson was a former McDonald's employee, with a love for Big Macs (Anderson Silva's pre-fight ritual is to eat two Big Macs the night before every fight) and a desire to open up a McDonald's franchise in Brazil.[134] No matter what his personal preference was in hamburgers, the influx of sponsorship dollars from blue-chip companies no doubt had Anderson "lovin' it."

Anderson "The Spider" Silva also had his vanity as a top-shelf fighter with such precision striking and unstoppable power that he would always remember the thrill of stopping opponent after opponent, long after he'd retired. Like his idol Spiderman ("he was the only hero who had bills to pay"), Silva was superhuman and electrified in performance; outside that venue, he withered into the margins like Peter Parker.

Anderson Silva has done all he needs to do to cement his legacy. He will always represent the measuring stick for perfection for generations of champions to come. He has become a reflection of his idol Bruce Lee—that unattainable picture of mental strength, martial arts and destruction.

22

THE GOOD LIFE

In the script of public perception, fighters are often typecast as the hard cases, coming from difficult lives and having worse upbringings. Like trained animals, they have turned to the professional circuit to direct the persistent rage burning inside to live opponents. Mixed martial arts showcases many exceptions to this stereotype, as there are many elite fighters who come from well-off families. These include (but are not limited to) Kenny Florian, Vitor Belfort, BJ Penn and Maurício "Shogun" Rua.

Born in Curitiba on November 25, 1981, of Portuguese and Italian descent, Maurício Milani Rua was the second of three boys, all of whom would later become involved in mixed martial arts. Maurício's mother was a track athlete and a marathon runner who genetically gifted her sons with athleticism.[135] In terms of family finances, Maurício's father was a successful businessman; the Rua family wasn't elite, but comfortably middle-class.

Maurício always credited his parents for a great upbringing, stating, "Both of our parents are very kind to us. They played soccer and swam with us since we were children," in an interview for the PRIDE website in 2005.

His mother always offered support and incentive for him in his journey. Maurício always felt indebted to her for the way she stood up for him throughout his life.

Like so many other Brazilian youngsters, the first dream to enter Maurício's head was that of the footballers. He played soccer with his father and neighborhood kids.

"I always played soccer when I was a kid," said Maurício. "I did play well up until my early teens. I used to play in big soccer clubs in Curitiba, even played in some big tournaments."[136]

Soccer was not the only sport that natural athlete Maurício excelled at. Although relatively unknown or unheralded in North America, there is a variant to volleyball known as "fistball" that originated in Europe. The major championships are dominated by Germany, Austria and Brazil, so exposure to the professional leagues existed for the young Maurício.

"I was close to going professional when I was around sixteen. But then I started doing Muay Thai and the rest is history," said Maurício, to the relief of MMA fans all around the world.

There was also a gig as a model for books, photos and even fashion shows that occupied Maurício's time. "I enjoyed the experience, but to be honest, I'm a fighter since I was 16," said Rua of his brief modeling career.[137]

Murilo Rua was Maurício's older brother by one year. Murilo might have shared many genetic traits with Maurício, but it was always clear that the two brothers were very different from each other.

Murilo was the inspiration for Maurício to commence training at the Chute Boxe academy. [138]

Said Maurício, "My brother used to get into a lot of fights in the street and get beat up, and one day at home, my parents said [to Murilo], 'You know we're going to put you in a school to learn martial arts and defend yourself.' "

At age 15, Maurício would sit on the sidelines and watch his brother train at the academy. Over time, he found himself more and more pulled into Chute Boxe, simply by exposure. By all accounts, Maurício was well-mannered and stayed far from trouble on the streets—so his motivation to start training was a little different from Murilo's.

"In the beginning, I was a little lazy to train, I just did it for fun," said Maurício. "When I started to like it and realized how good I was, I took it seriously."

When Maurício took up Muay Thai at 15 and Brazilian Jiu-Jitsu at 17, there was some resistance on the home front, as it was not something that his father initially approved of or saw the value in supporting.

"My father wanted me to work with him," said Maurício. "He represented sporting goods companies, right? I went around for a year, working with my father, and at every stop he would make around the country, I would train jiu-jitsu wherever I was. Train jiu-jitsu, train Muay Thai, whatever I trained, and I did that year, helping my father a lot, working, and I realized after that year that that was not what I wanted to do. I wanted to be a professional fighter and that was the end of that."

The Rua brothers deny any sibling rivalry between themselves. "We've never fought, even after getting upset. We've always gotten along," claimed Maurício.

Training was a different matter, with Maurício claiming that Murilo had always been better than he was in the early going, and that only recently did Maurício surpass Murilo as a fighter. Similar claims were floated by MMA and K-1 fighter Alistair Overeem regarding his older brother, Valentijn, at a Strikeforce presser.

"[Murilo] always got the better of our fights," Maurício told Dave Deibert of Postmedia News. "He's the older brother…and this age difference made a big difference. He was always bigger and stronger. Through my whole life, it was like that, so he would get the better of me. But recently, I became the bigger guy."[139]

Perhaps in the beginning there was some dominance by Murilo. However, it's a mark of Maurício's humble nature that he attributes recent success to his larger (205 pound) weight class over Murilo (183 pound). In 2005, Maurício was at the absolute height of his prowess, winning the PRIDE middleweight (205 pound) Grand Prix. By contrast, in 2004, Murilo had suffered a devastating first-round knockout to Russian Sergei Kharitonov contested at heavyweight—weight Murilo gained mostly in his midsection. 2005 saw Murilo drop to 183 pounds, where he was never able to regain his footing when matched with better-than-average fighters.

Brazilians are fun-loving people; a favorite activity involves assigning nicknames. The story of how Maurício was given his moniker is one he enjoyed retelling in English.

"I had at 15 years...one gi that [said] 'Shogun' (points to where the name brand would be on the sleeve). And my brother 'Ninja.' [People said,] 'Hey guys, you are Shogun!' 'Why?' 'Your brother 'Ninja' and you're 'Shogun!' "

What Maurício meant was that he had a gi where the brand name was "Shogun"; Murilo's gi was called "Ninja." Such a small detail ended up defining their respective nicknames, and perhaps adding to Maurício's allure when his popularity exploded abroad.

"I think certainly Shogun is the nickname that imposes more fear. It's a general of some sort in Japan, a very important war figure," explained Maurício. "Ninja is more of an ordinary warrior."

The additional benefit of Shogun's nickname was the cachet it held in Japan, where the term meant a "commander of force." The nickname was meaningless until Maurício breathed life into his career, but marketing could be improved if a fighter had a special name for public recognition. After all, what would Muhammad Ali have been in the all-time rankings without his moniker of "The Greatest"?

There was some nationalist ire drawn by Japanese opponent Akihiro Gono in 2004.

"Akihiro Gono, before our fight had said he was going to beat me, and then I would have to change my name," said Maurício. "I wouldn't be allowed to be called Shogun again, because Shogun is 'The General' in Japanese."

A soccer-kick-induced stoppage of Gono late in the first round of the fight ensured that Maurício would continue his ascension to his rightful place among MMA royalty.

"I still have the name, right?" Maurício smirked.

23

TRIAL BY FIRE

Stepping into a match where there is a guarantee of being hit back at full force is a difficult proposition to sell to most people. For many, training in martial arts is for fun, fitness or self-esteem. More serious practitioners are streamed in a different way: a process where students graduate from shadowboxing, pad work and hitting the heavy bag to hardcore sparring sessions. Eventually, fear of flying has to be pushed away when it comes to putting one's skills on the only stage that counts, the arena of competition.

Real fights—the purest test of skill—are classified into several different levels. Professional matches are the prominent face of MMA, boxing and Muay Thai. Before being able to earn money in these types of bouts, usually fighters start with unpaid amateur fights that are typically sanctioned under governing bodies. In amateur bouts, more protective gear is allowed, and rules often prohibit certain types of strikes. Yet there is another classification of fighting that is open to everyone and largely unregulated—"smokers." Gyms often organize bouts—using the same format as official fights—that resemble full-tilt sparring sessions, for new fighters to get experience without sacrificing their records.

In a grainy 1998 video, 16-year-old Maurício appears as unrefined as a lump of coal in a Muay Thai smoker held at then-Chute Boxe trainer Sergio Cunha's house academy.

"It was the kind of stuff that we always do in my hometown of Curitiba," said Cunha. "We put the gyms together to search for real fighters."

Maurício, representing Chute Boxe, and his opponent, Rodrigo Malheiros de Andrade, representing Cunha's affiliate academy, were the same weight, same age and at the same blue-belt level (Chute Boxe graded for belts in their Muay Thai system). The goal was to make a fair match for both competitors.

In the video, Maurício windmills his punches against his taller adversary, and appears to have rudimentary knowledge of how to clinch and throw knees. Cunha's student attempts push-kicks and roundhouse kicks, while Maurício prefers to close the distance and club with his right hand. The rounds are two minutes, with Maurício's corner, consisting of Murilo and Maurício's first trainer, José Seixas "Zito," fanning Maurício with towels to reduce his body heat. After a minute rest, the action resumes with Maurício aggressively attacking. Maurício appears to tire, pushing his punches and keeping his hands low, but he works through the lactic acid build-up to continually harass his opponent with arm punches. Although his technique and conditioning could have used refinement, Maurício was fighting with his heart. During the next minute rest, the fanning continued, with attempts by Maurício's corner to loosen up his shoulders (having relaxed shoulders is essential in boxing).

"When my student come to the corner, I told him, 'When he drop his hands, kick his head—hard,' " said Cunha of his advice to Rodrigo.

In the third and final round of the smoker, Maurício had moments of success—landing a right hand counter to a kick that had everyone cheering. Seconds later, Maurício got rocked by a head kick and fell onto his butt. As he tried to right himself to no avail, the bout was waved off, and Maurício tasted defeat.

Rodrigo, Maurício's opponent in the smoker, did not pursue a career as a professional fighter. Today, Rodrigo is a lawyer—one with an interesting story to tell in boardrooms and at cocktail parties.

As for Maurício, while he had lost via knock-out, he *had* shown the real qualities required to be a professional: aggression, plenty of heart and the desire to challenge himself.

"I thought that he would be a great fighter," said Cunha of his impression of Maurício, based on the smoker. "He was beating up my student—he was winning."

Maurício had to face the inevitability of loss at some point. That it happened in an unofficial bout that would not be recorded or count against his record perhaps made it easier to deal with; at the same time, Maurício would never forget how much he disliked the feeling of defeat.

Eventually, the time came for Maurício to fight in more organized Muay Thai events.

"In 2000, I had entered this fight event—I and Dida and Veio," said Shogun, of what might have been considered his first official Muay Thai match, along with childhood friends and Chute Boxe teammates Andre "Dida" Amado and his brother, Maurício "Veio" Amado. "Three friends, we all grew up together, and we all fought on the same card. It was our first fight for all of us, so we were all really super-nervous, we all basically slept in the same area that night together."

The pre-fight anxiety of the trio made the event memorable.

Said Maurício, "We were feeling sick going into the fight, nervous, you know, and I remember that day more than some of my biggest fights."

In the same vein, legendary Brazilian Formula One racecar driver Aryton Senna recalled his early go-karting experiences as the purest and most memorable because there was no money or politics involved.

According to Maurício's own account, he went 10-0 in Muay Thai bouts. They could not really be classified as amateur; they were just small professional events. To this day, Muay Thai striking is the backbone of Maurício's attack in MMA. He had these early events to thank for his expertise—and, no doubt, his wins continually fortified his confidence.

24

THE BIG TIME AND THE BIG MONEY

PRIDE Fighting Championships was the premiere league for MMA, having its first event in 1997 and meeting its demise in 2007. Earlier generations of MMA fans know that many of the greatest matches in the sport's existence occurred not within the hallowed halls of the UFC, but in front of tens of thousands of whisper-quiet fans in Japan. As much as martial arts like judo or karate were enshrined as part of Japanese culture, modern audiences were captivated on a boom-bust cycle of trends and fads that spiked to enormous heights and dissipated just as quickly. Since the final PRIDE show on April 8, 2007, the Japanese MMA scene has been irreparably damaged and hanging on life support, but this wasn't the case as Maurício "Shogun" Rua was ascending the ranks.

"I had a dream, a dream to be a professional fighter in Japan," said Maurício. "I saw the other people there and said 'I want to do that.' And that was all that I could think about."

Maurício's teammates at Chute Boxe inspired him, as their exploits in Japan were legendary. The greatest among them was Wanderlei "The Axe Murderer" Silva, a vicious striker with a preference for doing damage to opponents in the Thai clinch. Wanderlei had won the PRIDE middleweight (205 pound) title in 2001 and would have an impressive streak of 15 wins and one draw in PRIDE. Wanderlei did feast on Japanese cans—underweight and under-strength guys who were defeated by Wanderlei's fierce reputation before they entered the ring. At the same time, his best fights during that run included two knockouts of Quinton "Rampage" Jackson, three knockouts of Kazushi Sakuraba, a draw with heavyweight Mirko "Cro Cop" Filipović (Wanderlei dominated the match, but it was fought under special rules where the fight would be declared a draw if it went to decision) and a decision over Dan Henderson. Down the line, Rampage, Henderson and Cro Cop would get revenge; but this was Wanderlei's time and the golden era of Chute Boxe.

"All these guys from Chute Boxe were impressing me at the time," recalled PRIDE commentator Bas Rutten of Chute Boxe's dominance in MMA.

The fierce sparring sessions at Chute Boxe were the stuff of legend in the MMA community.

"I heard that they would pack up—like, put shin protection on, even body protection—and then every day, try to knock each other out," said Rutten. "They would take it to the next level…You can only imagine what goes on in that gym. Everything is full blast."

There was still some technical training on small details that would allow Chute Boxe fighters to be more efficient, although it seemed to be secondary to desired traits like fierceness and aggression.

"At night, always we got one other practice in," said Sergio Cunha. "We worked on other levels, like just jiu-jitsu, grappling, or just boxing."

The hard sparring sessions were the result of the "Chute Boxe mentality" that meant you had to prove yourself and show your teammates you had what it took to succeed in combat sports. As much as serious arts like boxing, Muay Thai, wrestling and Brazilian Jiu-Jitsu have made inroads in the world, the snake oil of traditional martial arts or the arrogance of weight-lifters and other "tough guys" still crossed paths with the reality of Chute Boxe—often with entertaining results.

"Chute Boxe always had a system—almost like a visa—you had to do to enter in," explained former team member Andre "Dida" Amado. "You had to earn your passport to be a part of them. If you walked in and said that you wanted to be a fighter, you had to prove that you could handle fighting. They would hand you one of their smaller but tougher guys—someone who would test you to see if you had heart. Because if you didn't have heart, you couldn't be a part of Chute Boxe."

"If someone said that they were good at jiu-jitsu, they would put him in with someone who was good at jiu-jitsu," said Dida. "If you walked in and said you were good at beating people up, 'Oh yeah—I'm good at beating people up, I'm a bouncer,' they would say, 'All right, here's a skinny sixteen-year old named Dida, why don't you train with him?' "

Chute Boxe trained a lot of security personnel, including bouncers and other muscle-bound meatheads. Dida often was tasked with initiating them into the Chute Boxe family. Dida was about 140 pounds—a teenager who appeared harmless. The heavyweight bouncers—many who scaled in around 220 to 250 pounds—were secretly delighted by their good fortune in being matched with easy prey.

Said Dida, " 'The guy would say, 'Are you sure? He's so skinny. I don't want to hurt him. Am I allowed to hit him?' And the coach would say, 'Go ahead, do what you have to do. He can handle it, hit him hard.' I would knock them down or knock them out and it would be a shock to everybody."

Giving and taking on a day-to-day basis were part of the membership dues charged by Chute Boxe. But in the bigger picture, Wanderlei's dominance was a major inspiration to the young blood of the team, including the unproven Maurício Rua.

"What Wanderlei means in my life is that he's my role model, inside and outside of the ring," said Maurício. "Even now to this day, I've always tried to mirror what he did."

Before Maurício could follow Wanderlei to PRIDE, he had to demonstrate his skill on the local circuit. Maurício did this by racking up wins at the Mecca World Vale Tudo (an event promoted by Chute Boxe owner Rudimar Fedrigo and future Anderson Silva co-manager Jorge Guimaraes) events number seven, eight and nine.

Shogun's first opponent was Rafael Freitas, known only as Rafael "Capoeira" to nickname-loving Brazilians. Shogun pressured his opponent from the start, and knocked Rafael out with a head kick just four minutes into the first round.

In Shogun's third fight, he beat Evangelista "Cyborg" Santos. Partially owing to this performance, Shogun was invited by MMA agent Koichi Kawasaki to fight in an American promotion, the IFC, to get some international experience before facing the big dogs of PRIDE.

The IFC, or International Fighting Championship, was a mid-level show that was holding a tournament in Denver, Colorado, on September 6, 2003. Brazilian Paulo Filho was intended to be Shogun's original opponent in the IFC tournament, but for whatever reason (such as Filho's unreliable, space-cadet nature), Filho didn't show up.

Shogun dispatched Filho's replacement, tournament alternate Erik Wanderley, a world jiu-jitsu champion making his pro debut, via second round stoppage. The next round of the tournament saw Shogun fight Renato "Babalu" Sobral, a Brazilian with a 22-5 record that included such luminary opponents as Fedor Emelianenko, Chuck Liddell and Dan Henderson. Shogun was susceptible to Babalu's takedowns, but kept the fight close until the third round, when Babalu submitted Shogun via guillotine choke, causing him to lose his first pro fight. Babalu went on to beat Jeremy Horn in the final round to win the tournament. A PRIDE representative was still sufficiently impressed by Shogun's performance in the tournament to grant him a chance to *compete in Japan.*

"Every fighter on the planet in that day and age wanted to be in PRIDE because of the way they got treated there," said Bas Rutten, of what was then the largest and best MMA organization in the world.

PRIDE, which aired on national television in Japan, was drawing tens of thousands of spectators and boasted incredible theatrics that were an event in themselves. The organization's fighters were elevated to the level of classical gods—showered with attention, put under high-powered spotlights, ushered into the ring by walking on a special elevator and raised platform. Fighting in PRIDE meant you were someone special, in that it was the closest thing MMA had to the major leagues of the NFL, NHL, MLB or NBA. All of the extras and intangibles provided, like incredible post-fight parties, helped PRIDE chisel out more of an edge in money negotiations.

On October 5, 2003—about two years after Shogun's brother Murilo "Ninja" Rua had made his PRIDE debut—Shogun would finally fight at the PRIDE Bushido 1 show against Akira Shoji. At 4-1 in MMA, Maurício was finally ready to follow in the footsteps of Wanderlei Silva and pursue the big time and the big money.

Shogun did not disappoint in PRIDE, as he stopped Akira Shoji with punches and a stomp in the first round. The list of impressive wins continued with Akihiro Gono (PRIDE Bushido 2), Yasuhito Namekawa (PRIDE Bushido 5) and Hiromitsu Kanehara (PRIDE 29) all being stopped with a vicious barrage of soccer kicks and stomps within the first round of each fight.

"He just tries to come in wild and tries to knock you out," says Bas Rutten of Shogun's style. "Coming forward, and he starts fighting. That's pretty much all the Chute Boxe guys."

When Murilo "Ninja" Rua dropped a controversial split decision to American Quinton Jackson at PRIDE 29, MMA agent Koichi Kawasaki revealed devious planning by the PRIDE brass in preparation for the 2005 middleweight (205 pound) Grand Prix.

"In my judgment, and many people's...Ninja won against Quinton Jackson," said Kawasaki. "PRIDE judges and promoter [didn't] want too many *Brasileiros* [in the Grand Prix]. So judges [gave] Quinton [the fight]."

Encouraged by Kawasaki, Shogun called out Jackson in the ring after the Murilo Rua-Quinton Jackson fight. The Dream Stage Entertainment (DSE, PRIDE's parent company) executives opted to give Shogun a chance against Quinton Jackson. There was some doubt from many sides over whether Shogun was even ready for the challenge that an established PRIDE veteran like Quinton Jackson would present, but the prospect for big money at this juncture was not something Maurício, Rudimar or the powerbrokers behind the scenes could ignore.

"I was the last guy put in," said Shogun, reflecting on the lead-up to the 2005 Grand Prix, a tournament that would consist of the best of the best. "No one else expected me to do anything. I wasn't one of the favorites. Most people—even in the magazines—didn't expect me to make it past the first round. It was just a dream to be in the Grand Prix as it was."

Quinton Jackson was eventually confirmed as Maurício's first opponent. After Jackson's epic wars with Wanderlei Silva in the 2003 middleweight Grand Prix and again in 2004 for the PRIDE middleweight title, Quinton Jackson was seen as a potential finalist and a clear favorite over Shogun. Jackson also pulled no punches in interviews; he was, after all, a guy PRIDE had once promoted as a homeless black dude at the start of his career.

"People in Japan believed it," said Jackson of the elaboration to his bio. "They tried to say that I was living on the streets, and eating out of trash cans."

He had a special incentive to stay silent on the marketing ploy.

"They were paying me cash money—I just went along with it."[140]

Eventually, Quinton Jackson spoke out in interviews and corrected the public regarding the demeaning and inaccurate factoid.

Entering the 2005 middleweight Grand Prix, Jackson seemed genuinely unconcerned with Murilo Rua's younger brother.

Said Jackson before the fight, "I'm going to teach Shogun how to ice himself after a fight because he's going to have to ice himself after this fight."[141]

Unlike the point-fighters who would populate MMA later on, Maurício Rua had unwavering sincerity in promising to deliver excitement in the bout, saying, "I will go for the KO because this is going to be the biggest fight of my career."[142]

The weigh-ins for the opening round of the Grand Prix were farcical, as Shogun, who initially scaled in at 93.5 kilograms, had unlimited time to make 92.9 kilos (versus the two-hour limit the day before the match to weigh in that most American athletic commissions grant).

"Every government body is corrupt in some way, shape or form," rationalized former PRIDE employee Jerry Millen of Japan's promotions lacking oversight from athletic commissions. "If you know the right people on the Nevada State Athletic Commission Board, you can get past a test."

As much as it was possible to bend the rules in the US, in Japan, promoters could literally make up the rules as they went along. It was unheard of for PRIDE fights held in Japan to be canceled over weight issues, nor were any PRIDE fighters officially punished for using performance-enhancing drugs. Rather, DSE employees often spoke about the need for fighters' bodies to look good, ostensibly for television.

The idea that each tournament participant was on equal footing was further dispelled by Japanese fighter Yuki Kondo weighing in the lightest of the tournament participants at 87 kilos and PRIDE president Sakakibara claiming that a visibly overweight Kazushi Sakuraba was in "the best shape of his life." The Japanese fighters were there to promote the samurai spirit of Japan—outnumbered and outgunned in a hopeless battle, cannon fodder for drawing in the Japanese public for television ratings.[143]

Before the fights, Maurício needed a way to relax and calm his mindset; therefore, he listened to music. According to Jerry Millen, during a visit to Curitiba, he uncovered Shogun's preference.

"I'm in Ninja's car. This car comes flying behind us, and comes to a screeching halt. Then you hear, 'Say you, say me,'—Lionel Richie coming out of the car. And it's Shogun pulled up. That's what he listens to—or did listen to—in his headphones before his fights, this slow love music."

The first round of the tournament, "PRIDE Total Elimination 2005," was held on April 23, 2005, in Osaka, Japan. In his fight with Quinton Jackson, Shogun wasted no time in clinching with him, forcing him into a corner of the ring and throwing hard knees to the body. Shogun succeeded in breaking down Jackson's midsection, which was a useful tactic in dousing any desire Jackson had to fight back effectively. Shogun soccer-kicked a downed Jackson for the stoppage at 4:47 of the opening round.

Jackson would later claim to have been injured going into the fight, saying[144] "I dislocated my ankle three weeks into training camp, and I couldn't run for three weeks, so my cardio was pretty bad and we had [a] 10-minute [opening] round."[145]

The next round of the sixteen-man tournament took place in June at PRIDE: Critical Countdown on June 26, 2005. Light-heavyweight Antônio Rogério Nogueira (11-1), the twin brother of former PRIDE heavyweight champion Antônio Rodrigo Nogueira, was a serious threat.

Rogério managed to knock Shogun down in the first round and had Shogun rocked near the end of the opening frame. Shogun was successful in taking the BJJ specialist down repeatedly throughout the fight, but it was still a close match, with Shogun scoring his own knockdown in the third round. Shogun won a judges' decision—the first time he'd ever won by anything besides knockout or stoppage.

The semi-finals and finals of the tournament were to be contested on the same night at PRIDE Final Conflict 2005, held on August 28. Having two fights in one night under a tournament format changes many variables, due to the possibility of one fighter having an easy first-round win and then facing someone who had just gone the distance in a war, perhaps incurring injuries along the way. For the tournament participants of PRIDE Final Conflict 2005, the event's rules were modified for only two rounds, to mitigate the wear and tear on the fighters.

Every Japanese fighter in the tournament had been eliminated before the semi-finals. The final brackets were interesting because reigning PRIDE middleweight champion and favorite to win, Wanderlei Silva, was in the opposite bracket to Shogun Rua. If Wanderlei defeated Brazil Top Team rival Ricardo Arona, and Shogun beat Alistair Overeem, the result would be an epic all-Chute Boxe teammate-versus-teammate final.

Unluckily for Wanderlei, Ricardo Arona was able to utilize his wrestling to win a decision. Arona was now 12-2 as a mixed martial arts fighter, with his first career loss coming by way of controversial decision to legendary heavyweight Fedor Emelianenko and the other via a slam that knocked him out cold courtesy of Quinton Jackson. Now Arona approached the summit of what could have been his greatest achievement as a mixed martial artist—a championship belt. All that stood in the way now was the winner of Shogun Rua vs. Alistair Overeem.

Shogun was facing the 205-pound version of Alistair Overeem, the Dutch striker from team Golden Glory. Overeem was 21-5 against respectable opposition; he had not yet descended into a slide of losses due to distractions or a lack of will, and was at a peak in his ability. At 6'5" to Rua's 6'1", Overeem was not going to be easy for Shogun to out-box or out-strength.

In the opening seconds, Overeem muscled Shogun to the ground and had side-control. As Shogun scrambled from his knees, Overeem attempted his patented guillotine choke. Two more takedowns followed, with Overeem getting top position each time. Again and again, Overeem attempted his patented guillotine that had finished his two previous opponents in the GP.

"He's got him! He's got him!" yelled an excited Bas Rutten after Overeem dropped to his back to get more leverage with the choke.

Seconds later, Shogun popped his head up—no longer in danger of being submitted, and now in Overeem's half-guard. Shogun now had top position to rain down strikes onto Overeem, who was winded from the guillotine attempts. Shogun stood up to utilize his soccer kicks and stomps; after getting to the feet and exchanging, they hit the mat again, with Shogun achieving top position. Shogun did bend the rules by grabbing the ropes while attempting kicks at a turtled Overeem; officials ran in to pull them away, but it was no use. Just as with Wanderlei Silva grabbing the ropes while stomping Dan Henderson in their first fight at PRIDE 12, Chute Boxe fighters sometimes allowed the heat of the moment to overrule any sense of fair play.

Shogun transitioned from inside Overeem's guard to side-control, then achieved full mount, where he pulverized Overeem with strikes. When he rode his right knee up on Overeem's left arm, it neutralized Overeem's ability to protect himself from the strikes; seconds later, the ref stopped the contest at 6:42 of the opening round.

The win, however impressive, did not come easy.

"[Alistair] Overeem is one of the strongest guys that I felt in my fights," Shogun later revealed. "I have a lot of respect for him in terms of his strength and how good he was. And he has an underrated ground game."

Thus the all-Brazilian final was set—Brazil Top Team's Ricardo Arona versus Chute Boxe's Maurício Rua. The rivalry between BTT and Chute Boxe added to the tension of the explosive tournament. When fight fans think of later attempts to create exciting tournaments—Showtime's Super-Six super-middleweight boxing event, or the Strikeforce MMA heavyweight tournament kicked off in early 2010—injuries, fouls, company events and politics had influenced who advanced, and ultimately, who was crowned tournament champion. That's what made PRIDE Final Conflict 2005's middleweight final so wild: both Arona and Shogun had won their three fights, with no alternates substituted into the tournament.

Shogun and Arona began their bout tentatively, waiting for the other to make the first move. Shogun threw a flashy "tornado kick" that missed, clinched with Arona, was taken down and ended up on the ground with Arona in his guard. Arona escaped an omoplata (shoulder lock), only to find himself the target of foot-stomps in the ensuing scramble; on the feet, Shogun was relentless with strikes and throwing knees in the Thai clinch. A takedown landed Shogun squarely in Arona's guard. First Shogun escaped to half-guard, then slithered into side-control; now with positional advantage, the pain would start. Elbowing Arona's unprotected ribcage, Shogun mixed up the strikes, but when he tried to pass and mount Arona, Arona forced Shogun off until Rua was back to standing. Then came Arona's tactical mistake of laying on his back, believing he could either stall or fend off Shogun—a strategy born out of exhaustion, miscalculation or poor instinct. Shogun never relented in attempting his stomps, eventually landing with one foot over Arona's head. He kneeled to lower himself into position and began to drop hammerfists to the head. After the fourth shot, the ref stepped in, the contest waved off at 2:54.

Wanderlei Silva, Murilo Rua, Chute Boxe BJJ coach Nino Schembri, Rudimar Fedrigo, Rafael Cordeiro and all the other Chute Boxe coaches, teammates and personnel present stormed the ring to mob Shogun. Confetti rained down on the entire stadium—the 2005 PRIDE Grand Prix winner was Maurício "Shogun" Rua.

In addition to a trophy and championship belt, the Grand Prix winner received a check for 20 million yen, about $200,000 US. Ricardo Arona had to make do with five million yen and a smaller trophy.[146] DSE itself earned around 400 to 600 million yen for the TV contract with Fuji TV, as well as one to two million dollars for a heavily papered live gate.

What was the reaction from Shogun on winning, now 23 years old, and on top of the world?

"I couldn't even believe what had just happened," said Shogun. "It was a few days afterwards when I realized 'Oh my god, I just won the Grand Prix! I can't believe I did this!' "

The good memory evoked by winning the toughest 205 pound tournament ever assembled in MMA history—a tournament that has never been equaled or surpassed by any other organization before or since—was symbolized by the title belt. Even months after his win, Shogun still carried the belt wherever he went.[147]

There was still the lingering question about who the best 205-pound fighter in the world was: Maurício Rua, Wanderlei Silva or Chuck Liddell. As of April 2005, Liddell had won the UFC belt with a KO of Randy Couture; August saw him cement his first defense with a win over journeyman Jeremy Horn. While Shogun would go on to stop Liddell in the UFC, we have to acknowledge that Chuck Liddell was far removed from his prime at the point that he finally met Shogun in 2009. No one can state with absolute certainty who would emerge victorious, but on paper, Shogun had achieved more at the end of 2005 than Chuck Liddell had.

Wanderlei Silva versus Shogun Rua was a dream match that carried its own mythology. After all, as training partners, there existed many stories and rumors that attempted to uncover who was more dominant.

"I heard a story about Shogun having pit bull puppies," recalls Bas Rutten of one tale. "Wanderlei wanted one, and Shogun said he had to pay $250 for it. 'Why don't we fight for it?' asked Silva. I heard in that fight, Wanderlei knocked him out in the training camp, and got himself a pit bull."

The story was also reported in a *FIGHT! Magazine* cover feature on Wanderlei Silva:

> **They would lace up 16-ounce boxing gloves and fight for as many rounds as it took before one of them was knocked out. If Silva lost, he'd shell out the cash and if Shogun lost, the puppy was free. All of their coaches and training partners gathered around to watch the dream bout that hardcore MMA fans would never have the chance to see on television. 'All I will say is that we went at it very hard and the fight ended in the first round,' recalls Silva, grinning from ear to ear. 'And I did not pay for that puppy.'[148]**

Bas Rutten had an interesting coda to the story, as he spoke to Maurício Rua in June 2012.

"I interviewed Maurício this morning, asked about the 'pit-bull story' ", said Rutten. "He started laughing and said it was not true. 'Haha,' he said he GAVE [Wanderlei] the dog, 'No KO' he said."

So perhaps it was all an urban legend, worthy of debunking on Snopes.com.

In terms of their regular sparring, Shogun himself was unwilling to disclose who consistently dominated: him or Wanderlei Silva.

"Training is training," said Shogun. "Some days I'm better, some days Wanderlei was better. At the end of the day, I don't really talk about what goes on in training, but in my opinion, Wanderlei is better than me."

Rutten agrees with Shogun's dismissive attitude toward what happens in practice.

"It doesn't matter [because] it's all about who can keep his composure during the [professional] fight," said Rutten. "I know these guys we all call 'The Dojo Fighters'. They do extremely well in the dojo, and they will tell the whole outside world who they tapped out, who they downed and everything, but if they had to fight themselves, there's so much pressure on them, they can't perform."

There was, however, a tape of Shogun and Wanderlei sparring around the time of the 2005 PRIDE Grand Prix that has been released to the public. Rudimar supervises his two charges as they spar while both wear boxing gloves and Wanderlei wears shin-guards in a contest of striking and takedowns. There are the fast, straightforward exchanges Chute Boxe is known for, but also, Shogun evades Wanderlei's pressure on the feet with multiple takedowns, which he can seemingly achieve at will. Wanderlei begins to come back with his own takedowns and ends the session with a knockdown of Shogun via body shot.

Again, the results of the video are inconclusive. The striking is very even, and although Wanderlei gets taken down, it was unusual for Wanderlei himself to look for takedowns in his own professional fights. After each furious exchange or takedown, the sparring partners break and reset on the feet, so we don't know who would get dominant position and go for a submission or stoppage.

Although closely matched in terms of both skill and will, Shogun seems much more versatile and dynamic in his fights than even prime Wanderlei. Take away the respect and admiration that Shogun held for Wanderlei as a mentor, and Shogun finds a way to win.

25

UFC GOLD

"I can't give my 'daughter' to a spoiled rich kid like
BodogFight or Elite XC (laughing). Ha, ha, ha! Stay away from
her (laughing)."

—*former DSE President Nobuyuki Sakakibara, on the sale of PRIDE*

PRIDEFC.com, March 28, 2007

In March 2007, Zuffa acquired PRIDE. The rumored price-tag was
$13 million US according to FightOpinion.com's Zach Arnold and
other sources.[149] Statements made by UFC president Dana White the
following month suggested that he had no idea that PRIDE was the
corpse of Bernie Lomax being animated by former PRIDE president
Nobuyuki Sakakibara à la *Weekend at Bernie's*.

Credit must be given to Sakakibara for maintaining such a flawless
act prior to the sale. Prospective buyer Ed Fishman, a casino magnate,
wanted 30 days to conduct due diligence on the company, but PRIDE
was completely uncooperative. DSE executives knew if Fishman looked

carefully, he wouldn't find a company valued at the $60-$65 million asking price.

When it was time to close the deal with the Fertittas, like any good grifter, Sakakibara continued to stall and feign hesitation to making the sale of his so-called "daughter."

"We didn't sign a contract till March. In Los Angeles," claimed Sakakibara. "I met their lawyers, my lawyer and Lorenzo [Fertitta] joined through the phone. We said 'All right, let's close the deal', but for some reasons, I couldn't sign right away."

Sakakibara then asked for 30 minutes to have a cup of coffee, and headed to Starbucks. While he recalls questioning his decision to sell PRIDE to the Fertittas, the real power behind PRIDE, a man named Mr. Ishizaka, would need to be consulted before the sale could be approved.[150] At this time, Mr. Ishizaka was hiding in Korea as a result of an outstanding arrest warrant in Japan, so Sakakibara likely called him during the break in negotiations in order to finalize the sale of PRIDE.

On the UFC 70 media conference call in April 2007, when addressing the acquisition of PRIDE, White was adamant that Shogun would continue to fight in PRIDE. "All of the guys who are in PRIDE will stay in PRIDE."

White was also explicit in stating that no PRIDE stars would migrate to the UFC until a "UFC vs. PRIDE Super Bowl" was held near the end of the year.[151]

Of course, all of this was magical thinking. There was no resurrecting the scandal-plagued PRIDE for a national television deal and less of a chance for a company that wasn't even fronted by a Japanese national who understood the realities of the now-damaged Japanese MMA marketplace. The Fertittas and Dana White might have known this all along, but acquiring PRIDE would achieve other strategic objectives for Zuffa to dominate the worldwide MMA landscape.

The first fighter with a PRIDE contract to be officially brought to the UFC was American Dan Henderson. Henderson reigned in two weight classes as the PRIDE champion, at both 205 and 183 pounds. It was announced on May 30, 2007, at the UFC 71 post-fight press conference that Henderson would square off with the new UFC 205-pound champion in Quinton "Rampage" Jackson at a fall date.[152]

As Dana White's tone about bringing PRIDE fighters to the UFC changed, the reality was that most of the contracts Zuffa had acquired from PRIDE were personal service contracts. This meant that most of the PRIDE stable could not be legally transferred to the UFC.

Speaking on the nonexclusive nature of the PRIDE contracts that allowed many PRIDE fighters to compete elsewhere, Dana White stated, "Yeah, it's a problem. I'm working on it. It's a big problem, but believe me, I'll fix it."[153] Every PRIDE fighter was rushed a UFC standard contract to bind them to their new masters.

It was rumored through the Chute Boxe website that Shogun was signed to the UFC in May and would debut at UFC 72,[154] but this did not come to pass. Initial reports also suggested that Shogun would be matched with Lyoto Machida; it wasn't until July that it was officially announced that he would debut against season one *TUF* winner Forrest Griffin. Jamie Pollack, a legal advisor Zuffa had appointed to run the Japanese operation, had arrived in Japan in May to take up his position at the PRIDE FC office in Tokyo.[155] Pollack had also brought his family—a sign that Zuffa was hopeful of making a long-term investment in the Japanese market. However, Pollack was harassed by former DSE employees whose loyalties lay elsewhere. In an absurd twist, former PRIDE president Nobuyuki Sakakibara continued to run business for pro-wrestling organization HUSTLE (which had no connection to the Fertittas whatsoever) out of the Fertitta-leased PRIDE offices.

When it came time for television networks to make decisions for new programming in October 2007 and no Japanese TV stations elected to give the new PRIDE a toss, the Fertittas declined to throw good money after bad. On October 4, the PRIDE FC office in Tokyo was shut down and all employees fired. Pollack delivered the announcement via telephone, without allowing the employees to return to the building to collect cell phones or personal computers.[156] While the send-off of PRIDE's employees may have been performed coldly, it was rumored that Pollack had been threatened by the yakuza (the Japanese organized crime), and that he had returned to the US in fear.

On February 1, 2008, PRIDE FC Worldwide, the company set up by Zuffa to run PRIDE, sued DSE for fraud.[157] One wonders what sort of due diligence the Fertittas performed prior to the purchase of the company. Avoiding involvement in a company like PRIDE that was connected to the yakuza would have been a smarter move for the Fertittas due to the gambling licenses they required to operate their Las Vegas casinos. Two months later, on April 2, 2008, Sakakibara, along with Ubon and Dream Stage Holdings (DSE), sued PRIDE FC Worldwide, as well as Lorenzo and Frank Fertitta, in US District Court in Las Vegas, Nevada. Sakakibara was, comically, counter-suing the Fertittas for failing to maintain the smoldering ashes of PRIDE as a "global top-level brand."[158]

It was also revealed that in addition to the asset buyout of PRIDE, Sakakibara had negotiated a consulting agreement where PRIDE FC Worldwide would pay him a monthly salary for 48 months. Behind the scenes, it was likely that Mr. Ishizaka, the true power behind PRIDE, had taken the entire $13 million that the Fertittas had paid for PRIDE. Therefore, Sakakibara structured the consulting agreement as a financial incentive for himself to broker the sale of PRIDE. In their lawsuit, the Fertittas were asking for the $1.5 million paid out to Sakakibara under the consulting agreement to be returned.

What services could Sakakibara have been performing for PRIDE FC Worldwide? Perhaps the consulting agreement was payment by the Fertittas for the former PRIDE president to stay out of the Japanese fight game and allow the Americans to attempt their Japanese sojourn unimpeded.

Nothing seemed to come of the litigation, as Sakakibara's lawsuit was dismissed in August 2010.[159] Neither side gained any ground. It was much better for the Fertittas that Sakakibara's connections to the yakuza didn't come up in open court. Some speculate the lawsuits were just to recover face and that both sides knew *caveat emptor* made it impossible to step backwards once the deal was done.

The upside of the deal was that Zuffa could pat itself on the back for conquering PRIDE. The Fertittas had also prevented any potential rivals from acquiring and running a large-scale competitor in Japan with PRIDE fighters. Zuffa also now held the rights to air the PRIDE tape library in the US, although Fuji TV still owned the rights to air the PRIDE library in Japan.

Forrest Griffin was formerly a police officer in Georgia. He'd earned quality wins against top opposition before winning the inaugural season of *The Ultimate Fighter*, including a decision over Jeff Monson in 2002 and beating Chael Sonnen by triangle choke in 2003.

In the public eye, Forrest rarely gave an answer to the media or fans that wasn't dripping with sarcasm or indifference. Trying to peel away Forrest's defense mechanism of humor was exceedingly difficult. There were a handful of clues to understanding what lay beneath the visible tip of the iceberg, like in his best-selling book *Got Fight?*, where he references watching *Good Will Hunting* 50,000 times in college while living in a shitty one-room apartment. When questioned about this, Forrest momentarily reverted to stating facts that were revealing in themselves.

"It was one of three video cassettes that I owned during a time in my life when I had no cable, no money and nothing," said Forrest. "It was awesome."

The 1997 film was a pivotal vehicle for Matt Damon and Ben Affleck, who sold the script with the same demand an unknown Sylvester Stallone made to Hollywood producers when he was trying to get *Rocky* made—that Damon and Affleck would star in the film.

"They kind of used *Rocky* as a maxim to get that film done and to do it themselves. They were offered money for the script, with different actors," said Forrest.

Everyone knows how *Rocky* turned out—Stallone played the lead role to commercial and critical acclaim, catapulting his career.

It's easy to find parallels with a good-hearted protagonist like Rocky Balboa and MMA fighters: in many ways, the then-unknown contestants of *The Ultimate Fighter*'s first season, like Forrest Griffin, played a leading role in the ensuing popularity of mixed martial arts in North America. Forrest came up the hard way with no breaks, but in 2010, thanks to his UFC earnings, he pegged his net worth at over $2 million. Forrest Griffin had come a long way from the nihilistic teenager who challenged himself by burning his arms with a lighter while listening to industrial rock group Nine Inch Nails in his room. Mixed martial arts was a big part of Forrest's new identity as an adult.

Going into the fight against Shogun, Forrest was regarded as a sacrificial lamb. At no point in his career had Forrest Griffin demonstrated the complete range of skills and dominance that Shogun possessed. Forrest had been stopped two fights previously by journeyman Keith Jardine; Forrest had also been knocked out by Jeremy Horn in his 10th pro fight. All Forrest had on his side was a full gas tank and a lot of heart.

Forrest later confirmed that he had entered the bout with an injured shoulder—a recurring injury that plagued him throughout his career.

"Going into a fight, everybody's hurt," he stated. "Train for a fight, and you get hurt."

Shogun didn't do himself any favors. According to some within his camp, he didn't even train for the Forrest Griffin bout. Later, it was revealed that he had hurt his ACL (knee ligament) prior to the match. Shogun was riding in with his proven skills and a misplaced belief that Forrest was an inferior reality show fighter who would simply fold up when the going got tough. No matter—Shogun also needed the paycheck the bout would bring.

Forrest Griffin had to contend with the terrifying image Shogun, an elite PRIDE fighter, projected going into the fight. At the same time, Forrest found a way to claim his disadvantage was actually something that would work in his favor:

"I've got a huge advantage when it comes to fear," said Griffin. "I'm afraid of everything…I'm more afraid on the flight to the fight than the actual fight."

On September 12, 2007, Maurício married Renata Ribeiro. Renata was a personal trainer whom Maurício had met on Orkut, a social networking website similar to Facebook, in 2005. It was reputed that Maurício had messaged her for three months and added her on MSN messenger before Renata looked at Maurício's profile and became interested in him. Initially, Renata's father had fears that Maurício might be a violent character—MMA was not understood to be a professional sport at this time, even in Brazil, where it was not yet mainstream.[160]

While the wedding to Renata might have been a day of joy for Shogun, he was cutting it razor-close to his fight against Forrest Griffin just ten days later. The marriage was a distraction that would divert Maurício Rua's attention from the critical job of making a splash in his UFC debut.

At UFC 76, held on September 22, 2007, in Anaheim, California, a visibly out-of-shape Shogun fought in a haphazard way, repeatedly giving up his back throughout the fight. The longer the fight went, the more confidence Forrest Griffin gained. During the fight, Shogun blew out his knee ligament, making a bad evening even worse.[161] With just 15 seconds left in the third and final round, Forrest did the impossible, submitting Shogun with a rear naked choke. It was an awful way for Shogun to debut in the UFC—and it would not be his last disappointing performance by a long shot.

In loss, Shogun's take was $150,000; Forrest got $45,000. You have to imagine that an elated Dana White, along with the Fertitta brothers, showered Forrest Griffin with an undisclosed "locker room bonus" outside Forrest's official pay for smashing PRIDE's 205-pound poster boy. Some believe Forrest was gifted with favoritism in his next bout where he won the UFC light-heavyweight title via controversial decision against former PRIDE fighter Quinton "Rampage" Jackson.

Forrest remained humble about the win against Shogun, saying, "It's all about the night. I was better that night, it doesn't really matter. Maybe on a different night—the week before, or the week after—he would have beaten me."

In August 2011, at UFC 134 hosted in Rio de Janeiro, the "real" Shogun would do just that, knocking out an unmotivated Forrest in just one round and proving Forrest Griffin to be right.

26

EXIT THE DRAGON

Lyoto Machida was born in Salvador on May 30, 1978. The son of a Japanese Shotokan karate master (Yoshizo) and a Brazilian woman (Ann Claudia), he had a distinctive Asian look and a highly-disciplined style that clashed with the easy-going nature of most Brazilians.

Yoshizo was a lord of discipline who inspired sibling rivalry between his sons Lyoto and Chinzo. Yoshizo had no qualms about allowing his sons to compete against each other, even believing that the one who beat the other in a karate match determined who would be most successful.

According to one source, "Lyoto and Chinzo fought in a karate tournament final [in 1998] that gave Chinzo a facial scar that is still visible."

Chinzo won the match between Lyoto and himself, but the prophecy by Yoshizo came to mean very little. In 2006, Chinzo became vice-champion in Shotokan Karate, but he failed as an MMA fighter with a 1-2 record. Lyoto, on the other hand, went all the way to the top in MMA.

The first big break Lyoto got in his career was a special mentorship from Japanese pro wrestling guru Antonio Inoki that opened up the doors to mixed martial arts promotions in Japan.

But why had Inoki chosen then-unknown Lyoto over other more viable prospects?

Said Lyoto, "[Inoki] came to Brazil, maybe 2001, and he was looking for one guy to represent his team. His brother is very good friends with my daddy, and [Inoki] met my daddy. He asked my daddy if he knew somebody who wanted to do MMA—to become an MMA fighter. My daddy told him, 'I have a son. He wants a lot to become an MMA fighter.' He thinks good things [will happen] if I met him."

At 24 years of age, Lyoto was invited to Japan to join Inoki's team. There, he flourished, with wins in organizations like New Japan Pro Wrestling, Inoki Bom-Ba-Ye, and K-1, all momentum underwritten by Inoki's influence as a manager with connections and resources.

However, like the impending demise of Japanese MMA's mass popularity, Inoki's management company collapsed in 2006, impeding Lyoto's ascent within Japan.

"I think in Japan, Inoki had a lot of problems in business," said Lyoto, "because the contract, it's not very clear. Everything is not very clear. That's why, I think, it was a big problem for the company."

The power broker who had previously backed Inoki (Tatsuo Kawamura, a gentleman who went to school with the late Hiromichi Momose, the purported yakuza boss that co-founded PRIDE) had backed away. Inoki cashed in his stake as a promoter and sold New Japan to cover his debts. Lyoto realized he wasn't being pushed hard enough in Japan, and Inoki really didn't have the power to help Lyoto anymore anyway.

Inoki still passed on some valuable learning experiences to Lyoto. Contrary to the popular belief that Lyoto practiced solely karate as the basis of his striking, Inoki had actually sent Lyoto to Thailand, where Muay Thai, the local style of full-contact kickboxing, was as entrenched in the culture as football was in America.

"Inoki sent me to Thailand," said Lyoto, "but it was a very short time—just 40 days."

The karate style Lyoto displayed fell within an unnatural and elusive rhythm that made him difficult to catch, and deadly when he landed. It was sure to generate waves in Thai gyms.

"When I arrived there, I brought a new style—I showed everyone my style," Lyoto said of his experiences at Muay Thai gyms in Thailand. "They talked a lot about my style, I think they liked it."

Throughout his MMA career, Lyoto's striking benefited from sparring and training with a variety of fighters from varied disciplines. Training partners during the latter part of Lyoto's career, like Anderson Silva and Antônio Rogério Nogueira, had striking systems based in Muay Thai and boxing respectively.

French-Canadian MMA fighter David Loiseau had the proper perspective on Lyoto's relationship to karate, "It's not necessarily the background itself, but the individual and his self-discipline. There's a lot of karate fighters that tried mixed martial arts. Machida is one of a kind. It's not because you're a karate fighter or a judo player that you're going to be successful. Machida is a black belt in BJJ. He has studied Muay Thai for years. He's studied wrestling for years. So Machida is not a karate-fighter. He promotes karate, his forte is karate, but he's also a BJJ black belt, which makes a hell of a difference in the fight game."

There was no promoter like Bob Arum thoughtfully guiding Lyoto through his early fights to maintain a perfect record. Rather, Inoki had little skill when it came to planning the careers of the fighters he managed. Lyoto's match with future UFC 185-pound champion Rich Franklin at the Inoki Bom-Ba-Ye (IBBY) New Year's Eve 2003 show is such an example. In 2003, Franklin was already a UFC veteran, undefeated at 14-0, with eight knockout stoppages and six submissions—a finish in every one of his wins.

The promoters of the IBBY show had just 60 days to find fighters for the show. Lyoto was a nobody with just two fights to his résumé, added to the card at the insistence of Inoki. Rich Franklin was one of the only opponents that could be found on such short notice.

Public opinion weighed heavily against Lyoto, with people trying to be helpful actually achieving the opposite effect.

"Many people came to tell me that if I stayed on my feet, I would be knocked out fast," Lyoto said.

Yoshizo was quick to rebut the critics, telling Lyoto, "It's not like that; go there and believe in our art."[162]

The first five-minute round saw the typically cautious Lyoto Machida edge out Franklin standing, secure a takedown, score a knockdown in the closing minute and then drop ground-and-pound in an attempt to finish Franklin at the opportune moment. After a restart to move the fighters away from the ropes, Franklin managed to sit up and escape to standing.

The second round saw both southpaws square off with hard exchanges. Fifty-five seconds in, Lyoto nailed Franklin with a hard straight left, pushed him away to create distance, then followed up with a front kick to the head that dropped Franklin. Following up with punches (just in case), Lyoto got the stoppage at 1:03.

After the fight, Inoki delivered his trademark slap to Lyoto. The act was born many years previously when a student punched Inoki twice during a school visit; after Inoki retaliated with a slap, the clip aired on Japanese television, and the tradition of celebrities and ordinary Japanese asking Inoki to slap them to instill courage became a ritual, with Inoki charging people between $1000 to $10,000 for his abuse.[163]

"Legend has it that when he does that, the fighter becomes successful," said Lyoto.

IBBY co-promoter Miro Mijatovic had a different explanation for the tactic.

"Inoki does nothing except promote himself," said Mijatovic. "He knows the slapping bullshit makes him part of the story—that's the only reason he does it."

Of course, in addition to his karate background, Lyoto also had the advantage of having been trained in sumo from the age of 12. He'd earned the title of vice-champion of Brazil in 2000 in the 115 kilo class.[164]

"In amateur sumo, you don't have to eat a lot. You don't have to get a lot of weight, because you have a class. You have a light class, you have a heavy class. You have a lot of classes," said Lyoto of the common perception many westerners have of sumo wrestlers being fat guys with bouncing titties chest bumping. "I think sumo is very good for your body. Very good for your legs, your hips—you can strengthen your hips."

Around the time that Lyoto Machida entered the UFC, he also strengthened his wrestling in order to compete with the new breed of fighters that were dominating MMA.

"I went to America to train wrestling with Rico Chiapparelli for a year [in 2007], and I improved a lot in my game."

Chiapparelli was an NCAA champion in college, and a USA national freestyle champion thereafter, so he knew his business and was employed as a coach by UFC legend Randy Couture. Lyoto would later utilize a jumping front kick to knock Couture into retirement at UFC 129 on April, 30, 2011; no doubt Lyoto's time with Chiapparelli factored into his confidence and ability to keep fights standing.

With his unorthodox karate moves and excellent grasp of wrestling for MMA, it wasn't long before "Machida furor" gripped the UFC's fan base. He was the mystical warrior everyone had been waiting for—and when he sent Rashad Evans into leg-shaking unconsciousness to claim the UFC light-heavyweight title at UFC 98, proclamations of the advent of "The Machida Era" began.

In the fall of 2009, Maurício Rua was slated to face undefeated Lyoto Machida (15-0). To suggest that people doubted Shogun's ability to win would be an understatement—many criticized whether Shogun even deserved to share the same octagon with Machida.

The time after the Griffin fight had been brutal for Shogun, as he underwent not just one, but two knee surgeries to repair his torn ACL.[165] Shogun made the mistake of training too soon after the first surgery in order to face Chuck Liddell at UFC 85, a fight he had to pull out of due to the re-injury of his ACL.

"This is when the second surgery had to happen, when I hurt my knee the second time," said a frustrated Shogun. "That was the lowest point in my career."

Orthopedic surgeon Sebastien Simard, who diagnosed Georges St-Pierre's ACL injury in December 2011, explained why re-injury can occur after surgery:

"The pain lasts for two or three months, and after that it doesn't hurt, but the healing isn't finished, which athletes don't understand."

An athlete needs six months of rehabilitation before resuming training, although returning after five months of rehab is possible in some cases.

"While the blood vessels are moving into the new ligament, it is fragile because it has holes like Swiss cheese. It isn't painful and you risk re-tearing, and if you need a second surgery, it takes even longer," said Simard.[166]

Shogun's recovery time increased as he sat on the sidelines for over 15 months before facing forty-four-year-old Mark Coleman, a UFC and PRIDE tournament champion, who himself hadn't fought in two years.

There was bad blood between Chute Boxe and Coleman's Hammer House squad, owing to a post-fight brawl after the first time Shogun Rua and Mark Coleman had fought at PRIDE 31 back in 2006. In their first encounter, Shogun posted his arm as he fell from a takedown, breaking his elbow. The referee immediately stopped the fight—with Coleman not immediately understanding or realizing the course of events. After Coleman pushed the referee away and continued to approach the downed Shogun with aggressive body language, Murilo Rua stepped in, with Coleman yelling at Shogun's brother. A slew of officials, trainers and security jumped into the ring to quell the explosive situation—this was when Wanderlei Silva entered the ring and went after Coleman; Hammer House teammate Phil Baroni took Wanderlei to the ground.

The official result of the fight was a TKO win for Mark Coleman.

"It was a sad situation when it happened—getting hurt—I wasn't happy about that," revealed Shogun. "The way that Coleman reacted was extremely upsetting to me and to everybody around me."

Backstage after the PRIDE show, Coleman apologized to the entire Chute Boxe team for his behavior. It was a tense moment, with Wanderlei still angered that Coleman had kicked him in the head during the ring scuffle.[167] Shogun accepted the apology, but later felt betrayed that Coleman viewed the TKO as indicative of skill, rather than Shogun suffering an accident.

"He started talking again, 'Oh [Shogun]'s nothing. I can beat him anytime,' " complained Maurício of Coleman.

Maurício was irritated that Coleman was personable and friendly in person ("Hey Shogun!"), yet in all his interviews, Coleman was disrespectful to the Brazilian.

Said Rua through an interpreter, "I would really love to fight him to shut him up...once and for all."

It would take until UFC 93 on January 17, 2009, for Shogun's wish to come true. Although Shogun won the fight via third-round stoppage, it was Coleman who won the event. With tenacity, takedowns and heart, Coleman had impressed the crowd, even in loss.

In the next fight, at UFC 97, a glimpse of the "old" Shogun from PRIDE resurfaced. There, Shogun beat former UFC light-heavyweight champion Chuck "The Iceman" Liddell with an awe-inspiring first-round finish. At the same time, Liddell was 1-3 in his previous four bouts, with knockout losses to Quinton Jackson and Rashad Evans. Liddell would fight just one more time—being knocked out by Rich Franklin in the first round, and then retiring, this time for good. Was Maurício Rua back to his old form, or would Lyoto Machida decimate him like he had done to so many others?

Perception of greatness, whispers of genius—and the inability of previous opponents to unlock Lyoto Machida's style—it all played into extreme favoritism for the champion.

Sherdog.com's Jake Rossen likened defeating Lyoto to opening a *Himitsu-Bak*, a Japanese puzzle box that required secret pressure application or a series of adjustments in proper sequence.[168]

As it turned out, Maurício had the combination. After all, there was more than passing familiarity between the two, as Lyoto had made visits to Chute Boxe in the past.

"People say that if I take the fight to the ground I'll win, but it isn't like that," said Shogun in the lead-up to the fight. "He's very good on the ground, I've trained with him, and sometimes that isn't the solution."[169]

A unique *Sport Science* television feature brought in Brandon Vera to test the power of the different types of kicks used by Lyoto Machida and Maurício Rua—karate versus Muay Thai. Vera could generate 66 G's of acceleration with a karate kick; the Muay Thai kick topped out at 80 G's—almost 21 percent more force. However, speed was one tradeoff for Muay Thai stylists, with the snapping karate kick clocking in 0.33 seconds faster than a Muay Thai kick.[170]

In order to prepare for Lyoto's unique karate kicks and unorthodox style, Maurício auditioned ten karate fighters, selecting seven-time karate champion João Gilherme Bendly as his sparring partner.

"I memorized Lyoto from the top to the bottom so that I can impose myself in front of Shogun," João told Tatame.com, of his job emulating Lyoto's style in sparring.[171]

There was also yet another change—Maurício did not ask trainer Sergio Cunha, who had helped prepare him for Chuck Liddell, to run his camp, choosing the services of K-1 and MMA fighter Andre "Dida" Amado and his brother Maurício "Veio" Amado instead.

"Friends," says Cunha of why Shogun chose Dida and Veio. "They're buddies. They trained together when they were younger, and they like each other. That's the thing."

There was also another reason, which would bite Maurício Rua in the ass later on in his career.

"I think with Dida and Veio, Shogun can do what he wants," said Cunha. "He don't need to follow what the coaches say…that's what I feel, maybe I'm wrong?"

At UFC 104 in October 24, 2009, Shogun took advantage of Lyoto's wide stance to repeatedly punish him with leg kicks. Believing he was up on the judges' scorecards, Shogun's coaches urged him to continue with the strategy, rather than looking for a finish. The end result was a controversial decision loss with all three ringside judges scoring the fight 48-47 for Lyoto Machida—perhaps the most disputed decision in the history of MMA.

"After analyzing the fight and thinking about the fight, I still feel the judges made the right choice," said Lyoto, several months after the fight.

Was it conceivable that Lyoto could acknowledge the prospect of defeat? After all, many times an athlete will acknowledge that the decision could have gone either way, as MMA fighter Jim Miller graciously admitted after a close call with Canadian Mark Bocek at UFC 111.

"I think it was a controversial fight," said Shogun, unwilling to appear bitter in public, but allowing those around him to understand that judging is subjective. "Some people thought I won the fight and some people thought I lost."[172]

Maurício was adamant that the judges' decision had been tainted by nefarious motives.

"It is difficult to know, but I believe it was in the particular interests of someone," Maurício told Tatame.com. "I do not say the UFC, however. Perhaps the people who work with betting exchanges."[173]

This was an angle that was very important to understand in the fight game, as legal gambling on events leaves MMA open to corruption. Fighters could always be coerced into tainting the result of a fight by purposely losing or carrying an opponent. The judges, referees or other officials could also be bought—however, allegations like this were always difficult (or dangerous) to prove.

There was a benefit from spending five rounds against Lyoto, since it helped Maurício get more experience that would be useful in a rematch. During the first fight, Maurício had detected a small weakness on the part of Lyoto regarding the placement of his hands in his guard. Due to the controversy over the fight and wide public interest in a rematch, it was announced that there would be a rematch between Shogun and Lyoto at UFC 113.

What Shogun Rua chose to do in preparation for the rematch would be pivotal to his legacy. He could train lightly and coast based on the belief that the decision should have gone his way; he could complain and moan that the rematch never should have been necessary in the first place, or he could work even harder to come back as a better fighter. Shogun decided to use the six months before the event, scheduled for May 2010, to make critical adjustments that would allow him to overcome Lyoto.

As with the first fight, Shogun employed João Gilherme Bendly as a sparring partner. Bendly was insistent that Lyoto Machida would taste defeat once again. The stylistic implications of karate were too deeply ingrained for Lyoto to approach the fight differently.

"You can't change ten years of practice in four months," said Bendly.

Two months before UFC 113, disaster struck when Shogun came down with appendicitis. Zuffa readied itself with a contingency plan: former UFC light-heavyweight and heavyweight champion Randy Couture was placed on standby to face Lyoto if Shogun could not fight.[174] After having his appendix removed, Shogun took a short rest. He began walking to get his body back into gear, and two weeks later, returned to his training camp.

Said Shogun of the ordeal, "The doctor and Dana warned me not to fight, but I took my risks, said I would be fine and [Dana] was glad with my attitude and complimented me."[175]

As for Lyoto Machida, he had recovered from a hand injury suffered in the first match that had delayed the date of the rematch. He was also still doing his typical training, along with the unique element of "urine therapy" that he had revealed using to the media in March 2009.

"I still drink my urine, a long times ago, a lot of doctors study about that, and they concluded that it is very good for your health. Because it's like a filter—everything you drink, everything you eat—you can put outside in your urine. You drink it to re-filter it, and you can get a lot of protein, a lot of things."

Lyoto first started drinking his urine when he had a persistent cough. Asking his father for advice, Yoshizo's prescription of drinking the first urine of the day cleared Lyoto's cough within a few weeks. Lyoto's father explained that it was like a vaccine, and that Japanese soldiers had used urine therapy during the war due to a lack of available medicines.[176] This was one case where the cure was much worse than the disease.

Perhaps Lyoto's cough would have dissipated on its own had he given it more time, but urine therapy was not unique to Lyoto Machida. Four-weight-division world champion boxer Juan Manuel Marquez also drank his own urine, but discontinued the practice prior to his third meeting with Manny Pacquiao in 2011, on the advice of his doctor.[177]

On the night of the Machida-Rua rematch at UFC 113 on May 8, 2010, Montreal's Bell Centre had an electric atmosphere, with over-whelming fan support for Shogun Rua. On this night, Shogun moved with a sense of urgency and traded strikes with no fear of Lyoto's power. Lyoto scored two takedowns from the clinch, but was unable to keep Shogun on the ground. Eventually, Lyoto rushed forward—the moment had arrived, like a target lining up in the crosshairs, with Shogun ready to gently squeeze the trigger. Shogun fired an overhand right, connected, and Lyoto went down. Shogun mounted and rained down strikes—mercifully stopping when he saw Lyoto was out. Shogun had won via knockout at 3:55 of the first round, breaking Lyoto's orbital bone in the process.

At the time he claimed the UFC light-heavyweight title against Rashad Evans at UFC 98, Lyoto's unique style of fighting had been considered invincible. After the knockout loss to Shogun Rua at UFC 113, Lyoto's father felt Lyoto's spirit had been diminished and would take seven years to recover. To add insult to the injury of loss, Yoshizo withdrew his support in an overt way, suggesting that Lyoto should retire from mixed martial arts. Lyoto was like the 2009 Lonely Island song "I'm On a Boat"—initially super-popular and revered, and then just a tacky and forgotten afterthought.

Shogun's win, on the other hand, was an incredible moment underscored by the Brazilian becoming just the third PRIDE champion to have won a title in the UFC, after Mark Coleman and Antônio Rodrigo Nogueira. Five years had passed since the defining moment of the 2005 Grand Prix win—now, in the biggest MMA organization in the world, Shogun was at the pinnacle.

27

DANCING DAYS

Many factors will shroud the legacy of Maurício Rua. His repeated knee surgeries sidelined him during critical periods in his career. Some of Maurício's wins actually earned him a reputation for being sloppy and unprepared. The emergence of Jon "Bones" Jones—an MMA super-prodigy—makes it appear that an even more consistent and dominant light-heavyweight has arrived.

When Shogun faced Jon Jones at UFC 128 on March 19, 2011, it seemed that time had caught up to Shogun, the way it catches up to all great fighters. Facing a fighter with superior reach, wrestling and athleticism, Shogun was forced to tap out to strikes in the third round against Jones, relinquishing his UFC title in his first defense.

Inside Maurício's mind, the idea that he has been surpassed as a fighter is a dark thought that must constantly be pushed away. The media and fans had declared that he was finished so many times previously—could he not make another triumphant comeback and reclaim the top spot? The truth is, like Mike Tyson, Maurício Rua was better at 24 than he became in his 30s.

Maurício proved against Forrest Griffin (win via first round KO), Dan Henderson (loss via five-round decision) and Brandon Vera (win via fourth round KO) the same thing that Wanderlei Silva has shown in his post-PRIDE outings: he can win some and lose some, he is a game fighter and can never be completely counted out. But Maurício has taken more and more damage in every fight, looking good when motivated, but sloppy the rest of the time. It's almost worse for Maurício than if he was simply being stopped cold by lighter-weight or lighter-hitting fighters as had happened to formerly iron-chinned Chuck Liddell. Maurício has even more reason to continue fighting, due to the flashes of brilliance that hark back to "the Shogun of old."

Recalling his submission win over American wrestler Kevin Randleman in 2003, Japanese fighter Kazushi Sakuraba explained the emotional response that made him continue to fight well past his prime:

"To win by submission is really a great feeling. It's the ultimate ecstasy. It wouldn't be going too far to say that this moment is why I keep training."[178]

No doubt Shogun himself had experienced many peaks that would set the baseline for his expectations of himself.

Asked to contemplate his life after retirement, in 2008, Maurício gave a light-hearted answer.

"Dancing!" he said, then, "I don't know?" followed by laughter.

His expression gave a different answer: shock at the idea that the ride could be over.

"I don't even let that thought come into my head right now, so all I want to do is fight. I don't think about anything else," said Shogun.

There are many fighters who soak up unbelievable amounts of punishment with little regard for future consequences. The repeated blows to the head prevalent in MMA and boxing can cause degenerative diseases in fighters. Canadian Gary Goodridge, a UFC, PRIDE and K-1 veteran, is the perfect example, as he was diagnosed in 2012 with chronic traumatic encephalopathy (CTE). CTE's symptoms include depression, memory loss, aggression and confusion.

"I have no regrets. I loved the way my life was, I lived a good life, and I'm happy with what I did," he told MMAWeekly.com in February 2012, rationalizing the quick-cash short-notice K-1 bouts and lackadaisical training routines that directly caused his situation.[179]

"My brain doesn't remember much these days," Goodridge told a *Toronto Star* reporter in 2011.[180]

Goodridge struggles on a daily basis with depression, memory loss and thyroid issues. Those contemplating a career in MMA cannot be oblivious to the realities of the game evidenced by Gary Goodridge's situation. In fact, many other figures have advised their charges wisely in accordance with an understanding of CTE or pugilistic dementia. Lyoto Machida is the perfect example of such a philosophy in action.

"I have taught my son to be as efficient as possible, to strike as much as possible but do not get hit in the head," said Lyoto's father, Yoshizo Machida, to *ESPN: The Magazine*. "If my son takes too much punishment to the head, I will have him stop fighting. There is no honor in ending up like that."

Through the ongoing Professional Fighters Brain Health Study being conducted by the Cleveland Clinic, findings released in 2012 showed that there were significant risks to both boxers and MMA fighters. The longer they stayed in the game, the greater the odds were against fighters emerging unscathed.

"There appears to be a threshold at which continued repetitive blows to the brain begin to cause measurable changes in memory and thinking, despite brain volume changes that can be found earlier," said study author Charles Bernick, MD, a member of the American Academy of Neurology.[181]

Even hockey and football players have shown symptoms and signs of CTE, but boxing and MMA have a pivotal difference: the goal in hockey and football is to score points, making head trauma incidental;

in fighting, one wins by attacking an opponent and intentionally inflicting head trauma.

Post-retirement financial planning was another area that fighters usually didn't address. For instance, former UFC champion Chuck Liddell's famous partying, along with poor investment strategy, necessitated his seeking employment with Zuffa in a token job as executive vice-president of business development after retirement. What Liddell's job consists of is anyone's guess, including his own.

"We haven't settled on all the specifics of my job, but I know they want me to be in on all of the meetings, giving my ideas for advancing the UFC," Liddell stated to SI.com in January 2011.[182]

It was a smart public relations move by the UFC to give Liddell employment. Not only did it keep Liddell from becoming a graphic example of a broke former fighter, but the move also encouraged other Zuffa fighters to play nice with the Fertittas in order to secure the possibility of post-retirement employment.

Maurício Rua owns rental properties, as well as his own gym in the Universidade da Luta. Perhaps with the rise of MMA in Brazil, he can supplement his income with commentating gigs. Also, since his family was middle-class to begin with, he has education, means and support that can help his handling of financial matters; Maurício likely won't have to resort to begging for handouts from the UFC post-career.

When Shogun retires for good, two things will be assured: he will never be the same as a person—and MMA as a sport will never showcase an explosive, tenacious and well-liked champion in his style ever again.

SECTION IV: RUSSIA

FEDOR EMELIANENKO

28

GOD'S GIFT

Fedor Emelianenko is not a pre-packaged celebrity with an easy-to-understand cookie-cutter storyline. His preference for zero recognition and geographical isolation in Stary Oskol, a town 300 miles south of Moscow, makes for a handful of clues that are difficult to piece together to solve the puzzle of his history and character.

Fedor was born September 28, 1976, in Rubizhne, a town in the province of Luhansk, Ukraine. At this time, the Ukraine was married in an unhappy union with the Soviet Union, but Fedor was ethnically Russian. Rubizhne boasted many chemical and pharmaceutical plants which produced jobs for local residents. Both of Fedor's parents had gainful employment. His mother, Olga Fedorovna, was a teacher, and his father, Vladimir Alexandrovich Emelianenko, was a welder.[183] Fedor also has three siblings: younger brothers Aleksander and Ivan and an older sister named Marina.

Vladimir moved to Stary Oskol, a Russian mining town about 100 kilometers (62.13 miles) from the Ukrainian border,[184] just after Fedor was born, to work in the production of construction materials.

Fedor was frequently ill as a child, having had a weak immune system. In 1978, doctors recommended a change of climate. Former PRIDE and M-1 Global employee Jerry Millen recalled Fedor's mother Olga telling him that the family had originally lived near a power plant. When Fedor became ill, his parents believed that the plant had something to do with his condition, so they opted to move away. Therefore, when Fedor was just two-and-a-half-years old, the rest of the family packed up to join Vladimir in Stary Oskol.

The family's new home boasted three All-Union Komsomol (communist party youth) construction sites in the 1980s including the Stoilensky and Lebedinsky ore mining and processing enterprises and the Oskolsky electrometallurgy enterprise.[185] The Emelianenko family lived in a communal apartment, in a room originally intended for drying clothes. They shared a kitchen and bathroom with other families on their floor.

Five-year-old Marina was entrusted with the care of two-year-old Fedor while their parents worked. Due to their jobs, Vladimir and Olga had little time to devote to their children.

"My soul was torn apart," recalls Olga. "I kept putting in requests to be moved to a different school, even as a cleaner but closer to my home, so that I would have an opportunity to come home during my lunch breaks. I was at the end of my tether when I was taken on as a teacher at School #22, and my children were given spaces in the school's kindergarten."

"My mom was a teacher, worked days and took the night shift," said Aleksander. "She came home no later than nine. Father worked in a factory, his shift was from early morning till late at night."[186]

Aleksander's earliest memory, around the age of four or five, is a tale of parental neglect:

"I can remember that I was forgotten in kindergarten. My parents had to pick me up, and I almost ended up staying the night with the night watchman because they forgot to," said Aleksander. "Finally my mother came at almost midnight."

Fedor took a different perspective, crediting his mother for her strength and support.

"My mother not only loves me as a son," said Fedor, "but respects me as a person."

Certainly Aleksander points to the negative aspects of his upbringing, but his family's situation was common in the disintegrating former Soviet Union. Having two working parents and experiencing neglect in the household was not exclusive to Eastern Europe, either.

Said Aleksander, "My mother was constantly suffering at work. I never saw my father. The streets brought us up. All these memories, everything that I am remembering of, I want to tell you about something happy, that I remember some happy moments, but there aren't any. They were times of change, hungry times, cold and I grew up on the streets."

Another one of Aleksander's recollections was that there was nothing to eat at home. He mentions making spaghetti or potatoes; in the best-case scenario, their mother would make a cabbage soup meant to last the week. Aleksander and Fedor might have gone hungry or subsisted on scraps, but they never appeared on the verge of starvation in any childhood photos made public of the duo.

Aleksander's memories sound like they were plagiarized from a Charles Dickens novel. The glass was usually half-empty, a viewpoint that became entrenched when his own career in MMA failed to take off.

The Emelianenko family hardly lived a life of luxury when contrasted with the ruling elite, oligarchies, black marketers, mobsters and their newly minted wealth created by the collapse of communism in 1991. The stories of life on the street, near-starvation and neglect were all rooted in hard truth; no doubt the negative experiences built the character of the Emelianenko kids, with Fedor and Aleksander choosing their own individual attitudes as they went through life. Fedor seemed to accept what he could not change and look for reconciliation with the unfairness of life. Aleksander might have coped for a time, but his inability to follow in his successful brother's footsteps triggered resentment and rage, and he began to displace blame for his own missteps onto others.

The marriage between Fedor's parents, Olga and Vladimir, eventually deteriorated, causing further hardship when Vladimir left the family.

A bitter Aleksander recounted, "Our father left us and didn't help at all. He said, 'I have my own destiny, and you live however you want.' "

Vladimir's departure opened up a rift between the brothers, as Fedor was away doing his national service in the army at the time of the separation. Aleksander claimed that Fedor was not affected in the same way by his father's absence, because he had not witnessed the fierce arguments between their parents, or the division of the apartment's furnishings.

The eventual dissolution of the marriage opens up questions about the family's dynamics. If Olga and Vladimir were unhappy, how much of their pre-separation dissonance did Fedor witness personally? Can we really believe Aleksander's suggestion that Fedor emerged unscathed from the situation because he was away in the army (hardly a picnic in itself) at the time of their separation?

Aleksander suggests that Fedor dealt with the situation much differently than he did: "My brother does have some relationship with [Vladimir]. But it's easier for him."

Of course, there are two sides to every story. While Vladimir's absence certainly left the family in dire straits financially, we cannot render judgment on his actions.

The self-interested side of human nature reared its ugly head when the boys—Aleksander and Fedor—became more and more successful, both in Sambo (a Russian form of wrestling) and in MMA. Their achievements rekindled Vladimir's desire to form a bond with his offspring in 2008 via telephone contact with Ivan, his youngest son.

"One time I couldn't take it, I grabbed the phone '[Ivan] is twenty years old, why are you teaching him like some school kid? You should've thought about it earlier,' " Aleksander reported.

Aleksander's antisocial tendencies can be traced back to his earliest days. He recalled fighting in school all the time, starting at the age of six, usually over trivial things.

Like Maurício's older brother Murilo Rua, the teenaged Aleksander was fond of street fights, even participating in a large-scale neighborhood-versus-neighborhood rumble.

"Some kid got robbed; his friends went back to see what happened, and it snowballed. Zhukov neighborhood went to war with Olimpiyskiy," said Aleksander.

He described a brawl of a thousand people against another thousand (in another interview, he claims it was 200 versus 200), turning over police cars, the city "standing on its ears" as a crowd fought with chains, rocks and iron pipes. More lethal weapons like knives were frowned upon, as they would have been taking it too far. Aleksander was lucky in this particular encounter, avoiding serious injury.

"Nobody really hit me," said Aleksander. "Although anything can happen when one crowd runs into another crowd."

Interestingly, the prospect of blood and gore didn't dampen his mood. Rather, it fed into his adrenaline addiction and risk-taking behavior.

Said Aleksander, "Fear was one thing that wasn't there. It was the other way around. You were filled with excitement."

Is it any wonder that Fedor spoke poorly of Aleksander, suggesting that he was always on the streets brawling, while Fedor was disciplined and stayed in the gym? The same pattern of mistakes and missed opportunities repeated itself throughout their respective careers.

For instance, at PRIDE: Final Conflict on August 15, 2004, Aleksander faced a shell-shocked version of kickboxer-turned-MMA-fighter Mirko "Cro Cop" Filipović. Cro Cop could have been easy pickings, as he had been knocked out by American fighter Kevin Randleman in April of the same year. Cro Cop was known to be intimidated by Aleksander, and might have been beaten on this particular night. Aleksander did not put in enough time in training and failed to adhere to his team's game-plan in the fight. Aleksander was stopped in the first round of the fight by Cro Cop, and an irate Fedor swore angrily as he watched his brother lose on the monitors backstage.[187]

Aleksander held promise, but failed to blossom, while Fedor was almost always successful to varying degrees in his endeavors, and held himself to a higher standard. Many people are like Aleksander—malleable to the conditions of their environment, able to gain few advantages; a mere handful adopts the attitudes of Fedor, doggedly pursuing a way out no matter what the circumstances.

A slide into a life of crime was the next stage in Aleksander's downward spiral. Aleksander was reputed to be involved in low-level gang activity such as extortion and debt collection. According to Fedor, Aleksander was sentenced to five years in prison. When quizzed about whether Aleksander was tried for robbery, Fedor mentioned that there were many other episodes. It wasn't in Fedor's character to elaborate about Aleksander's misdeeds, however.

"He lies that he hasn't been to prison," said former Russian Top Team teammate Sergei Kharitonov in an interview with ValeTudo.ru. "It's not true. He has."

Kharitonov charged Aleksander with not having a proper upbringing, branding Fedor's younger brother as a criminal, drug addict, alcoholic and general nuisance. Kharitonov also pointed to Fedor's hand in securing an early release from prison for Aleksander.

"I remember 2002 when Fedor said, 'I'd like Aleks to get out of jail somewhat quicker,' " said Kharitonov. "Fedor is the reason why Aleksander is free now. Actually, he owes his brother everything he has at the present moment."

In an interview, Fedor makes no mention of pulling strings, but he does point to his brother's early release.

"They gave him five years," Fedor explained, "but released him before that. After three and a half years."[188]

Aleksander has been the subject of discussion among MMA fans over the prolific series of tattoos he sports. Some viewed the tattoos as evidence of connection to the Russian mafia or of neo-Nazi views.

"There is a cathedral with five domes on my right arm," Aleksander said of the meaning of the tattoo, "and each dome denotes one year of imprisonment."[189]

Aleksander denied any connection to the mafia; a feature on his tattoos from *Fighters Only* magazine cast doubt on whether Aleksander embodied all of the other things his tattoos represented or typically stood for:

> **It is also worth noting that Aleks went to jail as a juvenile offender. Some of his tattoos indicate a high-ranking Vor, which is a status he would have been too young to achieve at the time of his imprisonment.**[190]

A more plausible explanation, from John O'Regan of *Fighters Only* magazine, is that these were the tattoos that Aleksander could get away with having in juvenile prison, where he was filled with youthful bravado. Later on, he would cover up the stars on his shoulders with other tattoos—something that no past or active Vor would ever do.

MMA fighter Sergei Kharitonov was not sold on Aleksander emerging as someone reformed by the prison system.

"Alex hasn't changed at all," said Kharitonov. "There were some cases when he could [return] to jail but Fedor stepped in again. There were also some cases when Fedor literally saved his life. Being honest, prison is the best place for Alex."[191]

Said Fedor of the effect of incarceration on Aleksander, "His outlook on life changed, I think, not for the better."

There were superficial similarities between Fedor and Aleksander. For instance, in his early years, Fedor himself had enjoyed fighting at school, although the intensity of these events doesn't appear to have been great. He believed that he participated in fights more than other children.

"He loved to fight. He fought everywhere with everybody," claimed his mother Olga. "In the kindergarten, at home, at school."

"In my school, there were friendly fights," said Fedor, before adding, "there were also more serious fights."

This did not affect Fedor's grades, as he excelled at all his subjects at the fine arts school he was enrolled in, with notable success in mathematics, literature and chemistry. Many who came into contact with Fedor throughout his career often remarked that he was among the most intelligent of the fighters within the industry.

The crucial event that altered the course of Fedor's life forever came with his introduction to judo and Sambo at around the age of 10 or 11 at the Alexander Nevinsky club. His mother was supportive, taking him to his first practice. In one interview, Emelianenko recounts that the gym was housed in a basement that was formerly a bomb shelter and that he wore simple work clothes at first, rather than having a Sambo outfit.[192]

Fedor's first judo coach was Vasiliy Ivanovich Gavrilov, a man who bought Fedor his first judo uniform and training shoes. Gavrilov was also key in imparting lifelong lessons to Fedor on how to be successful through hard work.[193]

Tragedy occurred when Gavrilov fell off a roof that he had been helping to repair and was killed. Vladimir Voronov, a Master of Sport in Sambo, then became Fedor's grappling coach. Voronov would never leave Fedor's side, from the time Fedor was 11 years of age, up until the end of his MMA career.

"Master of Sport" was a designation of the United Sports Classification System utilized initially by the USSR, and later, Russia. The titles in the tiered system, ranging from "Third-Class Junior Sportsman" to "Merited Master of Sport," were awarded based on competition results, and guaranteed various benefits to the athletes who secured them. Navigating this system to win and maintain titles was an important part of any serious Russian athlete's life.

There was nothing really remarkable about Fedor as a child—according to Voronov, Fedor was physically weak and demonstrated no innate talent for grappling.[194]

"He was small, puny, slender, but his eyes were burning," recalled Voronov.

Early identification of talent was a central point of the Soviet system that Fedor grew up under. Against the established benchmarks, Fedor did not stand out. Trainers wanted winners, even among the youngest boys.

Still—there was the deeper issue of character that would help separate Fedor from the rest.

"He never gave up and fought till the end," said Voronov.

Voronov's relationship with Fedor went deeper than typical, in that he took an interest in the boy's life outside the classroom.

"When training a boy you can't just finish the training session and say that whatever happens outside of the club is your problem," said Voronov. "You have to be interested in everything—the boy's relationship with his parents, his schoolwork, etc."

Voronov was not oblivious to the struggles of the Emelianenko household. He often chipped in by bringing bags of grain or potatoes to Fedor's mother.

As an adult, Fedor was known as a learned man of many interests, such as growing his own tea leaves or drawing cartoon-like images. As a child, he drew, worked with clay, danced, and was also musically inclined, playing the accordion. Time was at a premium, so he was forced to choose between musical aspirations and judo.

"Some people are born to play the accordion," reflected Fedor, "and some to listen. I think that I prefer to listen rather than play."

Judo, of course, won out.[195] It was not an activity without risk to Fedor's health, however.

"They stopped him doing sports because of high blood pressure," Olga told TV news channel Russia Today in 2009.

Olga was also supportive with helping Fedor increase his endurance by going jogging with him.

Andrey Bezruk, a judoka who trained with Fedor, remembered the resolve of the teenage Fedor.

"Even when it got really hard and painful, he used to shout, 'I'm going to be a world champion!' " said Bezruk, now a judo coach. "He was just 14 then."[196]

When Emelianenko finished high school in 1991, he decided to earn money to help his parents out. The principal of his sport school hired him as a security guard. Fedor would train at the school during the day and work security during the night shift, and the school became like a second home.

Fedor graduated with honors from a professional trade school in 1994. He became a certified auto technician.[197] Olga recollected that Fedor later graduated with an additional specialty as an electrician, even winning first place in an electrician competition.

In 1995, when he was 18, Fedor was conscripted into the Russian army. Few Russians were overly eager for their sons to face *dedovshchina,* the brutal hazing practice visited on the new fish by more senior soldiers (themselves eager to pay forward what was done to them). The salary of servicemen amounted to ten dollars a month—more a symbol of gratitude from Mother Russia, than real incentive. In any case, Fedor's family lacked the means to buy him out of the army.

"Draft-dodging is a national pastime," independent military analyst Alexander Golts told *TIME* magazine in 2009. "In Russia it's a million-dollar industry."[198]

There were brutal beatings to be dished out, money to be extorted, and other more cruel forms of abuse to be dished out to the new recruits. It was unfortunate that Fedor was assigned to the regular army forces, serving in a military firefighter brigade, rather than being placed in the "sports forces" where he could have trained in Sambo and judo rather than performing grunt work.

"I didn't have enough time to complete the requirements for the title of a Master of Sport before being drafted," reminisced Emelianenko. "Perhaps the draft committee did not look at my file closely enough," he coldly stated.[199]

For his part, Fedor understood how the strong brutalized the weak—typical in institutions like the military, prisons and many schools—and was prepared to stand up for himself.

"I came in March right in time for the fall draft," said Fedor. "Those who were there before me wanted to prove who's the boss in the place, [they] tried to [bring] everyone else down. I had to use my fists."

After a few confrontations, the predators in the ranks knew not to mess with Emelianenko. Fedor also made sure not to attract too much attention, as he had a quiet personality that could more easily avoid conflict. Despite these experiences, Fedor later refused to condemn the practices in the army, writing them off in a 2010 interview as acceptable conditions for modern Russia.

"During my military service, I had a very good experience," said Fedor. "Certainly we did have *dedovshchina*, but it was not really that huge, in that big extent. I wouldn't say that there was a lot of bullying; I would say that that was more teaching by the older soldiers of more younger [soldiers]."

It was a revisionist attitude, far removed from the truth he'd spoken of in previous years, but there was no room to be critical of the way the army was run in modern Russia; less so when considering the furthering of ties between Vladimir Putin and Fedor's manager, Vadim Finkelstein. Fedor's ties to Putin would eventually yield benefits, such as Fedor being appointed to the Presidential Sports Council in July 2012.[200]

Although there were dangers associated with his initial assignment in the firefighting unit, Fedor and his unit were never asked to undertake any suicide missions. The gung-ho attitude some of his fellow soldiers took exposed them to additional (and unnecessary) risks, however.

"As far as the firefighting is concerned, the most serious cases were burns on some of my colleagues," said Emelianenko of the inherent job hazards. "Some also got gas poisoning. They felt sick and lethargic for several days."

During Fedor's second year of service, he was transferred to a tank brigade.

There were no facilities for grappling available to Fedor. He was keen on maintaining his strength using whatever equipment was around and by creating a makeshift gym of his own.

"I had to settle for barbells, kettlebells and running long distance," said Emelianenko of his Spartan fitness routine in the army.

In 1997, Emelianenko's national service was over. He was no worse for wear, save for a few teeth he lost due to the lack of fluoride and proper dental treatment in the army.[201]

"It warms my soul that I went through it," Fedor said in interviews when questioned about his service. "I grew up. I developed my character there, toughened. I went in as a boy and came out a man with a hardened resolve."

Despite the hardships of his service, Fedor had managed to find greater discipline and he had enjoyed bonding with other men.

He was now free to pick up where he had left off with his Sambo and judo training. Hungry for grappling, Fedor trained obsessively, meeting within a year the requirements for the Master of Sport title that had eluded him before the draft. There was still the question of whether Fedor was among the elite of Russian athletes.

Fedor believed that he should have earned a place representing Russia on the Olympic team as a judoka. He certainly achieved results in competition. In 1997, Fedor took gold in the 100 kilo and above class at the European Sambo championships; 1998 saw him win bronze in the 100 kilo and below, as well as bronze in the open class at the Russian national judo championship; he also took bronze at the 1998 Russian national Sambo championship. Fedor placed bronze at the 1999 judo world cup tournaments of Sofia Liberation A-Team and the Moscow International Tournament.

At the age of 22, Fedor met the requirements for the International Master of Sport. Regardless of his tournament results, politics proved to be a major roadblock impeding Emelianenko from getting the opportunities he desired on the national judo team.

"I encountered the same unfairness in judging and team selection," said Fedor.

His account was partially corroborated by then-teammate Alexander Mikhaylin, who also pointed to the depth of talent of the Russian judo squad as being equally difficult for Fedor to surmount as the politics of the team.

"The competition among the super heavyweights in the Russian national team has always been exceptionally strong," said three-time judo world champion Alexander Mikhaylin. "It would have been very hard for him to overcome it, especially when it was combined with sports politics. In that situation, Fedor, to put it bluntly, got fed up."

Favoritism of certain individuals to the detriment of others can kill the spirit like nothing else can. As it was, Fedor had never enjoyed any status or connections in Russia; his only tool for improving his standing in society had been judo and Sambo. Now avenues for advancement within those areas had been denied to him.

Quitting the national judo team also had an economic imperative: the small amount of financial support that Fedor received from regional sports organizations wasn't enough to support him and his now-growing family.

Fedor married his first wife, Oksana, in 1999. The pair had met as teenagers in a pioneer summer camp where Fedor was participating in sports events and Oksana was a brigade leader.

"It is hard not to love him," said Oksana, who was taken by Fedor's humbleness and down-to-earth personality.[202]

Fedor and Oksana had a daughter, Masha, born in 1999.[203] As the head of the household, it was Fedor's duty to provide the kind of life where his family wouldn't have to struggle or suffer, as many Russians dealing with the rough post-Soviet economy did.

For the moment, the situation appeared bleak.

29

RUSSIAN OPTIMISM

According to former PRIDE FC and M-1 employee Jerry Millen, Fedor competed in local combat Sambo tournaments in order to maintain his "Master of Sport" rankings; these would afford special benefits for health care and pensions, although there were other interesting benefits. Combat Sambo was different from Sport Sambo in that it allowed striking and grappling, making it similar to amateur MMA.

"Fedor wasn't a really strong kid or a bully or any of that. He doesn't fight to beat people up—he views it as a competition," said Millen. "As a kid, Fedor and Aleksander first started competing in these Sambo competitions—fighting competitions. There wasn't a lot of money involved in Russia, so they would win strange things. One time he won a car; another time, he won a German shepherd—a specially trained fighting dog. And, he was living in an apartment at the time, his mother was in a house. He said to his mom, 'Will you take this German shepherd? I have no room for it.' He was walking the dog to his mother's house, some people saw him and stopped him—got upset and started crying, and all because they had lost a dog that was the same as that German shepherd. Fedor gave the dog up on the street instead of giving it to his mother."

Up until this time, there had been a few successful Russians or individuals from the former Soviet Republics in mixed martial arts (then referred to as "No-Holds-Barred"). Oleg Taktarov had won the UFC 6 tournament in 1995; Igor Zinoviev had fought Frank Shamrock for the UFC light-heavyweight title in 1996 (Zinoviev lost in just 22 seconds via a slam that knocked him out and caused a career-ending collarbone injury); Ukrainian Igor Vovchanchyn had won numerous smaller tournaments and made it to the finals of the PRIDE 2000 open-weight Grand Prix. Although the sport was unknown in Russia, there was growing international interest in MMA. There, Fedor had the potential to earn more money as a professional fighter than the small stipend he had received for competing in Sambo and judo. In the post-Soviet transition period, other prospects were available, such as mafia groups who were always hiring nationally ranked wrestlers and boxers as hired muscle—but MMA seemed a much better fit by comparison.

"It was hard for me," said Vladimir Voronov, "but I didn't object. Why? Because I thought that Fedor can also be successful in MMA."

"I had big doubts," said Fedor, "because I was a member of the national judo and Sambo team. It was difficult to decide to leave it."

Inertia can be a silent killer for most people. Being too familiar or comfortable with one's surroundings can cause long-term stagnation or tacit acceptance of compromise. The process can go on for years—co-dependence on a partner in a flawed relationship, working for bosses who make too many demands. And what guarantees existed that making dramatic changes will improve one's situation for the better?

Fedor was optimistic about entering MMA. He really believed that he could achieve great things. There was no way of knowing whether Fedor was better off transitioning to MMA. Better credentialed athletes such as 1992 Olympic gold medalist in freestyle wrestling, Kevin Jackson, had failed to make a viable career in MMA. There were many pitfalls and dangers, but the advantage of MMA was that it was a venue where Fedor could utilize and demonstrate his judo and Sambo skills.

Oksana was supportive, but full of anxiety. At this time, no one really understood the health risks associated with MMA, and to the layman, it appeared to be a barbaric sport that could cripple—or kill—Fedor.

"I'm always afraid he will get some injuries," she stated. "He convinces me before every fight that he can handle it—that he is better than his opponent."

Volk Han, a veteran of MMA organization RINGS and fellow-Sambo fighter, recruited Fedor to Russian Top Team. There, he passed on his experience to Emelianenko.[204]

Fedor was managed by Vladimir Pogodin. At this time, Pogodin was the vice-president of the Russian Sambo federation, as well as the promoter behind RINGS in Russia.[205] It seemed to be a good match, as Pogodin was able to get Fedor numerous fights in RINGS.

Although Fedor would be criticized for facing lesser-tier competition later in his career, his first professional fight was against one of the strongest opponents any debuting fighter could have faced—Bulgarian Martin Lazarov, a wrestler with excellent showings in international wrestling competitions.

Techno-music, spotlights and cheerleaders provided a strange ambiance for the event, held on May 21, 2000, in Ekaterinburg, Sverdlovsk Oblast, Russia. At the start of the fight, Lazarov, who had forgone wearing MMA gloves and had donned wrestling shoes, secured a takedown that landed him in Fedor's half-guard. No strikes to the head were allowed to downed opponents in RINGS, so Fedor was both protected and constrained (depending on his position) by the modified rule set. After a stand-up by the referee, Lazarov went for a single leg and paid the price with Fedor sinking in a guillotine choke. At 2:24, the bout was called and Fedor had his first taste of victory in MMA.

From there, everything seemed to be going well. Fedor went 3-0 in RINGS, with two submissions and one knockout.

"My next fights lifted me higher and higher in MMA," recalled Fedor.

At RINGS King of Kings 2000 Block B tournament in held in Osaka, Japan, Fedor faced Brazilian Ricardo Arona, with the fight a draw after two five-minute rounds. An overtime five-minute round decided the fight, which was awarded to Fedor by the judges. The Arona fight revealed weakness in Fedor's takedown defense, with the result being controversial. Arona had clearly dominated the fight, but was robbed of the victory.

Tsuyoshi Kohsaka, a veteran of 31 fights, was Fedor's next opponent that night. The bout began with Kohsaka throwing a right hook, which missed, grazing Fedor with Kohsaka's elbow. Kohsaka's elbow had opened up a pre-existing cut that Fedor had received in the Arona fight, prompting a doctor's stoppage just 17 seconds into the first round. Kohsaka was awarded the victory in what should have been a no-contest. Many pundits and fans have written off the elbow as an illegal move disallowed by the rules of RINGS (elbow strikes were permitted only if the fighter was wearing elbow pads).

"It's not a good memory," said Fedor of the fight. "I was cut by Kohsaka's illegal strike (elbow). There was blood coming from my eyebrow and I couldn't finish the fight. The RINGS' judges gave the victory to Kohsaka and wouldn't give me a revenge match. I don't think it was fair."[206]

Despite what Fedor and others believed, the elbow was not intentional and was merely proper striking technique on the part of Kohsaka.

"If a good hook misses, the elbow lands," boxing trainer Freddie Roach once explained in a left hook tutorial. "I'm not saying 'be a dirty fighter' or anything like that, but it's a tendency of the hook to follow through with the elbow."[207]

Because of the tournament format, Kohsaka was declared the winner, as RINGS needed someone to advance to the next round.

Six more wins followed Fedor's first official loss. Among these victories, a win over Renato "Babalu" Sobral had earned Fedor the RINGS openweight championship on August 11, 2001. (Bobby Hoffman was the tournament finalist, but he refused to face Fedor, claiming injury. Fedor states that the Japanese doctor had cleared Hoffman to fight, meaning Hoffman was terrified of losing to Fedor.) Beating Australian

Chris Haseman on February 15, 2002, made Fedor the last ever RINGS Absolute Class tournament winner.

Quizzed by a Russian television journalist over whether the victory over Haseman was difficult, Fedor was his typical curt self.

"Not really," he said of the win. "All of the [tournament] fights didn't differ too much from each other in hardness."

It was mostly true—outside of Ricardo Arona, Fedor had not yet stepped into the deep waters of MMA competition against a comparable class of fighters. Fedor's opponents were usually outmatched from the get-go. It was a trend that would change dramatically in the near future, and if Fedor wanted to keep winning, he would have to change as well.

Although Fedor had some striking training and had access to sparring with Russian boxers, he needed to up his stand-up game. Alexander Michkov, a former amateur boxer and Master of Sport, became Fedor's coach in striking, under the recommendation of Voronov around 2000.

"We started from scratch," said Michkov in the 2009 documentary, *Fedor: Baddest Man on the Planet.* "Nevertheless, [Fedor] was very coordinated. He quickly learned proper striking technique and defense maneuvers."

In May 2002, Fedor took gold in the Russian combat Sambo championships held in Moscow. Fedor had been sponsored in the Sambo tournament by the Oskol Electrometallurgical Kombinat, a plant in Stary Oskol. He was one of the few athletes from his region to receive such support over the years.

"It's not easy to sponsor an athlete like Fedor," stated Voronov, "because big sport means big money."

With an underdeveloped system for providing for athletes in the Belograd Oblast region, Fedor and Voronov made appeals for the state and industry to sponsor more athletes. Interestingly, at this time, their argument was that more sponsorship should be mandatory to *prevent* local athletes from resorting to careers in MMA.

To truly reap the rewards of a career in MMA, Fedor needed to fight in Japan's PRIDE Fighting Championship. Only the Japanese were paying the kind of money that made the risks tolerable. In PRIDE, Fedor was successful from the start, needing just two wins over opponents Semmy Schilt and Heath Herring to earn a title shot against Brazilian Antônio Rodrigo Nogueira at PRIDE 25.

There were no special training partners brought in for these fights; in fact, Fedor prepared for Schilt, Herring and Nogueira using two welterweight judo players who were only "Candidates for the Master of Sport," nationally-ranked athletes.

Although Fedor was the underdog against Nogueira, he had previously formulated a theory about his chances against fighters of other nationalities, based not on how their skills matched up on paper, but from a philosophical viewpoint.

"There is confrontation between Russian and Brazilian fighters in most tournaments," said Fedor. "Russian school is considered one of the spiritually strongest schools. The character. If our skills are not enough, we are still able to win by using our character."[208]

Character is one of the intangibles that becomes necessary when the going gets tough. The 1961 black-and-white film *The Hustler* illustrated this perfectly when pool player Eddie Felson (played by Paul Newman) attempted to take on Minnesota Fats (Jackie Gleason). Although Felson starts off by winning many sets handily in the first meeting, he pisses away his momentum by gloating and drinking—enjoying the sensation of victory too much—and Fats comes back to clean him out. After Felson experiences being beaten up by hoods, getting his thumbs broken and having his girlfriend commit suicide, the journey has sufficiently hardened Felson's resolve to enable him to defeat Minnesota Fats in their next meeting. This time around, there is no stopping to pose and admire his handiwork; Eddie Felson has the character to win.

Nogueira was the 19-1-1 PRIDE heavyweight champion, Brazilian Top Team member and a major proponent of Brazilian Jiu-Jitsu. He bore a large scar and noticeable indentation on his back from being accidentally run over by a truck at the age of 10. That he survived the incident, let alone became an MMA champion, was a testament to Nogueira's own depth of character.[209]

Fedor shocked the MMA world by upsetting Nogueira and claiming the PRIDE belt. This was a monumental moment in MMA history that no one saw coming—not the least being the brass at DSE and the executives at Fuji TV. The MMA landscape had forever changed, with all parties scarcely believing that this obscure Russian had so easily dominated one of PRIDE's biggest stars.

On the surface, it seemed that Fedor had it made: he was now ranked among the best in PRIDE, situated with Russian Top Team, granted a raise in his purses and blessed with a powerful man like Pogodin as his management—his future was secure.

Nothing could have been further from the truth.

30

STARY OSKOL

Part of Fedor Emelianenko's mystique lies in his inaccessibility. The difficulty in understanding who he is is exacerbated geographically by the inconvenience it takes to get to his hometown of Stary Oskol. While his family, friends and coaches live in Stary Oskol, the M-1 staff rarely visits, if at all. Former PRIDE and M-1 Global employee Jerry Millen claimed that Fedor's manager, Vadim Finkelstein, had only visited Fedor in Stary Oskol once or twice. Finkelstein made many overtures to have Fedor move to Saint Petersburg, but this only attracted Fedor's lesser-talented brother, Aleksander.

"Getting there is like going to another planet. The first trip was the worst because I didn't know what to expect," reminisced Millen. "The transportation system is not like in America or Canada or anywhere else. It's old school. Fly into Moscow, and then you have to go to the train station."

Although planes to Stary Oskol are available, even Fedor takes a longer (12- to 14-hour) train ride due to the unsafe flight record of many older Russian aircraft.

"The train is from *Petticoat Junction*, that old ['60s] television show, and it goes *slow*, 'Chug, chug. Chug, chug.' It's definitely a culture shock," says Millen.

The first trip by Millen occurred during his tenure as PRIDE employee. Millen went to Russia to get some video footage of Fedor as well as his medicals for PRIDE's upcoming October 21, 2006, show to be held in Las Vegas, Nevada.

Fedor's grappling coach, Vladimir Voronov, picked Millen up and drove him to a kids' summer camp. The training partners and visitors stayed in cabins. Millen fondly remembers plugging a production light into a socket, which blew out the fuse. Conditions were cold and damp—but the atmosphere was secondary to the fighter's purpose.

Said Millen, "This is fall, and there are a couple guys shadow-boxing in rain suits in the cold rain in this amphitheatre. And I remember thinking, 'This is weird.' "

Videos of Fedor training in a random playground were a source of laughter and ridicule by fans when the videos surfaced on the Internet, but Millen pointed to the different cultural values espoused by the Russians.

"They don't have Bow-Flexes or Nordic-Tracks. That's just the way they train," said Millen (not that North American MMA fighters required those brands of home-orientated fitness equipment to train effectively; typically spinning bikes and elliptical trainers are useful).

Alexander Michkov pointed out the rationale behind the minimalist nature of Russians.

"We do not have enough money," said Michkov, laughing. "We are simple and clean because it's what we have to work with; we must think of the most advantageous means to use what is available. That makes us strong, adaptable, train harder. Because we think it may be a disadvantage, it's extra motivation. Even though we would like some fancy equipment, I'll never understand treadmills. They are stupid. Fedor and the rest of our fighters prefer the street. At least there are distractions. Nature as they say is always more tasty. A treadmill I think is just brainless."[210]

Jerry Millen's second trip to Stary Oskol occurred when he was an M-1 Global employee and Fedor was fighting in the MMA promotion Affliction in 2008. At that time, the iron-ore company that supports Oskol was building the new, modern facility that Fedor would later train in.

"They wanted to name that gym after Fedor, and he refused. He said, 'No, don't name it after me,' " said Millen, extolling Fedor's humbleness.

The facility was eventually named "St. Alexander Nevsky Sport Palace" after the prince of Novgorod who ruled the region during the 13th century.

Another local training facility utilized by Fedor was a boxing gym on the upper floor of an old building. The scene reminded Millen of the gyms in use during the 1920s and '30s, where the blood and sweat of toiling pugilists poured onto the ground.

"What I thought was interesting was that Fedor would actually take classes with the actual students of the boxing gym. He's training, jumping rope—next to an eight-year-old kid," said Millen.

According to Millen, this was not done for a photo-op or PR stunt. Fedor really trained next to kids, taking public gym classes and then working with boxing coach Alexander Michkov.

Fedor had managed to train with the elite kickboxers of Golden Glory earlier in his PRIDE career, but due to management issues, his camp's relationship with Golden Glory owner Bas Boon soured, diminishing Fedor's ability to evolve as a fighter with it. As has been repeatedly noted by fans and pundits, Emelianenko usually lacked training partners of equal or greater strength in the various disciplines MMA is composed of.

"Fedor trains with all the young guys out there," said Millen of his time in Stary Oskol, "like Kirill and all those cats. Kids, not big guys."

As expected, Fedor got the better of his training partners, including heavyweight Kirill Sidelnikov, who was nicknamed "Baby Fedor." Although Kirill would eventually claim gold in Combat Sambo in 2010 and 2011, in MMA, he had no more in common with Fedor than Patty and Selma from *The Simpsons* had with Carrie Bradshaw from *Sex and the City*. Training with low-tier opposition would eventually work against Fedor down the line.

In 2009, before facing former UFC heavyweight champion Andre Arlovski, Fedor spoke highly of his training routine in Stary Oskol, although he seemed unconcerned with the advances being made at other modern MMA camps by this point.

"I believe I train harder than anyone else in the world," Fedor told Fiveouncesofpain.com's Sam Caplan. "The strength and power I obtain can only [be done so] here in Russia."[211]

At one point, Fedor's daily training routine was said to consist of two to three training sessions, various bodyweight exercises and two runs with a combined distance of 12–15 kilometers (7 to 10 miles). High-altitude training took place at Kislovodsk once or twice a year.

The inevitable super-fight with K-1 star Mirko "Cro Cop" Filipović, which took place on August 28, 2005, required Fedor to tune up his striking game, especially with regard to his kicks. Fedor left his comfort zone to train in Muay Thai with kickboxer Ernesto Hoost at the Vos Gym in Netherlands and added a Muay Thai coach, Ruslan Nagnibeda, to his team.

Improvements with regard to sport science, supplements or training methods seemed to dawdle behind other camps, however.

"[Fedor and Mirko "Cro Cop" Filipović] came from relatively small towns in Europe," said Fedor's former manager Miro Mijatovic. "They weren't exposed to sport science; they weren't exposed to nutritional stuff, right?"

Said Mijatovic of PRIDE's number one contender, "Mirko, like a 10-year-old kid, refused to eat any vegetables or salad."

"For my diet, it's simple," Fedor revealed in a 2005 interview. "I eat everything. I take no particular supplement, just mixtures of vitamins: Vitrum, Centrum. You can find them in any pharmacy."[212]

During his PRIDE days, one of Fedor's favorite restaurants was the McDonald's near his Shinjuku hotel.

"The Dutch were different—the Golden Glory guys," said Mijatovic. "They had a lot more protein, creatine, nutrients, that sort of stuff. They were a lot more tuned in to what we think is normal. Guys like Fedor and Mirko—it was low-tech."

Jerry Millen's third trip to Fedor's hometown was for the CBS television network, which was planning to broadcast one of Fedor's fights in Strikeforce, acting as a consultant to smooth things over and help the American film crew avoid a faux pas.

"They wanted Fedor to pick up these five gallon drums and throw them. [Fedor] said 'I don't train that way.' I said, 'They want to film it for the promo,' and [Fedor] said, 'Yes, but I don't train that way. I'm not going to do it.' [The film crew] were like, 'Make him do it.' "

The crew relented in their demands, with Fedor pulling some pulleys and hitting punching bags for the promo rather than performing staged acts.

Millen mainly acted like a diplomat, ensuring the crew didn't overstep Fedor's personal boundaries. Emelianenko would give Millen a wink when he wanted privacy and Millen would clear the room. Millen's banter suggests that he was the actual right hand next to the Russian legend—thoughtfully guiding the artist through skilled management, while Fedor's official handlers screwed around. While Millen may not have had much of a decision-making role to influence Fedor, he was much more adept than Vadim or Apy at handling public relations.

Of special interest during Millen's third trip to Stary Oskol was a visit to Fedor's church. There was also a ritual for spiritual cleansing where Millen, Fedor and Fedor's childhood friend Denis Kurilov all stripped down to their underwear and jumped into a freezing cold river, in a "baptism" of sorts overseen by Fedor's priest, Father Andrey.

Although Fedor hadn't appeared overly religious early in his career, something had triggered a change in his attitude.

"The way that I had lived before, I wasn't living my life the right way," Fedor told *FIGHT! Magazine*'s Neal Taflinger in 2009. "Today, it's a conscious decision, not like before, to follow certain principles of the church. To pray, to ask for forgiveness for my sins."[213]

Was it guilt over the 2006 end of his first marriage that left Fedor vulnerable to the overtures of religion? Many people embroiled in personal crises could be nudged toward spiritual groups who claimed to offer guidance.

Denis Kurilov's family owned a sauna in the town, which Millen describes as being hot as hell.

"It was the hottest thing ever—like fire on your skin," says Millen. The fun didn't stop there: "[Fedor] beat me with these Eucalyptus leaves. It felt like I was being hit with fire." The session ended with water being thrown on Millen, who—while still a careerist enmeshed within the superficial culture of Los Angeles—perceived himself as being closer to the Russian through this ritual.

As for the final verdict on Fedor staying close to his friends and family in Stary Oskol, he got a lot of personal enjoyment out of staying close to his roots. A more professional camp in a bigger city might have prolonged Fedor's career, but at the cost of diminishing personal returns.

31

CROATIAN CONTENDER

Japan—ever obsessed with fads—had latched onto kickboxing and mixed martial arts, as traditional martial arts had long been revered in Japanese culture. From the late '90s into the millennium, there were two major organizations of note in the country: PRIDE FC, an MMA promotion of titanic proportions, and K-1, a kickboxing organization that dabbled in MMA.

Croatian kickboxer Mirko "Cro Cop" Filipović, a K-1 fighter, would eventually become the number one contender to face Fedor Emelianenko in PRIDE. However, Cro Cop's switch from K-1 kick-boxing to a full-time career in MMA was not a given.

In 2002, the typical payday for Cro Cop's K-1 fights was around $30-40,000. The K-1 Grand Prix tournament winner got $200,000; bigger K-1 stars like Ernesto Hoost, Peter Aerts, Ray Sefo and Jerome LeBanner made just $60,000 per fight. With three K-1 wins under his belt in 2002, Cro Cop's management team began to demand an increase in his salary.

After long and hard negotiations, it was agreed that Cro Cop would fight on August 28, 2002 in an MMA bout against Japanese star

Kazushi Sakuraba. The event, called *Dynamite!*, was co-promoted between K-1 and PRIDE, with Cro Cop to receive a purse of $150,000. The powerbrokers of K-1 expected Cro Cop, who was 2-0-2 in MMA at this point, to lose, and thus become easier to negotiate with.

When Cro Cop saw the huge number of spectators in attendance (supposedly pegged at 91,107—Tokyo National stadium was configured for 80,000 without a sell-out[214]) on the night of the fight, he refused to enter the ring until his pay was doubled. K-1 actually relented, giving him $300,000 total. It was a big surprise when the larger but relatively inexperienced MMA fighter Cro Cop fractured Sakuraba's orbital bone in the second round, prompting a stoppage of the fight.[215]

Of course, the increasing number of demands from Cro Cop plus his unwillingness to do media or PR made him more trouble than he was worth. Holding the main card at *Dynamite!* hostage was the final insult that pushed the K-1 management over the edge, with K-1 president Kazuyoshi Ishii making the decision to blacklist Cro Cop from K-1.

Croatian-born Australian Miro Mijatovic was an international lawyer who had arrived in Japan in 1992 to work on mega-projects building infrastructure such as power stations, toll roads or oil pipelines—financially secure and rewarding work that eventually became boring. At the start of the millennium, he began to turn his focus to the glamorous world of the sports and entertainment business, representing Croatian kickboxer Mirko "Cro Cop" Filipović in a managerial capacity in late 2002.

Mijatovic's first order of business was to gain Cro Cop entry back into the big leagues of K-1. He managed this by using intelligence and legal maneuvering: K-1 had teamed up with Japanese video game manufacturer Konami to create a game that used the names and likenesses of K-1 fighters. One hitch stuck out to the lawyer in Mijatovic—the absence of any contracts where the K-1 fighters agreed to participate in this venture. The threat of a lawsuit was effective as K-1 was already reeling from bad PR due to K-1 president Kazuyoshi Ishii being charged with tax evasion and sentenced to 10 months in prison.

After negotiations, K-1 arranged a fight for Cro Cop—under MMA rules—against Japanese heavyweight Kazuyuki Fujita for a purse of $100,000. There was no compromising on the issue of Cro Cop competing in the 2002 K-1 Grand Prix, as K-1 president Ishii could not lose face over his decision to punish Cro Cop.

To the surprise of K-1 and the Japanese public, Cro Cop beat Fujita for a second time, and began to shift his focus toward MMA rather than kickboxing. With that decision, not only would Cro Cop soon build himself into a powerful contender to face Fedor Emelianenko for the heavyweight throne of PRIDE, but his stardom would help raise PRIDE's fortunes.

As for PRIDE itself, to the public, the company's integrity and stability were merely an illusion. The balance of power within PRIDE had shifted dramatically with the suicide of PRIDE founder and Dream Stage Entertainment (DSE) president Naoto Morishita, on January 13, 2003. Forty-two-year-old Morishita was found dead hanging by his neck in his hotel room at the Shinjuku Hilton; the reason offered up for his suicide was Morishita's mistress telling him that she wanted to end their affair. Attaching sexual scandal to the suicide helped make Morishita's widow ashamed of asking too many questions. Nobuyuki Sakakibara quickly assumed presidency; Sakakibara and Mr. Ishizaka (aka Mr. I, or Kim Dok Soo) also acquired Morishita's shares in PRIDE parent company Dream Stage Entertainment (DSE), rather than the shares going to the next of kin, Morishita's wife.

Behind the scenes, a power struggle was then waged between PRIDE producer Hiromichi Momose's group and Ishizaka's people.

"Momose and Ishizaka represented different subgroups of the Yamaguchi-gumi (the largest and most infamous yakuza group in Japan), and the battle for control of PRIDE was also a battle for which Yamaguchi-gumi subgroup would be taking the lead in Yamaguchi-gumi's expansion into Tokyo," said Mijatovic.

Organized crime groups were attracted to the fight industry of Japan like traditional mafia groups had controlled boxing in the US up until the late '50s. Momose was a Yamaguchi-gumi representative who was working with the Shizuoka-based Goto Gumi, a subgroup of the Yamaguchi-gumi. Ishizaka represented the Ota Kogyo, then a dangerous and powerful Osaka-based subgroup also of the Yamaguchi-gumi. The strategic objective for both gangs was simple—consolidate bases in Tokyo, infiltrate the major television broadcasters and begin running the fight promotions.

At PRIDE Final Conflict, held on November 9, 2003, Mijatovic witnessed a scene of "100-to-200 armed yakuza guys from two different groups basically looking like they were setting up battle lines and ready to start open warfare."[216]

The upshot of this backstage tension was PRIDE producer Hiromichi Momose being pushed out of DSE, and many power brokers deciding that DSE itself was unstable. It was understood that Mr. Ishizaka, a former loan shark of Korean blood, became the real power behind PRIDE.[217] Sakakibara carried out Ishizaka's orders, airbrushing former DSE president Naoto Morishita out of the official PRIDE history and stamping the organization with his own brand of narcissism, evidenced at PRIDE 34 on April 8, 2007, where Sakakibara had pictures of himself plastered all around the arena; Sakakibara also made the fighters give speeches honoring his greatness. The new PRIDE president, like many top players in the Japanese entertainment industry, used people around him to gratify his own needs first and foremost. The consequences of this regime change would send ripples all over the world with regards to MMA.

A win over commercial phenomenon Bob Sapp, a 330-pound former NFLer, capped Mirko Cro Cop's career in K-1. Cro Cop earned a fearsome reputation from this fight, as he had broken Sapp's zygomatic (cheek) bone, leaving Sapp crying in pain on the canvas.[218]

"Mirko Cro Cop became, without a doubt, the single hottest property in martial arts," said Mijatovic.

PRIDE became his new home. With Cro Cop's move, in 2003 PRIDE went from airing in the early morning hours to getting prime-time television slots.

American Heath Herring, a well-regarded journeyman, was Mirko Cro Cop's first opponent at PRIDE 26 on June 8, 2003. DSE had mastered the art of using information as a weapon to afford their favored fighter—in this case, Cro Cop—the best chance of winning. For three months, Herring had been told by DSE that he was fighting a grappler.

"With the Cro Cop fight, for two weeks before it I had no idea I was fighting him. So when it happened I wasn't ready mentally for the fight," Herring later told MMAWeekly.com after losing via first round TKO to Cro Cop.[219]

Everything was roses as Cro Cop won two more fights and earned a title shot against Antônio Rodrigo Nogueira for the interim heavyweight title. Cro Cop wanted to face Fedor Emelianenko, but Fedor claimed that a broken hand made him unavailable for the November date.

So overconfident was Mirko Cro Cop before the Nogueira fight, he was reported to have said "Has my belt been made for me?" via telephone to Sakakibara before boarding his flight to Japan.[220]

Where it counted, Cro Cop was on-point for the first round of his November 9, 2003 fight with Nogueira, controlling the fight, escaping all submission attempts, easily shrugging off takedowns, bloodying Nogueira's nose and brutalizing his opponent with a head kick that knocked him down at the end of the round. In the second, Cro Cop was taken down, mounted and submitted via armbar. Whether Cro Cop had it in him to win on this night will always be a subject of contention; what he ended up doing is recorded in the history books.

Legendary boxing trainer Cus D'Amato had a quote that summed up the series of decisions Cro Cop made throughout his career in a nutshell, "No matter what anyone says, no matter the excuse or explanation, whatever a person does in the end is what he intended to do all along."

Cro Cop had seemed like an unstoppable freight train, but after being derailed by Nogueira, he would have to start climbing from the very bottom of the ladder to secure a blockbuster match-up with Fedor Emelianenko.

32

NEW YEAR'S EVIL

Due to the yakuza-tainted nature of both K-1 and PRIDE, the opportunity arose for a third promotion in the fledgling Japanese MMA market. Competition among promoters would have driven the salaries for all MMA fighters up—for this, and other reasons, PRIDE would take extreme measures to lock up both Mirko Cro Cop and Fedor Emelianenko within their exclusive grasp.

The promotion Inoki Bom-Ba-Ye (IBBY) was recast with Japan's second largest TV network, Nippon TV, sponsoring what was believed could become the number-one promotion in Japan. President of production company K-Confidence, Seiya Kawamata, and Miro Mijatovic were the promoters of IBBY (Antonio Inoki lent his name to the promotion for 100 million yen, or about $1 million). PRIDE's biggest star, Mirko Cro Cop, was scheduled to face Japanese pro wrestler Takayama on the promotion's debut on December 31, 2003, for an easy score of $150,000.

There was anger and fear from DSE and PRIDE's broadcaster, Fuji TV, that the bigger-budgeted IBBY 2003 show (800 million yen—twice what Fuji TV had offered DSE) would undercut PRIDE's entire business model. Something had to be done to crush the threat—actions undertaken by PRIDE president Sakakibara that would ultimately help undo PRIDE itself.

The bad news for Miro Mijatovic and many others was that IBBY 2003 co-promoter Seiya Kawamata was, in fact, a yakuza fixer whose job description included placating the gangs who frequented MMA shows. The heat was on him for booking Mirko Cro Cop—considered DSE's property—onto the IBBY NYE show.

In order to sabotage the IBBY show, DSE paid PRIDE employee Ken Imai $500,000 to convince Mirko Cro Cop not to fight on the IBBY card. Sources indicated that Ken Imai had given Cro Cop $300,000 to break ties with then-manager Miro Mijatovic. Cro Cop pulled out of the IBBY, claiming a back injury, but he recuperated quickly to have two fights in February 2004 and six more fights during that year.

The dirty and underhanded maneuver of stealing Cro Cop from IBBY, engineered by DSE, inspired Mijatovic to step his own game up and approach the biggest fighter in PRIDE—heavyweight champion Fedor Emelianenko—to headline IBBY 2003. At the time, Fedor was considered relatively unknown in Japan, and for the brass at DSE and Fuji TV, the ordinary-looking Russian was unmarketable.

"It was common knowledge for a long time that Fedor was being paid absolute peanuts. His fight money was $10,000 to $15,000 at that time. Nogueira was making $120,000 a fight," said Mijatovic, contrasting the purses between current and former PRIDE heavyweight champions.

Problems with Fedor's manager—Russian Top Team boss Vladimir Pogodin—were also well known. Pogodin was only giving Fedor a fraction of the money PRIDE had been paying Pogodin.

"It was pretty obvious that Pogodin had been skimming off the top and underpaying Fedor for a year or so," said former PRIDE and M-1 employee Jerry Millen.

There was also pressure on Fedor from Pogodin to use steroids and other stimulants—something Fedor abhorred. Many fighters looked for an edge; it was common knowledge that steroids could be purchased over the counter in places like Brazil. PRIDE certainly didn't discourage drug use through its testing procedures—fighters pissing into open coffee cups with a DSE official waiting outside the bathroom door—with no follow-up regarding the results.

Fedor was well aware of how Pogodin could try to utilize his connections with PRIDE to cripple Fedor's career in MMA, or alternatively, Pogodin might use his power as vice-president of the World Sambo Federation to strip Fedor of his Sambo titles as a "Master of Sport."

"Roughly speaking, Pogodin tries 'to keep' a sportsman using his official position [as vice-president of the World Sambo Federation], because he is rather weak as the manager, and as it was found out, is a dishonorable person," said Fedor. "The fact that Pogodin has simply deceived guys from Russian team and me with money became one more reason of transition [to] 'Red Devil.' "

Leaving Pogodin would expose Fedor to other more nefarious types of threats.

"When Fedor wanted to leave Pogodin, he was very concerned about the possible impacts it could have on him in Russia," explained Mijatovic. "There was some concern initially about a physical threat."

There was also the question of his titles in Sambo, which meant a lot to Fedor in terms of both his personal pride as a sportsman, and the benefits accrued to such titles.

"That's why combat Sambo was so important for him—he needed to maintain participation to maintain his Russian sporting titles up," said Mijatovic. "What that meant was that it gave him access to a lot of privileges, including pensions after he's done fighting, all that sort of stuff. He was worried that Pogodin could get those stripped away from him as well."

On December 3, 2003, Miro Mijatovic flew into Saint Petersburg, Russia and negotiated a deal with Fedor. Mijatovic would be Fedor's promoter, creating a four-fight deal that would guarantee Emelianenko $150,000 for his participation in IBBY 2003 and escalate to $200,000 for future fights. The Red Devil team, run by Vadim Finkelstein and Apy Echteld, would become Fedor's new managerial representation. Mijatovic proffered reassurance that he could get Fedor back in the good graces of PRIDE, while Russian businessman Vadim Finkelstein was necessary, as he promised Fedor that he could handle any threats from Pogodin.

Vladimir Pogodin and Russian Top Team felt the sting of Fedor's "betrayal," and would later attempt to groom two-time Sambo champion Suren Balachinskiy as a viable challenger to take Fedor's PRIDE crown. Balachinskiy held two Sambo victories over Fedor; when RINGS founder Akira Maeda had traveled to Russia to hold tryouts for RINGS, Maeda had rated Balachinskiy the highest; Maeda's comments concerning Fedor were "with some polish, he might shine, a runner-up." Balachinskiy's career never made it off the ground: when the 0-1 Balachinskiy was purportedly going to appear at PRIDE 28 in October 2004, injuries scrubbed the RTT hope from the card. Balachinskiy's MMA record stands at 0-1 today.[221]

Vladimir Pogodin eventually disappeared from the picture, dying in a 2008 plane crash while en-route to a Sambo tournament in Perm, Russia.[222]

Fedor's new manager, Vadim Finkelstein, was described by Mijatovic as "your typical dodgy Russian businessman" from Saint Petersburg, Russia. Finkelstein had made his fortune in real estate development, launched an energy drink, was involved in meat importation and had a side interest as a small-time fight promoter. Although the Red Devil team officially became Emelianenko's new home, Fedor never moved to their headquarters in Saint Petersburg.

"Vadim didn't have a clue about sports business, or management, or anything like that," says Mijatovic of his impression. "[Red Devil co-owner] Apy Echteld doesn't have two brain cells to rub together," words perhaps colored by the acrimonious split of Mijatovic from the

Fedor camp that would occur later on. "Vadim and Apy were basically dishonest, incompetent, corrupt (laughter)."

Miro Mijatovic yielded many interesting details about his time with Fedor. Perhaps the biggest headache Fedor faced throughout his career (besides bad management) was the status of his fragile hands, which were prone to frequent injuries.

"He has got very small hands for a fighter, very delicate hands," said Mijatovic. "Obviously one of the big differences in fight preparation with Fedor was the taping of the hands that Cro Cop did that Fedor didn't do."

All boxers and kickboxers know to tape their hands in order to protect the bones in the hand from breaking on impact with hard surfaces like the skull. Some cornermen have special ways of wrapping, like trainer Felix Trinidad Sr. did for his son, welterweight boxer Felix Trinidad, that padded the knuckles and gave mental reinforcement because it allowed the boxer to punch at full power without fear of hurting their hands. James Toback's documentary *Tyson* revealed the edge that Mike Tyson chiseled out as his pre-fight ritual:

"While I'm in the dressing room, five minutes before I come out, my gloves are laced up. I'm breaking my gloves down, I'm pushing the leather at the back of my gloves," coldly narrated a scheming Tyson. "I'm breaking the middle of the glove so my knuckle can pierce through the leather/I feel my knuckle piercing against the tight leather glove on that Everlast boxing glove."

Fedor came from a different tradition of martial arts; his trainers, Michkov and Voronov, had a different rationale behind their methods relating to his gloves and hand wraps (or lack thereof).

"Fedor had almost no taping on his hands," said Mijatovic. "Fedor having the background of Sambo wanted to be able to use his hands or use holds or those techniques and favored that over protecting his hands."

Fedor punched with extreme force in a specific style. There was no way around injuries. PRIDE commentator Bas Rutten took notice of the unorthodox nature of Fedor's punching.

"His style—it's sloppy and it's kind of weird. His striking is not super-technical, because that's why he broke his hands so many times, because he throws this crazy overhand, and he hits at the wrong angle, and it's like it breaks your hand, because your bones are not inline if you hit like that," says Rutten.

"I was wondering if he does that on purpose to trick his opponents," suggested Rutten, as the unique angles utilized by Fedor would stun opponents who could not brace for the impact.

Said Rutten, "We should also talk about the power that Fedor had. He's got a lot of power. So then hitting a skull—the top of a skull—at a wrong angle, that will break your hand."

The impeccable technique and timing of Emelianenko's strikes were certainly effective in PRIDE, where he went 11-0, with one no-contest.

"Whenever he hits, it's on the money," said Rutten. "There is no load up in the punch, you see it in where his hands are at that moment—that's where it starts punching. And a lot of guys don't do that; 90 percent [don't] do that."

Another trainer who picked up on the stylistic weakness inherent in Fedor's style of striking was legendary boxing trainer Freddie Roach, who was preparing Andre Arlovski to face Fedor at MMA promotion Affliction's "Day of Reckoning" show.

"He's flat-footed, has no technique, but he can punch," Roach told SI.com's Josh Gross in January 2009, paying Fedor a backhanded compliment. "He's accurate. He'll follow you right to the floor, so he's aggressive."[223]

Aggression aside, inflicting unnecessary punishment in fights was never a goal of Fedor Emelianenko.

"He's got that aura, he's the good guy, the nice guy," said Rutten. "Generally a good guy, generally 'not want to hurt his opponent, but it's all part of the game, so I have to do it.' "

Mental preparation—or disposition—seemed to separate the Russian PRIDE champion from others.

"Fedor was very calm. Sort of the guy who is very analytical," observed Mijatovic. "When things got really, really tough, he was centered, cool and calm before his fights, or after his fights. Guys like Mirko, before a fight, felt an incredible amount of stress and tension."

The fight secured for Fedor on the Inoki-Bom-Ba-Ye's 2003 New Year's Eve show was against pro-wrestler Yuji Nagata. Almost immediately, PRIDE president Nobuyuki Sakakibara began issuing threats through various channels with the demand that Fedor pull out of his appearance in the competing promotion. According to IBBY co-promoter Miro Mijatovic, there were threats of lawsuits, and visits to Mijatovic's office from yakuza members. The fact that Sakakibara was aligned with yakuza boss Ishizaka, a top officer in the Yamaguchi Syndicate, made the threats that much more terrifying.

NTV expressed interest in backing the new MMA promotion for as many as four shows in 2004. The contract with broadcast giant NTV essentially allayed any previous doubts Mijatovic might have had in his co-promoter, Seiya Kawamata, as the backing of a major TV network made the enterprise seem completely legitimate.

The truth was, Kawamata was not really doing his job as a promoter. He'd promised to bring Japanese judo star turned MMA fighter Hidehiko Yoshida to IBBY, but failed. In September 2003, it was announced that Yoshida would appear on PRIDE's NYE show.

During December 2003, Kawamata spent much of his time holed up at the five-star Beverly Hills Hotel in Los Angeles (where the price of the *least expensive* suites ranged from $825 to $2300 per night plus applicable taxes) until he was forced to return to Japan for press conferences related to IBBY. The various factions behind the scenes were livid at the threat from the enemy at the gates; as the Japanese guy with connections to various yakuza groups, Kawamata did nothing to head off the impending disaster.

Said Mijatovic, "Kawamata knew the shit was going to hit the fan, but he didn't have any control over anybody."

Kawamata himself had also done a deal with DSE's yakuza, claiming he had been threatened by Mr. Ishizaka and PRIDE president Sakakibara into agreeing that Fedor would not fight at the IBBY NYE show. Again, it was important for PRIDE to eliminate the threat of a new MMA promotion cutting into their market share; sabotaging the IBBY 2003 main event was critical to PRIDE's strategic objectives. So confident was Sakakibara that he had the situation under control, he issued a press release on December 28 saying that Fedor would not appear on the IBBY show.[224]

The pressure began to mount on Mijatovic, with more threats as NYE approached:

"In the next 10 days leading up from December 20 through the actual event itself, things got very, very hot. People, guys were turning up into my house, you know, 2:00 A.M., 3:00 A.M., big groups, three or four guys. I don't know who they were but they certainly weren't friends of mine, you know, and I took other measures. I moved my family away from where we were living and started to [book] myself into hotels and other places as the event got closer and closer."

Mijatovic refused to bend to the pressure and the IBBY NYE show went on as scheduled, with Fedor headlining against Nagata. As a pro wrestler with an 0-1 record going into the Fedor match (Nagata's first loss being to Mirko Cro Cop), Nagata posed almost no challenge; a harder opponent like Tsuyoshi Kohsaka was considered, but Fedor's previously injured hand from his fight with Kazuyuki Fujita was still sore, and Kohsaka had a very hard head.

Fedor was dominant, beating Nagata via stoppage at 1:03 of the first round. There were 44,000 people in attendance—but due to the frequent main event changes from Cro Cop to Fedor, television ratings were dismal, at just four percent, putting IBBY in last place in the competition with K-1 and PRIDE's NYE shows.

Celebrations for the foreign (non-Japanese) fighters were held at a club rented out for the occasion.

"We booked a club in Kobe," said Mijatovic. "Together Fedor, Aleksander, Amar Suloev, Stefan Leko and Alistair Overeem—we celebrated until about 7:00 A.M."

While the participants of IBBY wound down after the show, behind the scenes, the criminal element that was fused to DSE management was in motion to re-establish the status quo and eliminate the threat of a third promotion.

Kawamata took $4 million of the $6 million paid out by NTV, and without a word to his co-promoter Mijatovic, he dropped off the radar. Another $2 million was payable from NTV to the promoters after the event; Kawamata later sued NTV to get it, but the courts eventually ruled that NTV did not have to pay the money out.

On January 2, 2004, Mijatovic took Fedor and his entourage to Universal Studios in Osaka while simultaneously trying to locate Kawamata (who had stealthily flown the coop to Hawaii) so he could get the $1 million he was owed to pay the fighters he'd booked, and take his cut of the profits from the show.

The next morning, Mijatovic arranged for the Russians to do some shopping in Osaka before they were to fly out. Near lunchtime, Mijatovic was wandering around the lobby of the upscale Kobe Okura hotel when two Japanese men approached him, informing him that PRIDE president Sakakibara and Mr. Ishizaka wanted to see him.

The men, named Sakamoto and Koyama, were Goto Gumi, then a subgroup of the Yamaguchi-gumi yakuza. They escorted Mijatovic to the hotel's bar, which was closed to customers at this time. There, Sakakibara, Mr. Ishizaka and a senior member of Ota Kogyo, another Yamaguchi-gumi subgroup, were awaiting Mijatovic. Sakamoto and Koyama flanked Mijatovic at the table, where he faced Mr. Ishizaka, meeting the shadowy figure behind DSE for the first time.

"I felt like this was a pretty shitty situation," says Mijatovic, "and things were about to get worse."

The first question asked by the PRIDE power brokers was regarding IBBY co-promoter Kawamata's whereabouts. Sakakibara and Ishizaka's anger magnified as Mijatovic told them that he had no idea where

Kawamata was. As Sakamoto and Koyama—the evening's muscle—bowed forward to apologize for letting Kawamata slip through their grasp, Mijatovic noticed both had holstered guns concealed under their jackets.

"I want to get Kawamata and cut his balls off!" screamed Sakakibara.

The next item on the agenda for the meeting was Fedor. It would take about 45 minutes for him to return from his shopping excursion; in the meantime, Sakakibara produced a two-page contract in Japanese that claimed Mijatovic's promotional contract with Fedor was invalid and stipulated Fedor would return to PRIDE for his old price of $30,000 per fight. Kawamata had already signed it on December 28; the PRIDE boss just needed Mijatovic's signature for this face-saving gesture to be completed.

Mijatovic then brought up how Mirko Cro Cop had been paid off by PRIDE not to fight on the IBBY show. Mijatovic told the table that this was why he had plucked Fedor away from PRIDE. Ishizaka was overcome with rage when he heard this.

"One of the guys pulled out his gun, put it on the table," said Mijatovic. "We continued to talk and when I continued to push back—insisting the whole problem started when they went after Cro Cop—he picked the gun up and aimed it to my head and said, 'You know what's going to happen if you don't sign?'"

The gun was a Beretta 9000, a semi-automatic pistol.

Sakakibara was furious, and reminded Mijatovic that this was not a negotiation. Koyama raised his pistol and pointed it at Mijatovic's head.

"You know you aren't leaving Kobe unless you sign," he told the burly Australian. "You don't sign, you're dead."

"I was fairly confident they weren't going to shoot me in the Okura hotel," said Mijatovic. "That's a bit difficult to deal with getting a body out of, especially a body of my size, out of the walls so I felt I had a bit of room to push back."

Mijatovic acknowledged that the stakes were serious, and that the yakuza could have ended his life. Obstacles to yakuza interests in PRIDE had been eliminated in the past, without any legal consequences. Mijatovic still wouldn't sign the contract transferring Fedor to PRIDE, insisting that because it was in Japanese (which he couldn't read), it would not be legally binding.

Fedor and his manager Vadim Finkelstein then phoned Mijatovic to let him know that they had arrived back at the hotel. Mijatovic was accompanied by the two goons—Sakamoto and Koyama—as he went down to collect Fedor. Finkelstein nearly fainted as Mijatovic told him Sakakibara and the yakuza were awaiting them in a hotel room. Finkelstein wanted to get his bodyguard—a scary-looking Russian who was still at the shops in Osaka—but Mijatovic told him that the situation would be fine as long as Finkelstein went up to the hotel room and explained Fedor's contractual status.

"We haven't cheated anybody," Finkelstein later said, responding to PRIDE's accusations that they held a contract to promote Fedor. "I'm Fedor's new manager – according to Fedor's contract with Pride, and our contract with him we haven't break anything."

There were now several yakuza goons outside the hotel room. Inside was a Japanese girl who would act as an interpreter for Finkelstein (Mijatovic spoke fluent Japanese). Sakakibara produced a contract for Fedor's services to PRIDE, which being written in English, Fedor slowly worked his way through.

As Fedor got to the clause about fight money, a smile came over his face, and he began to laugh. The contract stipulated Fedor was to be paid $30,000 per fight and a bonus for being champion. Fedor told PRIDE president Sakakibara that he had only been getting $20,000 and had never received the champion's bonus; he had never seen this contract (his signature on it was a forgery), nor had he ever signed a contract with PRIDE. Fedor's former manager Vladimir Pogodin had been ripping Fedor off, and Sakakibara only demonstrated the untrustworthy nature of DSE. After all, it was Sakakibara's signature next to Fedor's forged signature. Adding madness to injury, Mr. Ishizaka was yelling in the background that he'd seen Fedor sign the contract himself.

Fedor and Finkelstein got off easy—they had a plane to catch, and Sakakibara allowed them to go. Mijatovic took advantage of the confusion between Sakakibara and Mr. Ishizaka to get the talks moved to Tokyo, telling them that he had dinner guests that evening.

Discussions continued on January 4–5 at the Westin Hotel in Ebisu, Tokyo. At the conclusion of the talks, Mijatovic was forced to sign a contract to return Fedor to PRIDE, with no compensation or agent's commission paid to him. Giving in to the yakuza's demands was a bitter pill to swallow, but it was the only way for Mijatovic to escape unharmed.

As is the case for most victims, the crime perpetrated against them is just the first of many ordeals to follow. The trial waged in public opinion following their trauma becomes a vicious, wounding battle in itself. Thus, Mijatovic had his reputation slandered, not openly in the mainstream press, but in the yakuza-controlled press and on public message boards where anonymity was king and the allegations verged on obscene. By tainting his name with ridiculous accusations—that he was a representative of the Dutch or Russian mafia, that he had stolen the event money for IBBY himself or that the Russian special forces were hunting him down—the yakuza groups further damaged Mijatovic's credibility. It was as insulting and rage-inducing as a group of rapists labeling their victim as "a whore," "dressed like a slut," who "was asking for it" or "enjoyed it."

With any luck, the yakuza and DSE hoped that Mijatovic would fade into the margins without ever being heard from again.

33

UNSTOPPABLE

From 2004 onward, the myth of Fedor's invincibility began to take root. In his April 24, 2004, PRIDE comeback fight after the IBBY mess, he faced American wrestler Mark "The Hammer" Coleman (13-5) in the opening round of the 2004 Heavyweight Grand Prix. Coleman had won the 2000 PRIDE Open Weight Grand Prix and had finished seventh at the 1992 Barcelona Olympics in freestyle wrestling. Sakakibara wanted to punish Fedor for his "desertion and betrayal" of PRIDE, and set the match up because he felt that wrestlers were a weakness of Emelianenko (Later in 2005, PRIDE would try to lure Olympic Greco-Roman wrestling gold medalist Rulon Gardner into a fight with Fedor for a $1 million purse[225]); Fedor's team knew the reputation of Coleman, but they also knew about the lack of submission defense taught at Coleman's team, Hammer House.

The fight was not without moments of peril for Fedor—Coleman secured the takedown and took Fedor's back with both hooks in. It was the perfect position for Coleman to secure a rear naked choke or transition to another submission, but Brazilian Jiu-Jitsu was never a strong point of Hammer House and at 2:11 of the first round, Fedor armbarred Coleman.

As Coleman exited the arena, he was inconsolable in defeat. Backstage, he swore and punched a wall, eventually breaking into sobs.

After the fight, Fedor was in good spirits—he shook hands with Kazushi Sakuraba, and fielded a congratulatory telephone call on a cell phone from Miro Mijatovic.

"Thank you very much, Miro," gushed Emelianenko (in English) into the phone, still wearing his MMA gloves, slowly readjusting after the adrenaline dump in the ring.

Far from disappearing, Miro Mijatovic was back in the fight game, representing Fedor Emelianenko as an agent. In early 2004, Fedor had pushed hard for Mijatovic to represent him, as his manager Vadim Finkelstein had little clue about the Japanese fight game. A new contract had been created for Mijatovic to represent Fedor, with Mijatovic receiving a 10 percent commission on Fedor's fights.

As co-promoter of IBBY, Mijatovic was also was responsible for the payment to Bas Boon's Golden Glory fighters that Kawamata had absconded with. Mijatovic paid back half of the money owed with his own funds and worked for Bas Boon as a manager of his Golden Glory stable in exchange for no commission to repay the rest of the debt.

In order to save face over Mijatovic's actions in acquiring PRIDE's heavyweight champion for IBBY, the powers behind the scenes had devised special rules for handling Mijatovic.

"I was not allowed to move around the arena in 2004," said Mijatovic. "I was being held in a corporate box with two of Ishizaka's bodyguards outside the front door to make sure I didn't circulate."

Therefore, during events, Miro Mijatovic was to remain out of sight and his only contact with fighters was via cell phone.

At the news of Mijatovic signing to represent Fedor, Mirko Cro Cop had a devious way to twist the story to his advantage. Cro Cop claimed that he was soured by the knowledge that Mijatovic had entered into an agreement to represent Fedor. Cro Cop omitted the part where he had stopped communicating with his manager in November 2003, thus breaking their business relationship.

In a letter to Mijatovic, also published on the front page of sports newspaper *Saneki Sports*, Cro Cop wrote, "I cannot imagine nor understand that Mr. Miro Mijatovic, as my manager, concluded an agency agreement with Fedor with whom I plan to fight in the near future."[226]

Fedor, quizzed about Cro Cop's comments about Mijatovic, took a different stance:

"I think there is no problem even if Mr. Miro manages a number of fighters. On the contrary, I cannot understand why this issue becomes a problem."

To onlookers with no knowledge of the undercurrents between DSE, Miro Mijatovic and Mirko, Cro Cop had an airtight alibi. The reality was that by accepting DSE's payoff and refusing to fight on the IBBY show, Cro Cop had long abandoned Miro Mijatovic for PRIDE employee Ken Imai to work as his new manager.

As an employee of PRIDE, Ken Imai had even more power to handpick Cro Cop's opponents, so Cro Cop's anxieties over his fight career could be further assuaged. Ken Imai also appealed to Cro Cop's flashy side by offering to assist in producing a movie with Cro Cop (who was a huge fan of Jean-Claude Van Damme) as the star. He was conniving in getting Cro Cop himself to put up some of the money to produce a low-budget action film called *Ultimate Force*.[227] The straight-to-DVD release had its premiere the day after Cro Cop dropped his title fight to Fedor at PRIDE Final Conflict 2005.

"Mirko Cro Cop turned up to the launch all battered and bruised and looking sad after losing," says Mijatovic. "Cro Cop was never great at hiding his emotions or doing any PR—[a] bit funny for a guy who wanted to be an actor."

On June 20, 2004, Emelianenko squared off with Coleman's teammate, Kevin "The Monster" Randleman. Randleman was a two-time

Division 1 NCAA wrestling champion, as well as a former UFC heavyweight champion. Using his wrestling, Randleman scored a takedown just seconds into their bout. After Fedor scrambled up, this was followed by a suplex (a wrestling move where one wrestler picks up their opponent and uses their bodyweight to drive them to the mat) that seemed to spike Fedor directly onto his head.

"I was not so much thinking as having a heart attack," said a horrified Alexander Michkov, Fedor's striking coach, who was watching from the ring corner.[228]

Aided by his judo instincts, Fedor knew to tuck his head and avoid serious danger; moments later, Fedor reversed Randleman to take side-control; rained down punches to Randleman's head (32 strikes, according to Michkov) until Randleman released his clasped arms. Fedor took Randleman's arm and submitted the American with a kimura.

Controlling the final brackets of the heavyweight Grand Prix between Fedor Emelianenko, Antônio Rodrigo Nogueira, Sergei Kharitonov and Naoya Ogawa was a point of contention between different interests.

"PRIDE wanted to do Fedor versus Kharitonov, and Nogueira versus Ogawa," said Mijatovic. "They were closer to Nogueira's management than me and Fedor at the time, and basically wanted to give Fedor a hard time. I basically insisted that we get Ogawa because we'd given Ogawa an injured Stefan Leko in the first round and given him his passage through. There was also a lot of benefit for Fedor beating an Olympic champ and the great Japanese hope."

Naoya Ogawa was a big asset to PRIDE because he was Japanese; a former judo world champion and was a silver medalist in judo at the 1992 Barcelona Olympic Games. Canadian Gary Goodridge claimed that he had been offered $20,000 to lose to Ogawa (then 1-0 in MMA) before their bout at PRIDE 6; Goodridge declined the alleged bribe and went on to lose to Ogawa via second-round submission anyway, but the situation demonstrated that someone important was looking out for Ogawa.[229]

Even though Stefan Leko was a highly-touted K-1 kickboxer, he'd had minimal training for MMA. About a week before the Ogawa bout, Leko was unlucky to suffer a back injury that almost completely immobilized him. PRIDE offered to double Leko's purse (bringing his total take to about $300,000), Leko was injected with painkillers and the fight went on, with Ogawa winning via arm-triangle choke at 1:34 of the first round. It was a fishy situation—Leko had been offered financial incentive to take a fight that he simply could not win, let alone be competitive in.

Ogawa's next fight in the Grand Prix had been against the monstrously-sized Paulo Cesar Silva—also known as "Giant Silva." The 7'3" Brazilian super-heavyweight had been a pro wrestler with the WWF and New Japan Pro Wrestling before transitioning to MMA in 2003; although he still worked for DSE-owned HUSTLE doing wrestling shows throughout 2004. Ogawa steamrolled over the 1-1 Giant Silva, stopping him at 3:29 of the first round.

That Naoya Ogawa was an easier opponent than Russian Top Team fighter Sergei Kharitonov (then 9-0) was not the only reason Fedor's management desired Ogawa as an opponent. There was the matter of marketability, as the Japanese judo player was a much bigger star than the other tournament finalists.

"It was really good for Fedor's name recognition in Japan," said Mijatovic. "That was the featured main event for the Japanese audience of the heavyweight Grand Prix finals."

On August 15, 2004, Fedor entered the ring against Ogawa. That his opponent was a judo superstar held special significance for Fedor, who had never been close to qualifying for the Russian Olympic judo squad. Fedor also viewed judo as much more elite than Sambo. The Japanese opponent refused to touch gloves with Emelianenko before the fight. Fedor showed no emotion and responded by submitting Ogawa via armbar at 0:54 of the first round.

In the opposite bracket, Antônio Rodrigo Nogueira had won a decision over Sergei Kharitonov after one 10-minute round (followed by two minutes of rest) and one five-minute round. Nogueira was set to meet Fedor in the Grand Prix final that would provide the climax for the show.

Far from accepting his first loss to Fedor in 2003, Nogueira would tell author Sam Sheridan that he had been suffering from persistent back problems and two hernias that he had gotten from surfing.

"For like, two months, I was not walking well. I was coming down in my shape, and he was in the best shape he's ever been in," said Nogueira of his condition before losing his PRIDE championship to Fedor.

This time around, Nogueira's back was better, and he carried the belief that Fedor was not in great shape going into the fight.[230]

From the start of their fight, Nogueira was active from the guard, going for leg locks and triangle attempts. The commentators noted how important it was for Nogueira to go for submissions early before Fedor became sweaty, making it easier to escape Nogueira's submission attempts. Nogueira threw a punch, followed by an upkick (in the US, this would have been illegal as Fedor was technically a grounded fighter; in PRIDE, it was fair game), with Fedor standing up as blood from a cut above his eye streamed down his face. Nogueira's corner became animated as the doctor stopped the contest to survey the damage. A stoppage due to a cut inflicted by Nogueira's strikes would make Nogueira the Grand Prix winner, and allow him to regain the undisputed PRIDE heavyweight championship, as well.

Instant replay showed that the cut occurred when Fedor had knocked heads with Nogueira when Fedor was in the Brazilian's guard. After a few minutes of deliberations, the judges ruled the match a no contest. The epic finale of the Grand Prix was inconclusive, but there would be a rematch between Nogueira and Fedor where both men would be completely fresh.

Every major win by Fedor was capped with a celebration by his team. Disliking the smoke-filled clubs, neither a player nor an attention-seeker, Fedor did not seek out sexual conquests to the same degree that other PRIDE fighters did.

"Most of the foreign fighters liked foreign women," said Mijatovic. "Generally most of the guys went to the gaijin hostess/lap dancing bars (famous clubs like One Eyed Jacks, Seventh Heaven and Tantra) were where you could usually find fighters looking for fun."

Fedor had his own special way of cutting loose after fights.

"Fedor liked to drink," said Mijatovic. "We would hang around in the hotel and myself, him and his coaches would get absolutely shit-faced drinking vodka."

After Fedor's fight against Mark Coleman at PRIDE Total Elimination 2004, Fedor made small-talk with Coleman's teammate, American wrestler Kevin Randleman. Fedor asked Randleman what he was doing after his fight (Randleman had notched a spectacular first round knockout of Mirko Cro Cop). Randleman suggested that they have a beer together; Fedor replied that he only drank vodka.

Fedor's drinking entourage was often small—usually just Michkov, Voronov, Mijatovic, a Russian translator and other team staff members. The Russians could each put away a one-liter duty-free bottle (bought upon exiting Russia for Japan), sipping it throughout the night in coffee mugs (there weren't enough glasses to go around in a hotel room).

"They don't drink it mixed with orange juice," said Mijatovic. "They drink it like tea."

Fedor could be classified as a happy drunk, often breaking out into laughter as the night progressed.

There was also the matter of the classic "changing of the guard" typical in successful men where Fedor broke away from the woman who had supported him and brought him to success in order to trade up for a model with fewer miles on the odometer.

Fedor had always spent time away from his wife Oksana, whether it was for judo and Sambo competitions earlier in his career, or MMA fights starting with Fedor's time in RINGS. The commitment required by PRIDE turned the crevice between Fedor and Oksana into a canyon.

"It's not easy when he's not at home," said Oksana. "It's hard when he's in a training camp."

As a devoted father, Emelianenko brought small gifts for his wife and daughter, such as stuffed animals, or a toy dog from Japan. While these displays demonstrated affection, Fedor was never eager to have Oksana alongside him when he traveled for fights.

"Here in Russia, Fedor doesn't want to take me to tournaments," complained Oksana, during the time when Fedor fought in RINGS. "He says that if I would be in the arena, he would think about me, and it would distract him from thinking about his opponent."

There was a more obvious reason why Fedor did not want his wife with him when he traveled abroad.

"In the old days, he used to bring his wife Oksana [to Japan]," said Mijatovic, "then he started to bring his mistress, Marina."

What Mijatovic also noted were the similarities in appearance between Marina and Oksana.

Fedor would go on to divorce Oksana in 2006; Marina bore him their first child on December 27, 2007. In October 2009, Fedor married Marina during a ceremony held at the Church of St. Nicholas in Stary Oskol.[231]

Asked whether Fedor indulged in dalliances with Japanese girls, Mijatovic stated, "He did, but he wasn't into it as much as some of the other guys were."

Many PRIDE fighters enjoyed the spoils of war. Sam Sheridan recounts a scene where shy Japanese girls swarmed Antônio Rodrigo Nogueira, seeking autographs and photos with him; he obliged, in exchange for phone numbers.

"I make a lot of sacrifice, but the only thing I cannot stop is girls," Nogueira told Sheridan.[232]

Quinton "Rampage" Jackson gleefully recounted his own Japanese conquests in an interview:

"I like Asian women. I've just been over in Japan with Pride - I was like a kid in a candy store, I should've been paying them to keep me out there," Jackson had told *The Guardian* in 2007.[233]

As Fedor became a growing star in PRIDE, there were certainly more opportunities—of many varieties—available to the Russian. With 2004 nearing its close, Fedor's popularity in Japan was soaring.

Says Mijatovic, "[Fedor] couldn't stop and walk down the streets without being mobbed by autograph hunters."

A large percentage of the Japanese population might have known who Fedor was, but this did not translate into commercial appeal or greater sponsorship opportunities. The massive live attendance numbers of PRIDE were considered misleading indicators of MMA's popularity in Japan, as shows were produced in limited numbers, with audience sizes no superior to concerts occurring every weekend.

"Fedor was not easy for Japanese to identify with," said Mijatovic, "so commercial opportunities were limited."

"We actually did a deal with a liquor company," said Mijatovic of the first endorsement he scored outside T-shirts or figurines. "They produced a Fedor-endorsed bottle of liquor."

A 3D image of Fedor appeared on a bottle of Zipang shochu, a Japanese spirit; other editions were made featuring Kazushi Sakuraba, Wanderlei Silva and Nobuhiko Takada. Today, the bottles might be considered a treasured keepsake among the myriad of mass-produced MMA trinkets that clutter the market, with one website selling all four bottles for $799.99.[234]

December 31, 2004 was the epic rematch between Nogueira and Fedor on PRIDE's NYE show. Much had changed over the course of a year to improve PRIDE's fortunes—the threat of an NTV-sponsored promotion had been destroyed; Fedor had been re-signed and PRIDE was easily the largest MMA organization in the world. On this night, Fedor would cement his claim as the best heavyweight in MMA (although he would never label himself as such) as he won a dominant three-round decision over Nogueira.

There were even more machinations taking place behind the scenes to consolidate PRIDE's hold over the Japanese MMA scene. PRIDE made a backroom deal with Fedor's management, Vadim Finkelstein and Apy Etcheld to get rid of Miro Mijatovic. In exchange, PRIDE promised to partner with Vadim and Apy to launch the PRIDE sub-brand in Europe and Russia.

"PRIDE's real interest was getting me out of the equation at the time," said Mijatovic.

Every negotiation where Mijatovic stepped up and insisted the promoters cough up cost PRIDE—as well as its yakuza associates—more and more money. The ties that bound Vadim Finkelstein and Fedor together in Russia were virtually unbreakable. Finkelstein's clique ran in the same circles as then-Russian prime-minister Vladimir Putin's clique; it was assumed that Finkelstein had other special "friends" in Russia who could help him out in a pinch. Although Mijatovic had a three-year contract with Fedor, inked at the start of 2004, he stood a snowball's chance in hell of winning a lawsuit on Russian soil.

"In my last discussion with Fedor, after I learned that Vadim and Apy had sold me out, I gave him one piece of advice—and that piece of advice was to never sign a lifetime contract," said Mijatovic. "Over the years, I watched what was happening with Fedor and how he was managed, the discussions with the UFC. I always had a chuckle because I always think about the one piece of advice that I left with him."

Vadim Finkelstein's desire to build a mega-promotion of his own in Europe would hang over negotiations with every organization he shopped Fedor to in the ensuing years. He had spoken frequently with Miro Mijatovic about building a "PRIDE Europe"; with PRIDE's supposed backing, he planned a show for early 2005.

"Bushido Europe: Rotterdam Rumble" took place on October 9, 2005, at Ahoy Rotterdam Arena, Rotterdam, Netherlands. The organizers originally claimed that Fedor Emelianenko versus Dutch fighter Bob Schreiber would be the main event.[235]

Yukino Kanda, then executive vice-president of DSE, was quick to disavow any notion that Vadim's European adventure was connected to PRIDE, despite the use of the PRIDE logo in advertisements:

"Fedor is fighting, but the promoter of that show is the manager of Fedor," Kanda explained to *Full-Contact Fighter*'s Loretta Hunt. "It has nothing to do with us as a promoter. We are not involved [in] any way financially."

There was some sort of arrangement between PRIDE and Vadim Finkelstein, as several PRIDE fighters were appearing on the card with the blessing of PRIDE.

"We talked to that promoter because they requested PRIDE fighters, just like other events around the world that always want to associate with PRIDE," said Kanda. "[We] sent Mark Coleman and Kevin Randleman. They're gonna use our fighters."[236]

It should have been no surprise that Fedor was scrubbed from the Rotterdam card. There had been early suspicion from members of the media that Fedor could not appear, as his hand had been damaged in an April rematch with Tsuyoshi Kohsaka at PRIDE Bushido 6, where Fedor brutalized Kohsaka until the fight was stopped after the first 10-minute round.

Aleksander Emelianenko, Fedor's brother, ended up headlining Vadim Finkelstein's "Rotterdam Rumble" show against opponent Rene Rooze, a disappointing bait-and-switch for the now-jaded fans.

Vadim Finkelstein's ambitious European expansion plans were stillborn. Finkelstein's future promotion, M-1 Global, was similarly impotent when it came to penetrating markets and captivating audiences, never mind turning a profit. Finkelstein's dream of a major European promotion—one on par with the UFC or PRIDE—could have helped many fighters worldwide, but it would never come to fruition.

***

Every great fighter has a defining fight that stands out from the rest of their career. Intangibles like the media build-up, exponentially larger public interest and the heightened stakes create challenges of their own, with lesser-willed fighters being sucked into the swirling vortex along the way. The first match between Sugar Ray Leonard and

Thomas Hearns in 1981 at Caesars Palace in Las Vegas was a pivotal moment that helped boxing fans associate Leonard with "greatness" for the rest of his life. Fedor Emelianenko meeting rival Mirko Cro Cop was similar in that it was the fight that would decide Emelianenko's legacy: was he merely a good fighter—or a great one?

In the years that built up to the Mirko Cro Cop fight, there had been rampant speculation that Fedor was terrified of Cro Cop. Fedor seemed to avoid Cro Cop in 2003, citing hand injuries. Cro Cop's failure to make it through the first round of the 2004 heavyweight Grand Prix scuttled another chance for the pair to meet. At PRIDE Final Conflict 2005, held on August 25, the truth would finally come out.

In the fight, Fedor did the improbable in choosing to stand with Cro Cop during the early parts of each round—a risky strategy, since striking was Cro Cop's forte as an elite kickboxer. Cro Cop had been prepared physically, but mentally he began to cave and started to back-pedal against Fedor's offense. Fedor's punches were coming in too fast and Cro Cop retreated too quickly to counter-strike. For the latter part of each round, Fedor took the fight to the ground, where Cro Cop did an admirable job of stalling Fedor and maintaining a strong guard. After three rounds, it all came down to the judges' decision—Fedor was announced as the winner, retaining his PRIDE title.

It was a hard-fought win—Fedor emerged with a nasty shiner, but the win was the pinnacle of his career. From here onward, a mix of weaker opponents and inactivity would result in the eventual decline of his momentum and skill as a mixed martial artist. Accepting fights against soft opposition would make him a subject of ridicule and diminish his legacy.

Wágner da Conceição Martins, better known as "Zuluzinho," was the son of Rei Zulu, a fighter the legendary Rickson Gracie had defeated twice in Brazil. Officially 4-0, on December 31, 2005, Zuluzinho went into the circus match with Fedor as little more than a cow on a conveyer belt headed for the slaughterhouse. The opening round saw Zuluzinho get knocked down and demonstrate the dexterity of a beached whale on the ground. The second time Zuluzinho visited the canvas, he was stopped with strikes on the ground. Even though he dispatched his opponent within 26 seconds of the first round, by stepping into the ring with such a pushover, Fedor did far more damage to his own reputation than he did to his opponent's.

Next came a rematch with Mark Coleman at PRIDE 32, scheduled to be held in Las Vegas in October 2006. That the very first PRIDE event ever held outside of Japan was occurring this late in the game was a fact lamented by PRIDE commentator Bas Rutten.

"The thing that I reminded them all of the time all the way from the beginning was that 'We got to go to America,' " Rutten told the management at DSE. " 'You got to get on pay-per-view over there. It's important, because that's where the big money is. Everything is bigger in America.' And they never saw that as a big thing."

Hideki Yamamoto and Yukino Kanda of PRIDE's US offices repeatedly assured Rutten that no US sojourns were necessary, as the company was consistently performing well in Japan.

Unfortunately for DSE, PRIDE, its employees and the fighters, the extortion of Miro Mijatovic set a chain of events into motion that would undo PRIDE completely. The yakuza were overconfident, as they had successfully eliminated many threats to their stranglehold over both PRIDE and the Japanese MMA scene; they had discounted the possibility that someone would be crazy enough to go to war with them.

In January 2004 when Mijatovic tracked IBBY 2003 co-promoter Seiya Kawamata down to Honolulu, Hawaii, DSE officials had been unable to contact him and had made the fatal mistake of involving Mijatovic's family.

"They sent around a couple of guys to my house and scared my wife in the middle of the night," said Mijatovic. "She called me and told me what had happened and I was furious."

Many people are dismissive of mixed martial arts as a form of sport or entertainment; the violence appears gratuitous and sickening. But ask someone if they would maim or kill in defense of their family or other loved ones? There is no contest; the desire to protect those closest to us is a hardwired animal instinct.

The Australian flew straight back to Tokyo and made the decision to take Ishizaka and Sakakibara on. His first act was to barge into a meeting involving Ishizaka, Sakakibara, Sakakibara's right-hand man Shinoda, American lawyer Michael Connette, Yukino Kanda and Golden Glory owner Bas Boon.

"I stormed into a meeting room and told Ishizaka that if he ever sent somebody to my house again, then he could expect to find me standing in his bedroom early one morning when he woke up," said Mijatovic.

Bas Boon had to physically restrain Mijatovic as he nearly came to blows with Ishizaka. PRIDE had gone too far in pushing Mijatovic. Now Mijatovic saw only one way out—him or them.

In 2004, Mijatovic sought legal action as a remedy for the kidnapping and extortion offense committed against him. Working with anti-yakuza crusader Toshiro Igari, a former prosecutor who felt the Japanese legal system was too soft on organized crime, and a team of seven young lawyers (working as volunteers for no pay), Mijatovic built a case. Rather than go to the Kanagawa police that IBBY co-promoter Kawamata was cooperating with, he chose to file his complaint through the Tokyo police and the National Police Agency (also known as the NPA, similar to the FBI's role in the US). After all, Kawamata was former yakuza and had repeatedly shown himself to be untrustworthy. Kawamata's actions and background tainted his complaint and eventually the Kanagawa prosecutors refused to take his case any further.

There was a widespread belief that a campaign waged through weekly general-interest magazine *Shukan Gendai* helped get PRIDE pulled from Fuji TV, but this was not the case. It was simply Kawamata speaking to *Shukan Gendai* after his police complaint fizzled out. Fuji TV successfully ignored over a year of regular attack articles concerning DSE's yakuza backers and their relations with Fuji TV employees. Everyone knew that Japanese TV producers had ties to the yakuza;

publicly speaking about said connections wasn't really effective in making any changes.

In 2005, Mijatovic openly challenged DSE with a press release:

"This year, just like in 2003 and 2004 in their actions in relation to Mirko Cro Cop, DSE and its President, Nobuyuki Sakakibara, have engaged in various illegal actions in attempts to interfere with my contractual relationships with Red Devil and Fedor Emelianenko."[237]

The investigation by the authorities into the yakuza and PRIDE took two years. During that time, Mijatovic was told by the NPA that there was a contract out on his life in 2005 and 2006 and that the yakuza groups were actively searching for him. Mijatovic, in hiding in Japan, had declined police protection, as he did not fully trust that his whereabouts would be kept secret from the yakuza.

Following interviews by the police, Sakakibara issued a comical statement in February 2006, implying that PRIDE had loaned Fedor to Mijatovic and Kawamata for the Inoki Bom-Ba-Ye 2003 New Year's Eve show:

"Back then we graciously endorsed, and sent Fedor to their show. I have no way of knowing what happened between them and I don't intend to know about it," wrote Sakakibara.[238]

As for the Tokyo police and the NPA, they wanted to use Mijatovic to hook the big fish—Kiyoshi Takayama, then the number one member of the Yamaguchi-gumi. Adding to his fearsome reputation, Takayama was nicknamed "Katame," meaning "one-eye"; it was rumored that he had lost his right eye in a sword fight during his youth. The room in Osaka where Mijatovic was held had been paid for with Takayama's credit card.

For his part, Mijatovic had clear goals in mind—three to five years in prison for Sakakibara, Ishizaka and the other three goons, and the destruction of DSE.

"As the Police started to shift to aim at Takayama, I became less enthusiastic since they were going after the top boss of the Japanese mob," said Mijatovic, who would have faced further repercussions had he taken a role in opposing Takayama.

Eventually, the police agreed on a compromise—PRIDE would be taken off the air, and the Yamaguchi-gumi would rescind the contract on Mijatovic's life. Therefore, neither the campaign in *Shukan Gendai* nor the acquisition of the company by the UFC that would come later caused PRIDE's collapse.

Said Mijatovic, "What had the influence was when Igari and the NPA and the Tokyo police turned up to [Fuji TV] and said, 'take [PRIDE] off TV.' It was an instruction that was given."

Toshiro Igari's anti-yakuza crusading was not without repercussions: in August 2010, he was found dead in a Manila, Philippines hotel room. Igari had handled many cases where he had taken on the yakuza head-on, making powerful enemies along the way. His wrists were found cut open, and various pills were littered around his body.[239] While his death was ruled a suicide, colleagues and friends suspected otherwise.[240]

The sudden and unexpected loss of the television contract with Fuji TV in June 2006 left PRIDE with only SkyPerfecTV, a pay-per-view carrier in Japan, as their only source of domestic television income; the US market, now booming with the breakout success of the UFC, suddenly became a top priority.

A US show was set for October 21, 2006—PRIDE 32: The Real Deal—held at the Thomas & Mack Center in Las Vegas where Fedor would rematch Mark Coleman. The rules changed to the unified rules utilized in North America, however, PRIDE prohibited elbows to the head. The Nevada State Athletic Commission (NSAC)'s judging criteria was also different than PRIDE, which favored effort to finish a fight via knockout or submission first and foremost followed by categories like "Damage"; "Standing combinations and ground control"; "Takedowns and defense"; "Aggressiveness" and "Weight differences."[241]

The judging criteria didn't affect the outcome of Fedor's fight. He smashed Coleman's face into a bloody pulp and finished the fight by submitting Coleman in the second round via armbar. But the carnage did not end there—Coleman went on to bring his (now sobbing) daughters into the ring.

"Daddy's OK…he feels great," Coleman reassured them, his left eye closing up, a cut over his eye and another cut on the bridge of his nose, leaving his girls with the unforgettable memory of their father being mauled.

PRIDE 32 drew a successful live audience of 11,727 fans (with just over 8,000 paying) yielding $2,056,044 in ticket sales. North American pay-per-view buys, however, were less than stellar, estimated by reporter Dave Meltzer at around 33,000 sales at $39.95 a pop.

According to official NSAC documents, Fedor was officially paid out $100,000, less $175 for licenses. Coleman made $70,000, although there could have been other payments made outside the official numbers in order to avoid taxes.

Also of interest was Kevin Randleman, who had lost via first-round kneebar to Shogun Rua at PRIDE 32, and was suspended for submitting a urine sample devoid of human hormones to the NSAC in the post-fight drug test. If anything, the incident demonstrated the steep learning curve of pharmacology many PRIDE fighters would face when transitioning to the UFC later on.[242]

Polish fighter Paweł Nastula, a 1996 Olympic gold medalist in judo, tested positive at PRIDE 32 after his loss to Josh Barnett via first round submission. Part of Nastula's defense to the NSAC was that his PRIDE contract allowed him to use illegal stimulants.

"[My] written contract with the promotion of Pride, which binds me worldwide, allows usage of doping," claimed Nastula in an affidavit.[243]

DSE staged a second US show in February 2007, PRIDE 33, which was headlined by a rematch between Wanderlei Silva and Dan Henderson. No official pay-per-view buy rates were released, but Dave Meltzer estimated that the show sold fewer pay-per-view's than PRIDE 32 with just 28,000 sales.[244] The low numbers meant that DSE had lost their investment and the initiative, as they had failed to crack the US market.

"Now it's too late. UFC is bigger—and it was already taking over," lamented Rutten of PRIDE's late entry into the US market. "It was a shame. They should have done it in 2001, it would have been big."

On December 31, 2006, Fedor faced super-heavyweight kickboxer Mark Hunt, a New Zealander of Samoan descent, who had made the switch from K-1 to MMA in 2004. Hunt did more than show up—after Fedor failed at an armbar attempt, Hunt had Fedor in side control early in the fight, and after a brief stand-up, got side control again. But the advantageous positions on the ground did Hunt no good, as he ended up being submitted via kimura at 8:16 of the first round.

A new era in mixed martial arts began when PRIDE was sold to the Fertitta brothers in March 2007. Some assumed that Fedor Emelianenko was part of the deal, but Fedor became an elusive fish that Zuffa would ultimately fail to hook. The post-PRIDE era would mark the changing winds of fortune for two parties—Fedor, who moved to fringe-status in the mainstream, an outlaw who fought worldwide in a game of musical chairs for fragile promotions; and Zuffa, who swept forward as an all-conquering force of nature to become the undisputed king of MMA.

When the subject of Fedor was broached, UFC president Dana White actually confirmed that Fedor's PRIDE contract allowed him to fight for other promotions.

"It's a non-exclusive contract, and I don't do non-exclusive contracts," said White on a teleconference in early April 2007.

The Zuffa brass had already escalated the situation with Fedor's camp by using legal threats, as White insisted he would stop Fedor from signing a non-exclusive contract with any other promoter.

"We would absolutely slap an injunction on that," threatened White.[245]

Injunction or not, White would have no realistic chance of success if he were to take on Vadim Finkelstein in Russia—and there would be other complications with Finkelstein's various connections.

Fedor also had legal loopholes to circumvent his PRIDE contract. There was a clause in Fedor's contract that allowed him to fight outside of PRIDE, but only if the fight was held on Russian soil. Fedor's former manager Miro Mijatovic had first introduced this unique clause to allow his client Mirko Cro Cop to fight in Croatia if the opportunity arose; now Fedor benefited from Mijatovic's foresight in having written this clause into Fedor's contract.

Fedor would face American wrestler Matt Lindland at BodogFIGHT on April 14, 2007, held in Saint Petersburg, Russia. BodogFIGHT was a promotion created to help market an online gambling site launched by Bodog founder Calvin Ayre in 1994. In February 2012, Bodog.com would be seized, with Ayre among those indicted for illegal gambling and money laundering.

Fedor won the fight via armbar at 2:58 of the first round. Because Matt Lindland was a natural 185-pound fighter, the win diminished Fedor's reputation rather than ameliorating his résumé. According to Dave Meltzer's guesstimate, Bodog got less than 15,000 pay-per-view buys; the promotion officially folded in mid-2008.[246]

As for how the win situated Fedor, rather than signing with the UFC and seeking greater recognition, Vadim Finkelstein had his own plans.

In October 2007, "M-1 Global" was born out of a bizarre union between several players: Vadim Finkelstein and Apy Echteld, who managed Fedor; MMA manager Monte Cox, who managed top UFC fighters like Matt Hughes and Rich Franklin and Mitchell Maxwell, president and CEO of Sibling Entertainment Group, a theater company.[247]

"I got a call from a guy that was representing Sibling Entertainment Group, and they were a group out of New York that had put on Broadway shows," said Cox. "They had a guy who was a benefactor of theirs who was a wealthy Russian businessman, and he had somehow connected with Vadim [Finkelstein]."

Vadim Finkelstein had told the Russian businessmen about his problem—that he had the best fighter on the planet, but couldn't get anything done with Fedor. Mitchell Maxwell of Sibling told Finkelstein that he had no experience with combat sports, so he called manager Monte Cox with a proposition.

Said Cox, "They asked me, 'If we put a group together, and had Fedor at our disposal, would I be interested in running that company?'"

After a meeting in Amsterdam, the company "M-1 Global" was formed, with Cox being installed as the president and CEO. Finkelstein and Maxwell were to act as advisors, and more importantly, finance the company.

"Both sides were supposed to put in $10 million, and we were going to start with $20 million," said Cox. "The New York side put in money, but we always struggled getting the Russians to put money in."

The first event planned for Fedor by M-1 Global was a fight against Korean Hong Man Choi, a massive 300-pound, 7'2" goliath of a man. The show was called "Yarennoka!" (roughly translated as "We can do it!") held on December 31, 2007, as a co-promotion between several former PRIDE staffers and M-1 Global. Although this was Choi's second MMA fight, he owned a 12-4 record in K-1.

The fight was short, but it was anything but easy for Fedor. A takedown attempt by Fedor ended with Choi on top of him. After an armbar attempt, Fedor scrambled up with a noticeably marked-up face from Choi's punches. Fedor moved to strike with Choi in order to close the distance and attempt another takedown; once again, Choi simply powered Fedor to the floor and the Korean had top position. Struggling with Choi's size and strength, as Choi began to ground-and-pound Fedor, the Russian pulled off an armbar at 1:54 in the first round.

As a bonus, action star Jean-Claude Van Damme entered the ring to deliver an overly friendly congratulatory hug to Fedor. Van Damme had once promised Fedor a role in one of his movies, but Fedor eventually realized that nothing would come of the actor's Hollywood promises.

"That was a big success," said Cox of the one-off show that would become the seed for Japanese promotion DREAM to emerge later.

Cox recalls securing Fedor a salary of about $1 million. As would be the case with MMA promotion Affliction's payment to Fedor later on, the funds went into M-1 Global's bank accounts rather than being directly given to Fedor.

A win over Hong Man Choi, K-1 experience and size aside, still did nothing for Fedor's legacy. One of Choi's only two career MMA wins would later come over former baseball player Jose Canseco; his other win, notched before facing Fedor, was against Nigerian-born Japanese TV personality Bobby Ologun.

The relationship between Monte Cox and Vadim Finkelstein quickly soured as Finkelstein believed his M-1 Challenge shows—small cards with virtually unknown fighters being held in marginal markets—were the future. The New York side agreed with Cox that there was no financial payoff in Finkelstein's plan to build M-1 Global up as the next PRIDE or UFC; they were further irritated that the Russians did not operate in good faith by producing their $10 million.

Cox saw Fedor as a commodity that could be sold to other promotions, outsourcing risk and bringing in cash. The only real initiative by M-1 Global was a press release offering Randy Couture a $1 million bonus (on top of his normal fight purse) to fight Fedor under the banner of any MMA promotion, M-1, UFC or otherwise.

"We pretty much just parted," said Cox of his relationship with Finkelstein. "They kept the name 'M-1 Global' and [Finkelstein and Apy] went on to negotiate with Affliction."

Cox and the New York partners ran several shows under the name "Adrenaline" in the US until they ran out of money. Vadim Finkelstein and M-1, on the other hand, always sought specific contractual items that conflicted with the UFC.

"For Vadim [Finkelstein], it was very important that the M-1 brand got recognition," said Cox. "The UFC wanted a straight 'Here's the money we'll pay you, you come and fight for us and that's the end of the line.' "

Cox also heard that there was a disagreement over the UFC's practice of making payment directly to the fighter, and not a management group.

"Vadim wanted the money to go directly to M-1 Global, like it does for all their other fights."

As Monte Cox understood the arrangement, M-1 Global paid Fedor some money from his purses while Finkelstein invested the rest of Fedor's money in other ventures.

Only Fedor himself knows whether he found this arrangement satisfactory.

34

EXPORTING FEDOR

In recent years, the Zuffa-owned version of the UFC attempted expansion in a series of foreign markets—The United Kingdom, Australia, Germany, Brazil and Japan. The goal was to create a larger presence utilizing the UFC product to generate foreign pay-per-view revenue, sales of television rights and other revenue streams outside the North American market. With a similar strategy in mind, Fedor—on the fringes of Russian national attention, a superstar in Asia and with cult-like status in North America—had to rely on M-1 Global in order to translate his star power to the booming American fight scene.

Former M-1 Global vice-president Jerry Millen used the 2010 documentary *Exporting Raymond* as the template for understanding the disconnect between how Russians and Americans conduct business. In the documentary, *Everybody Loves Raymond* creator Phil Rosenthal attempts to translate the show into a production titled *"Voroniny"* in Russia. From fears over crime in modern Russia—including the threat of kidnapping—to workplace issues like overworked writing staff and ignorant TV executives, Rosenthal is bewildered by the challenges inherent in the culture clash.

Said Millen, "I kind of understand what Rosenthal went through. They hired him to go and do *Raymond*…and the Russians tried to tell him how to do his TV show, basically."

One recent development in television is the viral-like contagion of so-called "reality" shows from CBS's *Survivor* to MTV's *The Real World*. TV networks loved the part where they didn't have to pay actors, develop sophisticated scripts or elaborate sets; narcissistic show participants enjoyed parlaying non-existent talent and acting ability into a source of attention. Zuffa itself had exceeded all expectations with *The Ultimate Fighter* becoming a sleeper hit on the male-orientated Spike cable channel. Could M-1 develop a similar type of show in order to raise Fedor's stock in the US?

M-1 Global announced in February 2008 that a reality show would determine Fedor's next challenger. Sixteen contenders would travel to Saint Petersburg, Russia to compete in a tournament against each other for a shot at the uncrowned king of heavyweight MMA.[248]

MMA promotion Affliction, who had signed Fedor as the star fighter for their cards, went along with the program. A television show that promoted Fedor would only help with obtaining pay-per-view buys.

"I really believe, in its own way, this will be a great success," said Affliction partner Donald Trump on the Fedor reality show at a New York press conference housed at the Trump Towers in October 2008.[249]

Rosenthal fought tooth and nail to get *Voroniny* made to his airtight specifications—it was no surprise that his translated American comedy was a hit in Russia; in a not-so-parallel development, neither M-1 nor their partners succeeded in getting the Fedor reality show off the ground. It was one more strike in an unforgiving marketplace where any MMA fighter not promoted by the UFC was at a huge disadvantage when it came to drawing large pay-per-view numbers.

Fedor's promoter, Affliction, had bet the farm on turning him into a marquee name that could draw the same massive pay-per-view buy rates that UFC stars like Tito Ortiz, Georges St-Pierre or Chuck Liddell could garner.

Fedor was matched with former UFC heavyweight champion Tim Sylvia on July 19, 2008, at Affliction's first event, "Banned" (so named because of the UFC's decision to ban Affliction as a sponsor after the organization applied for a promoter's license). He needed just 36 seconds to knock Sylvia down and submit him via rear naked choke.

At the second Affliction show, "Day of Reckoning," held on January 24, 2009, Fedor was out-boxed by former UFC heavyweight champion Andre Arlovski until Arlovski made the mistake of attempting a jumping knee strike that was met by Fedor's deadly accurate overhand right. Arlovski was knocked out, losing for the first time in five fights.

Reporter Dave Meltzer estimated that both Affliction shows did around 100,000 buys, with "Affliction: Day of Reckoning" doing slightly fewer buys than "Affliction: Banned." Although there were other former UFC and PRIDE stars on the Affliction cards, the marketing machine of the UFC was not something that Affliction could overcome by sheer star power. With the cost of production and higher fighter salaries, Affliction had lost money on their first two MMA events.

There was noise that filming of the Fedor reality show was slated to begin in April 2009, but by July 2009, Affliction had folded their MMA promotion, in part due to Fedor's scheduled opponent, Josh Barnett, testing positive for anabolic steroids 11 days before the August 1 event.[250]

M-1 Global then sued Affliction for breach of contract, with Affliction counter-suing. Thanks to a 55-page court decision, details about Fedor's relationship with M-1 were revealed. While Emelianenko's disclosed pay from Affliction was $300,000 per fight for the Sylvia and Arlovski fights, M-1 Global itself was paid $1.2 million as part of a "consulting agreement," supposedly designed for tax purposes.

There were contractual clauses where M-1 piggy-backed onto Fedor—like Affliction sponsoring the M-1 Challenge shows to the tune of $1 million; on the plus side, Finkelstein was reciprocating by investing $1 million into Affliction stores in Russia. M-1 was hoping to team up with Japanese promotion DREAM to run events in Japan; Affliction wisely had trepidations about the cost of such events, never mind the cast of characters that might have been involved in such a venture.[251]

There were other initiatives that could have given Fedor more traction in American markets—yet M-1's handling of their star fighter continued to be incompetent.

"He was supposed to go to the Super Bowl with [Strikeforce opponent] Brett Rogers," continued Millen. "M-1 fucked it up."

When video game developer Electronic Arts (EA) marketed their MMA game through 7-11 Slurpee cups, M-1 had one question before committing Fedor's likeness to the project.

" 'How much do we get paid to be on the Slurpee cups?' Nobody knows this guy [Fedor]," recalled Millen. "You put him on a million Slurpee cups, and you want to be paid?"

Millen was also critical of M-1 Global's dealings with potential sponsors for Fedor, claiming that M-1 screwed up deals with their ineptitude. More alarming, according to Millen, M-1 was burning through its cash on mostly unnecessary expenses.

"We call it 'living the MMA lifestyle.' When they overspend—people want to fly first class, you want to eat in these fancy restaurants—you can't be doing that when you're starting a company," said Jerry Millen.

The way the company was being run, from an investor's viewpoint, it was hard to see M-1 as anything more than a sinkhole to throw money into.

According to former *FIGHT! Magazine* editor Donovan Craig, in 2010, Emelianenko spoke highly of M-1's value in managing careers:

"[Fedor] tells me that early in his career he was involved in dead-end matches that exposed him to great risk but didn't really help his career," reported Craig. "He now realizes how important it is for fighters to be developed and promoted correctly right from the start."[252]

Was Fedor was referring to his time in RINGS—enmeshed with the villainous Pogodin—as slaving for no future reward? At this point, M-1 had little ability to manage Fedor's career and steer him toward big-money fights; rather, M-1 steered Fedor away from any potential windfall he could have earned in the UFC.

Fedor himself was comfortable with his lifestyle, and had felt that he had earned enough money as a champion during his PRIDE days. From 2004 onward, his management had negotiated better purses than he ever could have imagined. Fedor's easy-going nature made him prey for Vadim Finkelstein's schemes.

"Fedor liked getting paid, but he's not that massively motivated by money. He made a tidy amount, and by the end of his PRIDE fighting career, he got to the stage where he felt pretty happy where he was," said Mijatovic. "That was the space that allowed Vadim to maneuver on top of him. My reading of the situation is that Vadim sold Fedor on the whole M-1 dream—that M-1 would become the PRIDE or UFC of Europe."

It was true that Fedor had excelled in school, and had a keen awareness of those around him. Yet he was unwilling (or perhaps unable) to take charge of his financial outlook due to a lack of business knowledge.

Fedor also greatly values his family. Similar to St-Pierre paying his parents' mortgage, Emelianenko had his own way of giving back to the mother who had raised him.

"Fedor was given a new home by the company that runs the mines of Stary Oskol. He went and gave that home to his mother. So mother lives in this house; he gave it to her. That's how he is," said Jerry Millen.

"You'd be surprised at how modest the guy's home is," says Millen of his visit to Fedor's home in Stary Oskol. "He lives in an apartment—or he was. He's not really that extravagant. That's why when people make fun of the clothes he wears—how he always wears the same sweater—they don't understand the values."

Moscow has cosmopolitan values as does any major city, but Stary Oskol is an isolated mining town with a vastly different culture harking back to a simpler era.

"He drives around in a Lada that his city gave to him in recognition of being a model citizen or whatever it was," said Mijatovic.

Later on in his career, Fedor would acquire a Toyota Land Cruiser—a gift from the government.

"I'm not too picky when it comes to cars," Fedor stated when questioned about his preference in automobiles.

"He doesn't wear a Rolex; he's not into the bling. He's certainly not into fashion, as you've probably noticed," said Mijatovic. "He's not into fast women. He's not into drugs. The usual pitfalls of most athletes' careers that cost a lot of money Fedor's not into."

The biggest question mark with Fedor was his relationship with Vadim Finkelstein. The reality of the situation in Russia was different from that of the US or Western Europe. Since Finkelstein ran with a clique that was close to Russian president Vladimir Putin's people, Fedor could not easily disconnect from Vadim Finkelstein, no matter how badly his career was managed.

"He's very intelligent. He's clued in. That doesn't mean he has freedom to do what he wants," said Mijatovic.

There were darker undertones to Finkelstein's dealings. In the fall of 2009 when Golden Glory co-owner Bas Boon was representing fighter Alistair Overeem, Boon made harsh statements against Fedor's management, alleging that Vadim and Apy were linked to criminal elements:

"It hasn't escaped my notice that we are dealing with a bunch of crooks who wish to brand their name onto someone who has managed to build up a successful organization on his own with a good network deal," Boon wrote on a message board of M-1's parasitic intentions toward Strikeforce, a mid-tier San Jose-based MMA promotion.

In April 2010, the argument heated up, as Fedor's management repeatedly avoided attempts by Boon to arrange a Fedor-Overeem fight in Strikeforce. Boon penned an open letter that accused Vadim Finkelstein of having mafia ties:

"Apy and Vadim should be concerned about using the Russian mafia to threaten people," wrote Boon, among numerous accusations and allegations ranging from an incident where Apy Echteld threatened a European promoter that he would enlist contract killers, to M-1 rejecting a lucrative offer from K-1 for Fedor's services in exchange for PRIDE covering Finkelstein's losses from his ill-fated "Bushido Europe" show in Rotterdam.

The K-1 offer was for a purported $2.4 million for a multi-fight deal. The $600,000 per fight was $150,000 more than Fedor was receiving on his fight-by-fight PRIDE contract, at least according to K1Legend.wordpress.com's Dave Walsh, who reviewed the K-1 contracts provided by Bas Boon. There was also the additional opportunity for sponsorship by K-1 parent company Fighting and Entertainment Group (FEG) of Fedor, and the clause where Fedor would be paid $1 million if he was lent out to the UFC.[253] If Vadim countered the K-1 offer by getting DSE to cover the losses from his disastrous Bushido Europe show in Rotterdam, Fedor got the short end of the stick.

In his official response to Boon's letter, Vadim Finkelstein was overly defensive against Boon's allegations of mafia ties.

"What most displeases me about the open letter are the comments that accuse me of being a part of the Russian mafia," wrote Finkelstein. "Throughout my professional life, I've been a businessman, and I've created from scratch several companies. I'm very proud of what I've been able to accomplish, and I have a very respected standing not only in Russia, but in other countries, as well."[254]

Vadim also pointed to attendance by high-level Russian politicians at M-1 events as evidence of his upstanding nature. As many individuals with passing knowledge of modern Russia understood, running with the elites of Russian society suggests deep involvement with corruption rather than innocence.

35

STRIKEFORCE

PRIDE's folding left many top fighters as orphans easily recruited into the UFC machine. There were the usual vindictive attempts to smash the fighters tainted by association to the UFC's major competitor with both successes (Shogun Rua losing to Forrest Griffin, Gomi losing to Kenny Florian) and failures (Quinton Jackson smashing Chuck Liddell). Affliction's demise opened up similar opportunities for the UFC machine to crush its enemies, see them driven before them.

"Dana White's ego is so big and he wanted Fedor so bad that he would have given his left nut—if he even has one—to get Fedor," said Jerry Millen of the UFC's motivation to acquire Fedor after the demise of Affliction as an MMA promotion in July 2009.[255]

"Dana wanted to see all the PRIDE guys get their asses kicked when they came to the UFC, believe me," said Jerry Millen.

It was only fair that the UFC brass wanted to acquire fighters from other rival promotions in order to demonstrate the superiority of their product. The motives of the promoter have to be self-interested in order to protect the reputation of the promotion.

Negotiations began for the second time in late July 2009, with Millen being banished from the room by Vadim (due to either Millen's tumultuous relationship with the UFC, or Millen simply not having a managerial role at M-1) where the meeting was to take place. He listened in on a conference call, which turned out to be fortuitous for his purposes.

"In the second deal, I didn't want to see Fedor go to the UFC," said Millen. "I told Fedor upfront, 'You know what's best for you. You know that Dana White is a bad person. I know that you'll make the right decision.' He winked and he hugged me, and he said, 'I understand, Jerry.' "

Jerry Millen was on the conference call during the whole meeting. During the meeting, the UFC faxed a "cease and desist" order to Strikeforce saying they couldn't have M-1 managed Gegard Mousasi. According to Millen, "We bought Affliction, we own them" was the tone of the fax. It was obvious manipulation by Millen to call M-1 manager Apy Etcheld and point out that the UFC was screwing with their fighter, Gegard Mousasi.

"[The M-1 guys] flipped out and started screaming at them, 'We're meeting with you, and you're fucking lying! You're meeting with us here, and at the same time, you're sending us a fax saying that you own Gegard Mousasi," said Millen, who believed that he had thrown a monkey wrench into the Fedor-UFC negotiations.

Co-promotion with M-1 Global, a company where Fedor owned 8.5 percent, was seen as the decisive factor in the talks turning sour. A YouTube video[256] released at this time with caricature representations of Dana White and Vadim Finkelstein having a fictional dialog managed to capture Dana's worldview with himself parting the Red Sea to lead MMA to the Promised Land side-by-side with M-1's massive sense of entitlement in negotiations:

> **DW: Listen to me, you fucking drunk, vodka-drinking, pea-brained, ball-licking faggot. Me and Lorenzo built this piece of shit into what it is today not to have one of Fedor's high school**

dropout lowlife friends who think they are an agent come in here and tell Dana-fucking-White whose balls to lick.

VF: Sorry, I forgot, he also refuse to do any UFC Full Access show. All media marketing cleared with me first. I will disregard your disgusting language and filthy words. Dana, do we have a deal?

In short, it was a joke of an idea to imagine the UFC granting M-1 special concessions when the UFC had been judge, jury and executioner for so long.

Insults aside, Fedor was too valuable to the UFC, which held binding exclusive contracts over its fighters like a fat kid holds the cookie jar in a death grip. Recruiting Fedor to lose to UFC fighters would have served the UFC's interests. Whenever negotiations occurred, neither side really understood their prospective dance partner.

Another explanation for the impasse, suggested by Miro Mijatovic, was that Vadim Finkelstein fundamentally mistrusted the pay-per-view model whereby Fedor would have been offered a low guarantee with a percentage of each pay-per-view buy thrown in on top of that. DSE and PRIDE president Sakakibara had screwed Finkelstein around time and time again; there was no real reason Finkelstein could trust that Zuffa or the Fertittas would produce accurate figures for pay-per-view revenue when it was against their own interests to do so. Finkelstein didn't understand that pay-per-view numbers could be verified because in Russia, everything could be manipulated. Finkelstein really lacked business sophistication, and was also ignorant to the many other ways that the UFC profited from their fighters outside of pay-per-view revenue.

San Jose, California-based promotion Strikeforce was only too happy to pick up the slack by agreeing to M-1's demands of co-promotion and signing Fedor in August 2009. Strikeforce had also signed a pivotal three-year TV deal with Showtime in February 2009, giving them national reach and much more exposure. That the UFC had lost

Fedor delighted the many "enemies of Dana White" who felt animosity toward the UFC due to what they perceived as dirty business tactics.

White voiced the displeasure of a jealous rival who had seen his offer of courtship spurned with the news that Fedor had signed with Strikeforce over the UFC.

"Fedor is a fucking joke," said White. "He turns down a huge deal and the opportunity to face the best in the world to fight nobodies for no money!"[257]

Of course, it was a mix of M-1's mishandling, Zuffa's iron-fisted tactics and mutual distrust between both parties that had prevented any meeting of minds.

On November 7, 2009, Fedor met American Brett Rogers (then 10-0 with nine knockouts and one submission) on a Strikeforce event aired live on CBS. Fedor was doing well in the fight, until Rogers reversed Fedor on the ground and dropped some ground-and-pound on him, breaking Fedor's nose in the process. In the second round, Fedor dropped Rogers with a perfectly timed right hand, prompting the stoppage at 1:48.

Once again, Fedor won—and due to the low stature of Brett Rogers, the win did nothing to improve Emelianenko's legacy. Rogers would go 1-3 in his next four fights, his lone win a controversial decision over lightly-regarded journeyman Ruben Villareal (19-19-3 at the time of their fight), further discrediting Fedor's win over Rogers. Then again, it was possible that Fedor had so devastated his opponent, he'd taken a part of Rogers's soul.

After the Rogers fight, a smart manager would have capitalized on Fedor's momentum and quickly followed up with a second fight to further entrench Emelianenko in the US. After all, if Fedor succeeded in becoming a household name in the US, there were lucrative sponsorship opportunities and richer contracts that could have been negotiated down the road. M-1 Global, of course, took a different approach in allowing Fedor to drop off the radar, giving rise to the growing dissent that Fedor was a paper tiger.

There were rarely any challenges in the media to the script provided by Zuffa that the UFC was "firm-but-fair" in its attempts to acquire Fedor. No other individual or organization involved in MMA—M-1 Global, Fedor, Strikeforce or even Showtime/CBS—had the same hold over MMA reporters and journalists as Zuffa had. Even journalists who had been burned by Zuffa, forbidden to attend UFC shows and barred from UFC conference calls, had to play ball with the hope of being reinstated at some point. Mainstream stories about MMA in this time period rarely focused on the low pay scale and stringent contractual clauses enforced by Zuffa.

Most journalists dedicated to covering mixed martial arts from both mainstream and obscure outlets often intentionally avoided challenging the status quo. They were often self-interested cheerleaders in the pockets of promoters, necessary to market fights and combat the perception of MMA as a brutal blood sport to help open up markets where MMA was still illegal. From here onward, every time the media rolled over and gave up inches, Dana White raged with verbal pomposity to occupy a mile—all with the shameless compliance of media personalities, writers, reporters and editors who seemingly forgot how to ask hard questions or press the UFC on pivotal issues.

The upshot of playing the game were the myriad enticements that Zuffa could offer. Certain MMA reporters eventually landed jobs with UFC-related television programs; other reporters were given freelance work writing for *UFC magazine* and different UFC websites; MMA magazines received precious advertising dollars from Zuffa; some MMA websites partnered with the UFC in exchange for investment; other UFC-friendly MMA outlets received exclusive news scoops that helped elevate careers in the cutthroat world of journalism.

There were white knights among the media and fans who tried to defend Fedor's reputation as a fighter, but they could do little to stem the tide of criticism and negativity. Only a dominant performance from Fedor, witnessed by the masses, could allay the doubt in his ranking as the top heavyweight and top pound-for-pound fighter in the sport.

36

Fedor vs. M-1, the UFC and Werdum

After months of negotiations, the second bout on Fedor's three-fight Strikeforce contract would finally be fulfilled against Brazilian heavyweight and UFC cast-off Fabricio "Vai Cavalo" Werdum. There was little or no doubt in the minds of all experts that Fedor would crush Werdum on his way to bigger and better things.

Werdum had been beaten by Fedor-victims Antônio Rodrigo Nogueira and Andre Arlovski. His record was an unimpressive 13-4-1, and Fedor still carried the mystique of 28 straight wins (including one no-contest) going into the bout. Werdum had his strengths—he was 6'4", a two-time ADCC world submission champion and two-time world jiu-jitsu champion, but these details were overlooked in the lead-up to the fight.

Fedor was at an automatic disadvantage at almost every crossroads preceding the Werdum fight. Because M-1 had dragged out negotiations with Showtime and Strikeforce in the months preceding the bout, Fedor missed a crucial chance to gain network television exposure on an April 19 date on CBS.[258] The CBS card would end up being marred by an infamous Nashville brawl between the Cesar Gracie crew (Nick and Nate Diaz, Jake Shields, and Gilbert Melendez) and Jason "Mayhem" Miller which would sour CBS executives on airing MMA on their network in the future.[259]

Although Fedor was tied to Strikeforce contractually, this exclusivity was only for US-based fights. M-1 had the right to shop Fedor around to foreign partners for shows in the damaged Japanese market, or the nonexistent marketplace of Russia. While re-negotiating the contract with Strikeforce, Vadim Finkelstein opted to make statements declaring that Strikeforce had failed to make good on its contract of co-promotion with M-1.

The other crucial event that occurred during this time period came through the interference of the UFC, as Dana White hinted at ongoing negotiations with M-1 to acquire Fedor Emelianenko's services.[260]

"I want Fedor. I want to do it. And I never say never. They can call me right now, and we can start talking and figure this thing out," White said in early January 2010, at the UFC 108 presser.

"[The UFC] were negotiating with M-1 while Fedor was still under contract with Strikeforce," said Jerry Millen. "They made Fedor a six-fight $30 million offer."

Millen insisted that Fedor was then being guaranteed $5 million per fight by the UFC. Zuffa would never confirm this figure, as other high-level UFC fighters would demand a raise were they to learn that their loyalty and proven drawing power wasn't being rewarded with the same funds available to Fedor.

Millen also confirmed the two-faced nature of M-1 in negotiating with the UFC while still being under contract with Strikeforce:

"Why M-1 was negotiating with them was beyond me," said Millen. "That was just the way M-1 did business, 'Oh, we got a contract with you. That doesn't matter—we'll still see what kind of offer we can get from these other people.' "

As for the offer of $5 million per fight, many fans took this as a sign of Zuffa's generous nature in attempting to reward Fedor for a lifetime of dedication to the martial arts. This was a gross misreading of the situation.

"Dana White wasn't offering Fedor $30 million because he wanted him in the UFC in win, and be a champion, and be a star," said Millen. "[Dana] wanted to destroy the image of Fedor Emelianenko and any semblance that he had as the greatest heavyweight because he came from PRIDE."

In recent memory, White had sent a rising Lyoto Machida to annihilate a disobedient Tito Ortiz at UFC 84; this came full circle when Jon Jones was sent to destroy Lyoto Machida (after Machida had asked for "Anderson Silva money" to step in on short notice against Rashad Evans at UFC 133) at UFC 140. Jon Jones, in turn, would earn Dana White's animosity when Jones refused a short notice fight with Chael Sonnen, leading to the cancellation of UFC 151; one wondered who the UFC could set Jones up against at this point? However, no matter what the promoter's own personal agenda (and there always is one), the fighter has to rise to the challenge and beat the man or woman placed in front of them.

The official announcement for the Werdum-Fedor fight came out on May 3, 2010, with the bout scheduled for San Jose's HP Pavilion on June 26. That gave Fedor about seven weeks for his training camp, minus travel time to get from Russia to California.

A typical training camp for a top-rated opponent in MMA can be eight to twelve weeks, depending on the situation. The other factor of importance is the ongoing training that athletes should be doing year-round. Fedor had been inactive since his bout with Brett Rogers in November 2009—therefore, at the time of the June 26 bout with Werdum, he would have been out of action for just under nine months; hardly an ideal schedule for a man considered the most elite in the world.

Bad luck reared its head, as it was reported that Fedor broke his hand in his win against Brett Rogers.[261] Participation in the February 2010 "Russian Cup of Combat Sambo" tournament either aggravated or worsened the injury, leading Fedor to withdraw from the tournament after the semi-finals where Fedor placed fifth overall.[262]

Fedor's grappling coach, Vladimir Voronov, would comment after the Werdum fight about the way the repeated hand injuries had hampered Fedor's training camp, saying "The fact is that for the last months Fedor suffered from quite serious injuries that prevented to fully engage in preparation process."[263]

Fabricio Werdum chose not to view himself as a stepping stone for Fedor to march over. This was the greatest opportunity of Werdum's career, and he intended to make the most of it.

"The fight against Fedor is 99 percent confirmed to April 16th. I have three months to train to the most important fight of my life", Werdum told TATAME.com in January 2010, so optimistic that he began training for Fedor long before the official dates were set. "I already have a strategy set…I'll make history."[264]

There was much more to Werdum than his record or jiu-jitsu credentials. He had been thrown into the fire against American wrestler Tom Erikson in just his sixth professional fight, traveling to Japan to compete in PRIDE. Werdum had also trained with Mirko "Cro Cop" Filipović, at the time when Cro Cop was regarded as the number two or three heavyweight in the world after Fedor and Antônio Rodrigo Nogueira. Cro Cop used Werdum for his jiu-jitsu knowledge, but Werdum improved his own skills in the process.

"The first time, I just stay four months," Werdum recalled of his initial experience. "After, Mirko say, 'Stay here more, please. You help me, I help you.' And we stay two years in Croatia. It's very good this place, because Mirko is train a lot. He's good guy, good friend."

Cro Cop had given Fedor all he could handle in their August 2005 match, standing with the Russian giant, but backpedaling his way to a unanimous decision loss; the impact of Cro Cop's performance wasn't lost on Werdum, who was a less gifted striker compared to Cro Cop.

"Everybody try and stand-up with Fedor, try to block his punches, his kicks," said Werdum. "I saw in the videos everybody try—and everybody lost."

After his time with Cro Cop, Werdum trained with the world-famous Chute Boxe squad, leaving after two years of progress. He followed Chute Boxe trainer Rafael Cordeiro to California where Cordeiro's team, Kings MMA in Huntington Beach, became his current camp. Unlike Fedor, Werdum had not enjoyed continual success or recognition within the MMA community; therefore, the mere prospect of a fight with Fedor motivated him to do his best.

Werdum had already had a chance to shine on the big stages of the now-defunct PRIDE FC and the now-dominant UFC. After going 2-2 in the UFC, he was unceremoniously cut for refusing a pay decrease to his previously agreed-upon contract.

"They kind of used me, and threw me out," Werdum would later reflect on his tenure with the UFC to *PVT* magazine.[265]

Outside the UFC, Werdum had actually scored the opportunity of a lifetime. He could make himself a worthwhile investment for any MMA promotion if he were to beat Fedor.

On the MMA TV talk show *Inside MMA*, Werdum predicted a submission win for himself, "I go to the ground, because I believe in my jiu-jitsu," going on to say that it would happen in the first round because "there's no sweat [to impair getting a submission hold as happens in the later rounds]."

It was the kind of pre-fight statement even experts would laugh off, as Werdum had dictated victory within the narrowest of parameters.

The incompetence of M-1 crystallized into a perfect storm for Fedor. Due to what M-1 called "visa issues," he was late entering the US prior to the Werdum fight. The most likely reason Fedor's visa was delayed was perhaps due to M-1's administrative sloth, as M-1 fighter Magomed Shikhshabekov, who was scheduled to fight on the same June 26 Strikeforce/M-1 co-promoted show, failed to get his US visa in time to compete on the card.

The planned itinerary was for Emelianenko to get into the country early for a June 16 appearance at Strikeforce's Los Angeles show. He was then supposed to make an appearance at the E3 "Electronic Entertainment Expo" in Los Angeles in order to help promote the EA Sports MMA video game.

"The Russian heavyweight will arrive in the U.S. earlier than his usual schedule in an effort to spend more time with stateside fans," a report from Sherdog.com stated, quoting M-1 director of operations Evgeni Kogan.[266]

In the end, neither appearance materialized, as Fedor scrambled simply to arrive in the US. Jet-lagged from transit, stressed to the gills with pre-fight anxiety, and already annoyed with media obligations, upon arrival, Fedor was promptly trotted through a nearly two-hour media conference call on June 18. The call had originally been scheduled for Thursday June 17, but everything was pushed back because of Fedor's visa situation.

An additional headache—through no fault of M-1—came through the loss of a lucrative seven-figure (potentially—this depended on the number of shirts sold, each of which Fedor would earn a royalty from) one-year sponsorship deal with apparel company Tapout.

According to Vadim Finkelstein, there was only one culprit behind the deal tanking:

"It was our understanding that the T-shirt was in production," Vadim had told Sherdog.com through an interpreter. "However, at the beginning of this week, we were told by our sponsorship representative that Tapout had received a call from Dana [White] which involved him saying that if Fedor signs a T-shirt deal with Tapout, then Tapout would be out of the UFC."

There were other reasons why the UFC had pull with Tapout: it was believed that Zuffa had ownership over a percentage of Tapout. In 2012 there was a lawsuit levied against Tapout by Hitman Fight Gear's former owner, Dan Diaz, that alleged Tapout had both allowed suppliers to overcharge for goods sold and taken kickbacks from suppliers; both of these actions would have reduced the royalty payments to fighters. Dan Diaz's case against Tapout went to trial in the Superior Court of California in September 2012.[267]

Clothing company RVCA had also previously been a sponsor for Emelianenko for two of his fights, but M-1 stated that the relationship ended in the fall of 2009 when the UFC allegedly banned RVCA from sponsoring UFC athletes such as BJ Penn and Vitor Belfort if the company continued to support Fedor. Fedor was earning $10,000 per month, plus royalties from RVCA T-shirts; M-1 pegged the damages from the loss of RVCA's sponsorship in the range of $1 million.

Clinch Gear, a company founded by MMA fighter Dan Henderson and Aaron Crecy, ended up sponsoring Fedor for his walkout T-shirt for the Werdum fight. As Clinch Gear was already banned by the UFC—perhaps out of retaliation for Dan Henderson signing with Strikeforce in December 2009 instead of renewing his UFC contract for what Henderson saw as stilted wages—there were no threats that anyone could proffer to destroy Fedor's sponsorship deal.[268]

With him and his team staying at the posh Doubletree Hilton in Santa Monica, Fedor could not have been in a worse state to conduct in-person interviews with the media on June 18. After the strain of the conference call, and several hour-long blocks of time allotted to various media outlets, the Russian—described as a "prima donna" by one Strikeforce employee—simply shut his door, even refusing to answer for his translator, Tanya.

Fedor's entourage consisted of manager Vadim Finkelstein; M-1 director of operations Evgeni Kogan; grappling coach Vladimir Voronov; striking coach Alexander Michkov; Fedor's second wife Marina; Father Andrey, a Russian Orthodox priest of the Nizhniy Novgorod diocese; childhood friend Denis Kurilov; lawyer-turned-boxing promoter Steve Bash; and a photographer and videographer who both produced material for the M-1 website. Due to a need for photos and video material for the Showtime promos, in the evening everyone piled into two vehicles and headed to the M-1 Global affiliate gym in the Chatsworth district of Los Angeles—an area also known as the epicenter of the American porn industry.[269]

Fedor sulked as he exited the gym's change room. He began the demo workout with a pummeling drill with Voronov, which was followed by throwing several kicks (with shoes on). Fedor put on a pair of white MMA gloves and began to hit the pads held by Michkov with his speedy one-two's, calling for a towel to wipe the sweat from his brow. An unusual—perhaps involuntary—reaction of Fedor's is to repeatedly touch his nose.

Through it all, the Showtime photographer snapped away, directing the shoot with the vindictive and rude posture of a bitter old man. All the gym lighting suddenly switched off, as the photographer's lamps went on. The shadows cast across the room, Fedor perfectly silhouetted from the side à la Alfred Hitchcock.

With the shoot over, Fedor posed for obligatory photos with the gym owner, several members, local fighters and anyone else who wanted to imply association with greatness. A perturbed teenager asked, "Is he coming back in?" as Fedor filed out to the van, sitting and eagerly awaiting his departure from what seemed like a never-ending list of duties. On the ride back to an Italian eatery in Santa Monica, Marina gently rested her head on Fedor's shoulder as the torrent of noise and demands continued to swirl around them.

Watching Fedor depart the van, head drooping, he was dragged down by the circumstances of this trip. Three days later, on June 21, Fedor missed a scheduled call-in interview and was photographed visiting Hollywood, implying that he would rather take in sights than perform media duties. The truth was, Fedor needed a space of mental calm, and being prodded by journalists simply wasn't helpful to him at this time.

The open workouts for the media were held on Wednesday June 23 at American Kickboxing Academy in San Jose, California. Arriving early, one could catch fighters such as Cain Velasquez, Jon Fitch, Herschel Walker and Phil Davis working out. The walls were adorned with past and present AKA members who had been champions like BJ Penn and

Frank Shamrock.

Frank Shamrock emceed the open workouts, introducing women's 145-pound champion Cristiane "Cyborg" Santos; Josh Thomson, who could demo little since he'd just worked out and Cung Le, whose kicks were so powerful that they sounded like they reverberated three blocks down the street. When it was time for Fedor's appearance, the build-up of Emelianenko's mystique continued to promote the fight.

"He is—by far—considered the best pound-for-pound mixed martial arts fighter in the world," hyped Shamrock, "and really, the best mixed martial arts fighter—the greatest fighter—of all time."

After answering questions for the assembled media scrum, the photographers were given their op when Michkov held the focus mitts high—perhaps the location of 6'4" Werdum's chin—while Fedor bounced on his toes. There was no warm-up, no wrapping of hands and no wasting of time. Fedor threw a left jab, and then another, as Michkov reached out with the focus mitt each time to condition Fedor to slip the counter. After a few more different strikes, Michkov signaled the end of the demo by crossing his pads; Fedor bowed his head.

For a few minutes, people milled around while Fedor did one-on-ones and posed kneeling and shirtless. When it was all over, pockets of media still lingering, the comedian in Shamrock politely cleared the gym.

"Show's over. You don't have to go home, but you can't stay here."

When the fighters assembled for the Thursday press conference held two days before the fight, there was a tremendously different attitude and aura emitted from the Russians versus the Brazilians. Werdum and his team arrived early, found a mic at the presser, and began enjoying themselves by singing into it as if they were on stage at a club. Fedor's team showed up on-time, but closer to the wire, marching rushed and avoiding contact with others.

The media question and answer period was dry. Journalists overlooked Werdum, rarely qualifying him as a top challenger. A question about whether Fedor disliked interviews and media attention drew his honest answer.

"To tell the truth, I prefer to stay in the shade," said Fedor.

The aftermath of the fight would see M-1 scapegoat excessive media intrusion for Fedor's performance. He was overawed by the attention and spectacle of US sporting events, perhaps as gap-toothed and aloof as Soviet experiment Ivan Drago had felt when he'd witnessed Apollo Creed's entrance to James Brown with flashy dancers and other special effects in *Rocky IV*.

When it was time for Fedor and Werdum to square off for the photographers, you could sense a tremor shiver through Werdum's body. Standing in front of an emotionless Fedor felt terrifying. Your body had an involuntary reaction, like an ice cube slowly traversing down your back. The photographers snapped away, eating it up.

After the press conference broke, Matt Lindland was on-hand to corner teammate Pat Healy. Matt Lindland had shared the cage with Fedor at the Saint Petersburg Bodog show on April 14, 2007. Lindland had once been a serious middleweight contender for the UFC title. Unfortunately, either due to his grinding fighting style, UFC politics or the need to make an example of somebody, in 2005 he'd been tossed out of the UFC and forced to pick from the wide array of table scraps in the fight world. His best success was a split-decision loss to Quinton Jackson at 205 pounds; against heavyweight Fedor, he'd given up even more weight just to stay employed.

"I was just excited for the opportunity that I was even considered for that fight," said Lindland of his situation.

Promoter Bodog had baited Lindland with the promise of a three-fight contract. A year later, with the gambling company's fight division a reported $38 million in the red, BodogFIGHT folded and Lindland's contract was unfulfilled.

"That was very disappointing, because a good part of that contract were the fights after the Fedor fight," said Lindland.

Only the UFC could boast a regular schedule of events whereby its fighters got consistent paychecks and exposure. The UFC has existed since 1993 whereas the upstart promotion like Bodog simply existed to help promote online gambling as a loss leader and had only put on fights from August 2006 to November 2007, before fizzling out. Lindland suffered a lot through his inactivity and search for a reliable show to appear in; over the years he had repeatedly called the UFC and begged Dana White to be let back in, to no avail.[270]

The circus match-up of Lindland vs. Fedor attracted some criticism, but Matt couldn't let it seed doubt within him.

"I knew that he would bring his skills, and that I would bring mine," said Lindland, "I don't really get too caught up with what other people are saying and focus on what my game plan is for that fight."

Lighter wrestlers like Ricardo Arona and Kevin Randleman had had success against Fedor. Lindland had won the silver medal in the 69-76 kilogram category at the 2000 Sydney Olympics in Greco-Roman wrestling, so he'd be well-equipped with tools to potentially beat Fedor.

Said Lindland, "If anybody watched the fight, they saw what my game plan was: go in there, throw strikes to close the distance, get close, body-lock, and try to get him to the ground."

When the first left-hook Lindland threw grazed Fedor's face, opening up a cut, it appeared fortune was smiling on the American. Matt managed to secure double underhooks and position Fedor for a throw, but what Fedor did next caused lasting bitterness for Lindland.

According to Lindland, "I think the ropes, in that instance, played a big factor in me [not] getting the fight to the ground."

What Lindland was referring to was the instances where Fedor grabbed the ropes to prevent being taken down. The referee repeatedly warned Emelianenko, but Fedor was cagey and did what was necessary while bending the rules. At the same time, Lindland had grabbed the ropes to propel himself into the clinch, but that part of the story was minimized in Lindland's version of events.

When the fight hit the ground, Lindland was armbarred in just under three minutes at 2:58 of the opening round. Lindland salved his wounds with small talk with Fedor backstage, and later that evening, over at Vladimir Putin's palace.

While the Lindland-Emelianenko bout was just a minor footnote in MMA history, the American wrestler had valuable insight into how the Werdum fight might play out.

"[Fedor's] good. I don't know if he has a ton of weaknesses. He hits hard on his feet—you don't want to get hit by him; and on the ground, he's got *phenomenal* speed for a guy his size," said Lindland.

In the same breath, Lindland also praised Werdum's submission skills:

"It could be interesting if it goes to the ground and Werdum is on top controlling positions. I don't see Fedor catching a submission from the bottom against a guy like Werdum."

Lindland was not overrating Fedor's ground skills. Against submission specialist Antônio Rodrigo Nogueira, Fedor had spent much time in Nogueira's guard—where Nogueira was most dangerous—without any serious trouble.

Perhaps the most insightful comment Lindland provided had to do with the cage utilized in Strikeforce versus the traditional boxing ring from PRIDE.

Said Lindland, "I think a cage would be a better environment for fighting Fedor in."

One thing that Jerry Millen had mentioned while disparaging M-1 as "being run by kindergarteners" was that as of his last trip to Stary Oskol in 2008, Fedor still wasn't training in a cage.

"The cage that they had brought over from some other place in Stary Oskol—it was a real tight wire mesh, real thick wire, not like fencing like a regular fight cage, but something like a barbeque grill grade cage," an incredulous Millen related.

The cage was useless—being thrown up against steel that hard and tight would have knocked out training partners; it was never even assembled. Were M-1 to approach any cage manufacturer in the world, they could have easily scored a free cage had they simply mentioned who would be training in it.

Shogun would later relate after a brutal loss to Forrest Griffin in the UFC, training in the cage makes a huge difference because the cage is bigger and requires more punches to put someone in a corner. Fedor needed to train in an exact replica of the conditions he'd be facing in MMA fights.

The weigh-ins at the HP Pavilion went without incident. Some fighters existed in a field of combustible gas that could ignite hostility with the slightest spark of disrespect, but both Werdum and Fedor carried themselves with grace and dignity. Werdum made a clown face, eliciting laughter and puzzlement, but that was the extent of the show. They were more than professionals in this respect—in a real way, Fedor and Werdum were friends. In the background, pretty Rockstar Energy Drink™ girls posed with glowing smiles.

Thanks to the tapering off of training days before the fight, Fedor was now in good spirits. He was at the very top of a rollercoaster. All he had to do now was get the ride over with, and he would quickly be back in his security blanket of Stary Oskol.

The next day was fight night in San Jose. The televised portion of the card was craftily designed to ensure fights with exciting finishes. Josh Thomson went to war with Pat Healy, securing a rear naked choke in round three, despite two broken ribs; Cristiane Santos knocked down sacrificial lamb/showcase opponent Jan Finney six times en route to a second-round TKO win and a motivated Cung Le initially outboxed Scott Smith before smashing him with a spinning back kick and following up with punches his way to a second-round TKO.

Attendance at the HP Pavilion was later officially announced as 11,757 in a venue that could have been configured to seat approximately 18,000. By no means was this the fault of anyone at Showtime, Strikeforce or M-1; the show was simply being held in an oversaturated market in a depressed economy with less marketing budget or brand visibility than the UFC provided for its own shows.

Favoritism for Fedor was evident everywhere, from his larger base of fan support at the arena to an ice carving in a private reception for Showtime/Strikeforce employees with Fedor's name displayed prominently in the ice while Werdum's name was in smaller letters below.

Even Strikeforce middleweight champion Jake Shields came out to see the fight, and was initially denied cageside seats from Strikeforce officials due to his apparent intention to sign with the UFC.

Werdum, as the challenger, walked the entrance ramp first. There were flames shooting up to the ceiling, then fireworks, with the arena screens and lights lit blue with Werdum's name appearing in white letters. Fabricio was dressed in his gi, tied with a black belt, shaking hands with spectators along the way to the cage as the crowd booed him as the villain.

Fedor's entrance strained both the arms of fans reaching into the sky with camera phones to capture the moment and the vocal cords of the audience, which was adept at mispronouncing his name. His stoic attitude, uncluttered walk-in T-shirt and ice-cold personality all hid the realities of his mangled preparations. In the background, the faint strains of "Oy, to ne vecher" (a Russian folk song about 17th century rebel Stepan Razin's dream that his captain interpreted as an omen of their defeat), performed by Fedor's priest Father Andrey, could be heard above the rising din from the crowd. Red lighting, perhaps inspired by the official color of the Communist Party in the Soviet Union, was the motif for Fedor's entrance. More fireworks exploded with the force of mortars landing, startling the journalists on press row.

While the announcers insisted that Werdum could send shockwaves through the sport with a win, Fedor slapped his face and his body, trying to shock the nervousness and numbness out of his system. Referee Big John McCarthy, working the competing promotion of Strikeforce, thanks to a falling out with the UFC, began the bout with his trademark phrase "Let's get it on!" while clapping his hands together.

For the first few seconds, both Fedor and Werdum were tentative. Ten seconds in, Werdum connected with a low kick and moved out of range as quickly as possible. Fedor crept back into range while Werdum tried to stay elusive and move his head. After a wild exchange, it *appeared* that Fedor had knocked Werdum down and was on his way to yet another first round TKO. With Fedor in his guard, Werdum went for an armbar, while Fedor successfully escaped danger only to roll off the cage back into Werdum's awaiting trap. This time, Werdum secured his legs for a triangle choke while still holding Fedor's arm.

At 1:09 of the first round, the unthinkable occurred. Fedor tapped in submission—the unstoppable Russian legend had given up. Werdum jumped up and mounted the octagon fence like a victorious King Kong while an official was tasked with urging him to come down.

Fedor's reign at the top was now officially over.

Outside the room used for the post-fight press conference, the celebrations from Werdum's camp were so loud, a Showtime representative had threatened Werdum's camp with sanctions from the athletic commission to get them to quiet down. Actor Forrest Whitaker participated in the cheering, along with Renato "Babalu" Sobral, Rafael Cordeiro and all of Werdum's other teammates and supporters.

At the post-fight press conference, Frank Shamrock announced his retirement from MMA to little fanfare. As the former UFC middleweight champion, he had burned brightly during an era that predated the *TUF*-fueled MMA boon that had occurred when his career was winding down. Only a few older, educated fans would give Shamrock his due, and Shamrock's status as an "enemy of Dana White" meant he'd been written out of the official UFC history.

Fedor, emotionless, but his face slightly marked up from Werdum's landed strikes, arrived and took his place with Vadim Finkelstein to his left and translator Tanya and Scott Coker to his right.[271]

"I made a mistake," claimed Emelianenko, saying later, "I relied on myself too much, and that's why I paid for it."

In the background, one could still hear the jubilation from the still-ecstatic Werdum camp. It was embarrassing for Fedor's camp, and it came across as blatant (although unintentional) disrespect that the Brazilians were so proud at the moment when Fedor was so vulnerable.

The question of who would take over as the next dominant heavyweight loomed large over the press conference. Perhaps it still has not been answered to this day.

37

END OF THE LINE

Antonio "Bigfoot" Silva was the first-round obstacle to Fedor Emelianenko advancing in the ultra-ambitious Strikeforce heavyweight Grand Prix that was slated to kick off in early 2011. A win could restore Fedor's luster and would be the first step to reclaiming his former stature at the top of MMA.

Bigfoot boasted a respectable record, including a fight narrowly (or controversially) dropped to Fabricio Werdum. To the brass at Strikeforce, Showtime and M-1, Bigfoot was a clumsy clay pigeon being set up as target practice for Emelianenko.

The consensus among MMA fans was that M-1 Global, Fedor's management company, was the reason why Emelianenko's career was losing steam. To squeeze every last concession out of Strikeforce and Showtime, after the loss to Werdum, M-1 had dragged on negotiations for months and negotiated a new four-fight contract for Fedor. Who could blame M-1 for trying to get as much as they could at this juncture, when the clock was ticking on Fedor's career?

The fight date with Bigfoot was set for February 12, 2011, at New Jersey's Izod Center.

A few days before the fight, the Roseland Ballroom in New York City was the site of the "Strikeforce Fan Experience." Professional MMA contests might have been prohibited in New York, but having fan events here could help build support for legalization on a grassroots level.

A few minutes before the official start-time of the event, Fedor coasted into the backstage area of the ballroom with his managers, coaches, priests and assorted personnel. Sitting near the large entourage was former UFC champion and Strikeforce Grand Prix tournament participant Josh Barnett, quiet and undisturbed in the corner. Barnett differed from Fedor in that Barnett was a showman, learned from experiences in pro-wrestling.

There was the all-important question at this time regarding Barnett's difficulties in obtaining a license in California due to three positive steroid tests (the final failed test having helped torpedo both Barnett's scheduled fight against Fedor Emelianenko in Affliction, as well as the promotion itself).

"I'm not fighting in California, so I'll get a license when I need to," said Barnett. "I've already done everything that [CSAC] required of me—and then some. I don't actually owe them anything at this point."

All Barnett had to do was show up with a lawyer for the commission's verdict. They could turn down his request for a license, leaving him free to fight elsewhere (like Texas, where Antonio Margarito, who had been caught with loaded hand wraps prior to his bout with Shane Mosley, was later licensed to fight Manny Pacquiao), but something about the hearing spooked—or upset—him.

As for the ambitious Strikeforce Grand Prix, if the organization successfully pulled it off, it would signify the emergence of a serious competitor to challenge the UFC. The Zuffa brass were petrified of the day when another MMA promotion would try to cut into their exclusive control of the pay-per-view market; Strikeforce seemed more and more intent on encroaching on the UFC's territory there.

When a fighter has an established name later in their career, like Muhammad Ali or Mike Tyson, the public always holds out hope that the young lion seen earlier will manifest itself. Fedor was no different in 2011 than Ali was in the late '70s or Tyson in the late '90s—someone who could no longer turn the clock back, no matter what expectations the audience projected onto him.

The night of the fight in East Rutherford, New Jersey, was no anomaly to the rule of great fighters declining. The first round did not provide a dominant display from the Russian. In the second round, as Bigfoot got top position and rained down punch after punch on Emelianenko, the audience began cheering at Fedor's escape attempts rather than any offense he put up. With tremendous will, Fedor survived the second round and made it back to his corner.

The doctors stopped the fight in between the second and third rounds due to a cut on Fedor.

"*Bullshit!*" "*Kill the doctor!*" "*Fuck this!*" "*Let him continue!*"—those were the alcohol-laced epithets of the venue spectators when the decision was announced and they were to be deprived of a third round. One spectator, someone with a low threshold for enduring frustration, threw a full bottle of water in the direction of the cage—with the missile landing near the bewildered official M-1 photographer.

Some made the excuse that Fedor could have turned the tide in the final round, but the fight itself told the story—Bigfoot had better takedowns, ground control and striking. It wasn't that Bigfoot was invulnerable or iron-chinned, as he would suffer back-to-back knockout losses in his next two fights.

"Something went wrong from the very beginning and I didn't readjust myself," Fedor told the crowd post-fight, "Maybe it's the time to leave."

But would those around him simply let him retire?

On March 12, 2011, the news broke that Zuffa had acquired Strikeforce, where Fedor was still under contract to fight (although M-1 would later claim that Fedor's contract was directly with Showtime). Dana White delivered the news by giving a valuable exclusive interview to a video journalist from MMAFighting.com.

"Strikeforce is going to run, business as usual," said White in a statement that would become a popular internet meme as Strikeforce was gutted like a fish with a rapid-fire succession of changes.[272]

Zuffa quickly opted to fire most of Strikeforce's employees from matchmakers to PR staff. The best fighters in the organization, like Nick Diaz and Cung Le, were signed to the UFC. The Strikeforce heavyweight division was to be phased out, with Strikeforce losing its strongest selling point. Despite all the changes, in December 2011, Showtime opted to renew their deal to broadcast Strikeforce shows.[273]

The loss of Strikeforce as an independent promotion was a sad event for all top-tier MMA fighters, who had lost one of their only sources of leverage in negotiations—the threat of going to a competing promotion. The media outlets and individuals barred from accreditation on press row at UFC events were now similarly barred from covering Strikeforce shows. MMA as a whole had lost some of its luster as the rivalries between promotions made for exciting developments. Rather than taking the sport to a whole new level, Zuffa was preparing to water it down to the saturation point in order to secure control and profits.

There was now the matter of Fedor's next opponent for the final fight on his Strikeforce contract. American Dan Henderson, who normally fought at either 185 or 205 pounds, was rumored to be in discussions to face Fedor at a catch weight of 220 pounds.

"If I did fight him, it would be no catch weight," Henderson said in a video released in April 2011, "I don't do those at all. If I'm going to fight him at his weight, I'm going to fight him at his weight."[274]

The fight—at heavyweight—was set for July 30 at the Sears Center in Hoffman Estates, Illinois. The action was close, with Fedor dropping Henderson with a good right hand and then following him to the ground; Henderson came back out of the scramble to take Fedor's back and nailed the Russian with a right uppercut, stopping Emelianenko on the ground with strikes. The decision to take the fight at heavyweight was a good decision by Henderson as he got full credit for the win with no excuses about Fedor being drained from cutting weight.

Fedor, now a loser of three fights in a row, needed to salve his pride somehow.

"I think [the stoppage] was early," complained Emelianenko. "I don't want to say anything bad about the referee, but I think it was early."

The decision makers at Zuffa opted not to renew Fedor's contract with Strikeforce. Fedor would now have to brave the wasteland of barren MMA promotions that lay outside of Zuffa's banner.

M-1 trotted out Jeff Monson (43-12) as a credible comeback opponent at an M-1 show held in Moscow on November 20, 2011. Monson was a decorated grappler, 9-1 in his last ten bouts, and most useful of all, he posed no challenge whatsoever to Fedor.

Fedor kept the fight standing, dropping Monson three times in the second round. After the fight, it was reported that the American's injuries from the fight included a broken femur, as well as a ruptured patella tendon.

Next up came a bout with Japanese judoka Satoshi Ishii at DREAM's "Fight For Japan: Genki Desu Ka Omisoka" to be held on December 31, 2011. Ishii was a gold medalist in judo at the 2008 Olympic games in Beijing, China, but his MMA career had been mismanaged, and he was only 4-1-1 at this point.

Fedor smashed Ishii, knocking him out at 2:29 of the first round. There were news reports after the fight that Ishii had suffered cerebral edema and would never fight again.

Training partner Ryo Chonan quickly denied the rumors about Ishii:

"Satoshi Ishii is just fine," said Chonan. "The people who spread these false rumors about other people's lives and livelihoods should just die."[275]

Whether Fedor was even interested in the caliber of opponent M-1 was setting him up with was one question; whether Fedor wanted to continue fighting was another. When M-1 planned a Saint Petersburg event on June 21, 2012, against Brazilian Pedro Rizzo, an interview suggested that Fedor would be retiring after facing Rizzo.

"It will be the last fight of my career," Fedor told Russian television outlet isport.ua. Later, Emelianenko said that he'd been misinterpreted, and that he had not decided on retirement yet.[276]

Pedro Rizzo (19-9) hadn't been on top of his game since beating Ricco Rodriguez at UFC 45 in 2003. He came into the bout with three wins over Jeff Monson, Gary Goodridge and Ken Shamrock—a stellar résumé, had the wins occurred several years earlier when those fighters were in their perceived prime. Rizzo's best days might have been long behind him, but the payday from facing Fedor was welcomed with open arms.

In the fight, held at Saint Petersburg's Ice Palace, Fedor stalked Rizzo from the opening bell. When Rizzo attempted to open up, Fedor calmly circled away from any danger. After a combination that started with a low-leg kick, Fedor landed his patented right hand punch, dropping Rizzo and following up with strikes on the ground until the referee stepped in. Fedor had taken just 84 seconds to end the bout.

In the wake of the fight, Fedor made the decision to retire from MMA competition.

"I think it is time I quit," Emelianenko said, citing his daughters' growing up without him as the reason for his departure.[277]

Fedor ending his career with three clear, dominant wins was a good way to go out. He would always remember his losses—bitterness over the cut stoppage against Tsuyoshi Kohsaka, falling for Fabricio Werdum's ploy, getting cut against Antonio Silva and the early stoppage against Dan Henderson. Capping his tremendous career with three wins meant the last thing Fedor had to remember the next time the notion of fighting entered his mind—driving past the gym where he used to train, hearing a news blurb about MMA on the television, feeling an old ache in his joints—was the silent feeling of inner triumph.

He couldn't rewrite the mistakes of the past. They were a part of his learning curve and his life's experiences. In every situation, Fedor could only perform his best under the circumstances; there was no ideal situation where he could emerge undefeated or unscathed from the dark side of the sport.

Was Fedor Emelianenko the greatest MMA fighter of all time? He would never attach the title to himself.

Fedor had succeeded in achieving the goal he spoke of on many occasions—simply being a good person, one who evoked warm thoughts when his name was spoken. To him, that was more important than his championships or other accolades.

CONCLUSION

The legacy of legendary careers often involves a slew of injuries, chronic pain and a loss of the "ease-of-body" that healthy people take for granted. On an episode of HDNet's *Inside MMA* that aired in November 2011, Rich Franklin catalogued a roadmap of pain across his body.

"I have the plate in my hand from the Loiseau fight, and I've been through a couple different surgeries," said the former middleweight champion. "The worst part is at night when I'm sleeping. There's just so much pain in the shoulder, it's just like a throbbing, dead pain the whole time, and it's traveling down my arm."

"I know," said Bas Rutten, empathizing with Franklin. "Every time I stand up, it's 'aaaaahhhh'…when I throw a ball with my daughters, I can't jump for it. If I jump this high (demonstrates three inches between his fingers), it hurts a lot. It's crazy, right? You would think cartilage, no cartilage in the kneecap, they go 'It's easy,' no it's not."

In a follow-up interview, Rutten did point to other reasons outside MMA for his body's state of disrepair.

"I think it came from me using a lot of cortisone as a kid. I think I got tendonitis from that," said Rutten, who noticed the onset of his knee problems as a track and field athlete in high school.

"There's no cartilage in my knee caps, but I don't know if that comes from fighting, or it's a genetic thing because although I'm on my knees a lot, it doesn't completely tear the cartilage off—it doesn't do that to other people."

Rutten lists off other minor injuries from his time as a fighter—a broken hand, a broken toe—nothing major, he says.

"It's about how you train," said Rutten of the incidence of injuries that cause long-term and chronic pain. "My training has always been insane. I have guys in my class—who have to fight two weeks later—who couldn't do the warm-up."

The hardest part of such injuries is the lack of sympathy given to athletes who have had their bodies used up in the pursuit of glory. The injuries to the tendons and joints are nothing compared to the possible repercussions from brain damage sustained in MMA due to strikes to the head. Despite the hard evidence presented by various studies, stakeholders within MMA use denial, incongruent comparisons and rationalizations as their defense against the realities of chronic traumatic encephalopathy.

"There has never been a death or serious injury in the UFC," proclaimed Dana White at the UFC 140 press conference. "When you take two healthy athletes, you get them medically cleared and checked out, the way that you're supposed to, you don't cut any corners; you go overboard on it; then you have the proper medical staff there while they're fighting; then you get them checked out after the fight is over, it's 100 percent a safe sport."

"People talk about concussions and Parkinson's and all these other things. This is life, things happen. You never know what's going to happen," rationalized White.

Easy for the man who has never had a professional fight in his life—nor any amateur boxing bouts—to say when the risk is completely offloaded to others.

"Yeah, we took risks," said Jon Jones, "but this is what we chose to do with our lives."

To Jon Jones, who has two brothers playing football, perhaps there are similar risks to the brain inherent in both sports. However, in 2012, thousands of former NFL players were able to launch a massive class-action lawsuit against the NFL over brain injury risks, with part of the suit's argument hinging on the fact that the NFL glorified violence to the media.[278] Clearly, MMA mythologizes violence at its very core, so former fighters would have little public sympathy were they to launch similar complaints.

All the glowing speeches praising the safety record of the UFC disregard the hard, underlying truth: in MMA, brain damage is a given, not a statistical anomaly.

"They take care of us," said Tito Ortiz, of the Fertittas flying fighters down to Vegas to get brain scans.

It was impossible to mention the obvious—that the fighters were as highly valued to the UFC as racehorses were to the Kentucky Derby. As long as Tito Ortiz's name could secure a return on investment through sales of pay-per-views, broadcast licensing, tickets, merchandise and other revenue streams, the Fertittas would take all the steps necessary to ensure that he was in a condition fit to enter the octagon.

"I'll enter the cage every day and brain damage is the least of my worries," said former UFC heavyweight champion Frank Mir.[279]

Perhaps Mir—or even athletic commissions themselves—should have been more concerned. When Mir fought Junior dos Santos at UFC 146, the ringside doctor asked him "Do you know where you are, sir?" as Mir rested between the first and second rounds. His answer was "Mandalay Bay"; in fact, he was at the MGM Grand Garden Arena. NSAC officials then allowed the fight to continue.

That there are no side-effects to fighting was something that fighters have to believe in order to perform without holding back, but there is no doubt that there will be future consequences for all MMA fighters who stay around the game long enough, period. That doesn't mean the sport has to be banned, but fighters should be going into MMA with their eyes open, not parroting the promoter's fiction designed to allay fears of genuine health risks, avoid political backlash and deceive the general public.

Fighting has its rewards—big money, attention, sexual conquests and, most of all, adrenaline and endorphins that catapult the winners into the stratosphere. The emotional epiphany experienced at the top, along with the lure of leaving an everlasting legacy, seems worth risking everything for.

The eventual fate of most MMA fighters when their careers are over is no secret. Many veteran fighters, superstars of the sport in their heyday, have fallen on hard times. The current crop of active fighters doesn't want to square up and look at the vanquished greats, any more than teenagers want to look at their parents and connect the dots to what their lives might end up resembling.

Australian sports commentator Michael Schiavello recalls the change he'd witnessed in his boyhood idol, heavyweight kickboxing champion Dennis Alexio.

> **When I was 17 I'd seen him as a Herculean figure with a physique and aura of almost mythological proportions. Now in his 50s, his once thick mane of jet black hair had whittled down to near baldness and he looked more like a lean super middleweight than the former, muscle-bound heavyweight champion of the world. His skin was as bronze as I remembered but now sagged a little in his cheeks and wrinkled around his eyes. He was just as tall as he'd always been, of course, but in my eyes he seemed shorter and far removed from the human skyscraper I'd view him as through teenage eyes. Most strikingly though, his aura of greatness had gone. Fifteen years ago that aura had burned so bright as to have blinded, but now all that remained was a small flame dancing on a skinny wick.**[280]

Alexio had changed, and although he didn't say it overtly, so had Michael Schiavello, who was no longer a seventeen-year-old boy. Only cultural icons who died young like Che Guevara or Jim Morrison could be remembered forever in their prime, because they never endured the ravages of aging.

There will always be new champions anointed as the next Ali, the next Tyson, the second coming of Jesus and so forth. This is usually something done to drum up business, and business is what MMA has become, but it doesn't guarantee that the next person to hold the belt will have the character to defend it multiple times—let alone become a legend. Fighters like GSP, BJ, Anderson, Shogun and Fedor are as rare as athletes like Tiger Woods, Michael Jordan or Wayne Gretzky.

For the pound-for-pound greats, one of their greatest achievements is the way they will be talked about and remembered for years to come, long after they leave the game. Not as men who were mere participants, or title-holders. They made it to the metaphorical top of a nameless mountain whose summit was always in flux, and it remained a matter of debate if they had really reached the top.

Their memories of glory—however fleeting—will last forever. Close your eyes, and for a split second, travel back to the beauty of the moment: crowd cheering, elation, relief. Transcendence over everything.

It was guys trying to reconcile what they have become with who they used to be that destroyed them inside. There is no going back. Not now, not ever. The tragedy with the pound-for-pound best is that they will feel every lost step in their decline. Their greatest strengths become their greatest weaknesses.

Despite the myth that conditions for fighters will improve with time, only government action will force organizations—both in North America and abroad—to enact laws designed to protect fighters from some of the dangers they are currently exposed to. Japan needs an athletic commission to oversee MMA and professional wrestling; the UK, Australia and Brazil need an athletic commissions to oversee MMA. The Muhammad Ali Reform Act and all its provisions, which currently apply to professional boxing in the United States, need to be applied to MMA.

There will be no "fighters union"; there isn't a single UFC fighter who openly admits to being signed with the "Mixed Martial Arts Fighters Association." Any active fighter signed to the major promotions who thinks about speaking out about topics like fighter pay, or the level of respect afforded to fighters, knows that he'll have his balls cut off and shoved down his throat by the powers that be. Many fighters could testify to this truth—if they were comfortable with the idea of never competing in the major leagues of MMA again.

"*You don't like it, don't fight,*" sneer some of the so-called "fans." Others claim that the salaries of even lower-tier UFC and Bellator fighters who have several fights in a year equal close to six figures *"when you include sponsorship."* Again, an incongruent comparison, as it fails to take into consideration the opportunity cost of training, medicals, non-paying amateur fights, low-paying fights in tiny organizations— even being stiffed for hundreds of thousands of dollars in purses, as K-1 has done to its best and most loyal kickboxers. Significant sponsorship is reserved for the established MMA elite, and there just aren't that many years for most fighters to collect those supposedly fat purses & bonus checks before their bodies stop functioning and taxes and alimony gut them financially.

In life, not everyone can be among the best at what they do. Most people need to resign themselves to mediocrity and lowered expectations just to continue living in an unfair and arbitrary universe. Ignoring the issues, consuming MMA as mere entertainment and skewering critics of the current landscape are all hallmarks of an ignorant populace, content with backsliding into decay.

Yet there is hope on the horizon. Educated fans are beginning to see through the grandiose lies and half-truths, and are refusing to act as sycophants backing the obvious agenda of promoters who take as much as possible while giving fighters back pennies on the dollar. Lawmakers in some states have tried to pass legislation that would help protect MMA fighters, like the poorly-conceived AB2100 bill in California, albeit with zero success thus far. The Federal Trade Commission has taken the time and resources to investigate Zuffa after its acquisition of Strikeforce parent company Explosion Entertainment; however, in February 2012, the case was closed, and the FTC stated "it now appears no further action is warranted by the Commission at this time."[281]

Nothing could be further from the truth. There are many unresolved issues within MMA that require immediate attention from parties with the power to force compliance from promotions. Anyone else who tries to speak up—fighters, the MMA media, sponsors and other stakeholders—can be silenced with threats or coerced with rewards.

As for the crooked promoters, the organized-crime groups, the dishonest managers and agents and all the other vermin that populate the industry, although they rarely realize it until it is too late, they have built castles of sand. Sooner or later, the tide will turn.

Until the time when a semblance of fairness comes to MMA, the pound-for-pound fighters, along with all the other men and women reaching for that title, will be doing what they have always tried to do: push through the shadows and perform. Fighting not for financial rewards or popularity, but for the love of a cruel sport. A love that is rarely reciprocated.

Photographs

(Where not otherwise indicated, all photo credits: Brian J. D'Souza)

Georges St-Pierre signing an autograph at The Striking Truth *premiere in Toronto, Ontario on February 25, 2011*

Georges St-Pierre sitting cageside at MFL 1 – The Beginning, held in Montreal, Quebec on October 17, 2009

Inside Montreal's Tristar Gym

BJ Penn (L) and his brother Regan Penn (R)
photo credit: Zdenek Mlika

BJ grappling
photo credit: Zdenek Mlika

(above) WEC and UFC champion Jose Aldo
being interviewed by reporter Paula Sack
at Shooto – Brazil 20 in Rio de Janeiro on
December 11, 2010

*An afternoon of sparring for team
Nova União during December 2010 at
the Upper Sport Club in the Flamengo
district of Rio de Janeiro, Brazil*

An indifferent Anderson Silva fields criticism at the post-fight presser for UFC 97 in Montreal on April 18, 2009

Fighter Ed "Monstro" Carlos (L) hits Thai pads held by trainer Luciano "Monge" Moreas (R) at the main Chute Boxe facility in Curitiba, Brazil in December 2010

*Anderson Silva steps on the scale at the UFC 97 weigh-ins on
April 17, 2009*

*Admiring fans pose with Anderson Silva at Rio de Janeiro's X-Gym in
December 2010*

Antônio Rogério Nogueira at the X-Gym in December 2010

Lyoto Machida being interviewed in the cage at WFE 8 – Platinum, held in Salvador, Brazil on December 15, 2010

Maurício "Shogun" Rua, at Robinson's Karate School in Newmarket, Ontario in May 2010

Maurício Rua and his Muay Thai coach, Andre "Dida" Amado

Murilo "Ninja" Rua (L) spars with K-1 fighter Glaube Feitosa (R) at the Universidade da luta in Curitiba, Brazil in December 2010

Brazilian ring card babes at Shooto – Brazil 20 in Rio de Janeiro

The Rockstar Energy Drink™ girls strike a pose at the weigh-ins for Strikeforce: Fedor vs. Werdum

*Left to right: Josh Barnett, Fedor Emelianenko and Alistair Overeem at the
Strikeforce Heavyweight Grand Prix press event hosted at Chelsea Piers in
New York City on February 9, 2011*

*Fedor Emelianenko kneels for a photo op at American Kickboxing
Academy in San Jose, California in June, 2010*

Fedor Emelianenko and Fabricio Werdum weigh-in the day before their June 26, 2010 fight at San Jose's HP Pavilion

Fabricio Werdum scales the fence after defeating Fedor Emelianenko on June 26, 2010

353

Acknowledgments

This book would not have been possible without the support of many individuals, who contributed their time, insight, expertise and kindness towards my cause. We all like to mythologize individual achievement and ascribe credit to a select few. Yet there are so many people who have lent their support to me, including:

Jeff Evans, for trusting me and letting me do things my way.

Alexandre Choko (futureofboxing.com), who started me on my MMA journey, and provided the answers that uncovered raw truth.

Tom Callos, the type of martial arts instructor every community in the world needs.

Miro Mijatovic, who faced treachery and betrayal, but came out on top.

Allison Lampert, whose work remains timeless and whose company is always welcome.

My brother Greg D'Souza, for making my website. Ananiy Vasyura (avdesignmedia.com) for designing my cover. Ralph Di Fiore and Scott Marler for proofreading. Karla Bobadilla of Lewis Birnberg Hanet for her legal services. Jonathan Scott for the paperback design. The Ontario Arts Council for supporting my writing through a Writers Reserve grant recommended by ECW Press.

Nilson de Castro, Rudimar Fedrigo, Roberto Batata and Cyborguinho for welcoming me to Chute Boxe.

Laise Menadro, Claudia Valente and Irmeson Cavalcante de Oliveira for showing me Curitiba.

Vilmari Pedrozo for finding my expensive DSLR camera that I accidently dropped in Curitiba, Brazil and returning it to me in Canada.

Ahmad "Alex" Zahabi (BurlingtonBJJ.ca), for the wrestling, jiu-jitsu and friendship.

The top-notch coaches and staff at Toronto BJJ (TorontoBJJ.com)— Josh Rapport for investing in the academy to bring us the best of the best; Professor Jorge Britto for giving us an anchor in jiu-jitsu; and all the other instructors, including Thomas Beach, Eduardo Dibb, Michael Zaniewski, Chris Sit, Donald Emerson, David Bodrug, Oscar Dewindt, Ryan O'Shea, Nathan Rector, Alessandro Roman and Jalan Lahoni. Also thanks to everyone else who showed me a tip, technique or trick over the years.

My special thanks to the sources, editors, PR staff and others who helped me out: Stephane Patry, Victor Vargotsky, Monte Cox, Bas Rutten, Sergio Cunha, Matt Lindland, Evgeni Kogan, Frank Shamrock, Robert Bentley, Bas Boon, Matt Hughes, Murilo Rua, Steve Bash, Jon Jones, Mark Hominick, Fabricio Werdum, Forrest Griffin, Eric O'Keefe, Andre Pederneiras, Kenny Florian, David Loiseau, Jerry Millen, Josh Barnett, Lyoto Machida, Michael Afromowitz, Chris DeBlasio, Jordan Breen, Dave Walsh, Dave Meltzer, Donovan Craig, Michael Woods,

João Paulo "Tuba" de Souza, Andre "Dida" Amado, Ben Goldstein, Jon Fitch, Jonathan Snowden, Zach Arnold, Zdenek Mlika and Loretta Hunt.

Last, but not least, thanks to the friends who I can enjoy and share my success with, as we have shared so many good times together: Suzanne, Kimberley, Cynthia, Jeremy Williams, Travis Sapp, Mike Pancino, Aleksa, Rui, Vinod, Clement Wai, Senem, Anne, Sidney, Terry, Leonard and all my other friends who encouraged me during my journey.

Endnotes

1 *FIGHT! Magazine*, April 2008
2 http://yamagazine.ca/?c=6&a=27
3 http://bleacherreport.com/articles/6502-an-interview-with-georges-rush-st-pierre-in-colorado
4 http://www.mmamania.com/2008/10/12/georges-st-pierre-earns-brazilian-jiu-jitsu-black-belt-under-bruno-fernandes/
5 http://www.lapresse.ca/sports/autres-sports/autres-sports/200903/30/01-841519-le-phenomene-georges-st-pierre.php
6 *The Montreal Gazette*, 04/03/06
7 http://hour.ca/2006/03/02/ufc-pq/
8 http://alcoholism.about.com/cs/adult/a/aa073097.htm
9 http://www.theparisreview.org/interviews/4779/the-art-of-fiction-no-22-james-jones
10 *The Striking Truth 3D*, 2010
11 http://www2.macleans.ca/2010/09/27/lord-of-the-ring/
12 *The Ultimate Fighter: Season 12*, Episode 5 'Disrespectful' 11/13/10
13 http://www.gspofficial.com/gsp-anti-bullying
14 http://ca.sports.yahoo.com/mma/news?slug=dw-wetzel_georges_st_pierre_addresses_bullying_042611
15 http://bleacherreport.com/articles/643105-ufc-129-watch-georges-st-pierres-mixed-martial-arts-debut-from-2002
16 *PRIDE FC Secret Files*, Kamipro Books, 2008
17 http://www.casinogaming.com/features/blackbook/index.html 10/18/2012
18 *Total MMA: Inside Ultimate Fighting*, Jonathan Snowden, ECW Press, 2008
19 http://articles.latimes.com/1993-11-11/news/mn-55577_1_carl-thomas-sr
20 http://www.adcombat.com/news/2008-04-18/nick-lembo-explodes-zuffa-myth-ufc-rules-history
21 http://sports.yahoo.com/video/player/news/26789328#news/26789328
22 *Dana White, King of MMA*, June White, Enterprises Unlimited, July 2, 2011

23 http://espn.go.com/boxing/story/_/id/7591458/stars-honor-muhammad-ali-70th-birthday-gala-vegas

24 *Tigers in the Mud: The Combat Career of German Panzer Commander Otto Carius*, Otto Carius, Stackpole Books, 2003.

25 http://fr.canoe.ca/sports/nouvelles/archives/2006/11/20061121-123200.html

26 http://www.t-nation.com/free_online_article/sports_body_training_performance_interviews/the_terror_speaks_matt_serra

27 *Financial Post Business* magazine, 05/07

28 *Tapped Out*, Matthew Polly, Gotham, 2011.

29 http://mmajunkie.com/news/22912/ufc-boss-says-new-champ-jon-jones-biggest-test-may-lie-outside-of-the-cage.mma

30 http://www.mensjournal.com/jon-bones-jones-is-sweet-and-vicious/2

31 http://www.xyience.com/index.cfm?fa=person.detail&pid=26

32 http://mmajunkie.com/news/4910/ufc-newcomer-jon-jones-to-replace-tomasz-drawl-at-ufc-87.mma

33 http://mmavalor.com/2011/01/11/ufc-news-jon-jones-officially-leaves-bombsquad/

34 http://www.mmaweekly.com/diego-sanchez-falling-down-to-learn-to-pick-himself-back-up-again

35 http://www.sanluisobispo.com/2010/01/13/988447/chuck-liddell-among-those-suing.html

36 http://fr.canoe.ca/sports/nouvelles/archives/2011/11/20111104-131226.html

37 http://www.sbnation.com/2012/6/7/3070029/bradley-vs-pacquiao-fight-2012-purses

38 http://www.philstar.com/sportsarticle.aspx?articleid=819433&publicationsubcategoryid=69 09/20/12

39 *New York Times*, "Unbeaten Boxer Pioneers Ways to Make Money Hand Over Fist," 09/16/11

40 http://www.guardian.co.uk/sport/2011/jul/09/lewis-hamilton-mclaren-sponsorship

41 *New York Times*, "Carrying a Flag for Mixed Martial Arts," 9/22/10

42 http://www.sportsnet.ca/mma/2010/04/27/showdown_quebec_bird/

43 http://www.heavy.com/mma/mma-news/2010/04/trainer-eric-okeefes-license-revoked-unable-to-corner-goulet-at-ufc-113/

44 http://www.cbc.ca/news/politics/inside-politics-blog/2010/05/georges-st-pierre-from-the-octagon-to-parliament-hill.html

45 http://www.mmafighting.com/2011/01/20/georges-st-pierre-manager-shari-l-spencer-part-ways

46 http://www.mmafighting.com/2011/02/09/frankie-edgar-splits-from-manager-shari-spencer

47 http://www.mmafighting.com/2011/05/25/finally-official-georges-st-pierres-rounds-won-streak-ends-at

48 http://sports.yahoo.com/mma/news?slug=ki-iole_georges_st_pierre_win_streak_ufc_129_042811

49 http://www.sportsnet.ca/video/36673754001/40310156001/GSP-a-finisher 11/01/11

50 http://tysontalk.com/tysontalk-exclusivesteve-lott-responds-your-questions/

51 *FIGHT! Magazine*, April 2008

52 http://sports.espn.go.com/extra/mma/news/story?id=3200399

53 http://mmajunkie.com/news/25814/ufc-137s-francis-carmont-repping-tristar-gym-in-georges-st-pierres-absence.mma

54 http://radio.thescore.com/episodes/the-mma-show-october-18?utm_source=feedburner&utm_medium=feed&utm_campaign=Feed%3A+Fight-Show+%28The+MMA+Show+with+Mauro+Ranallo%29

55 *Discover Hawai'i the Big Island*, Luci Yamamoto and Conner Gorry, Lonely Planet Publications, 2011

56 *Why I Fight*, BJ Penn and Dave Weintraub, William Morrow, 2010

57 http://www.openmatradio.com/2012/02/20/episode-8-bj-penn-pt-1/

58 *Why I Fight*, BJ Penn and David Weintraub, William Morrow, 2010.

59 http://mmaweekly.com/featherweight-champ-jose-aldo-injured-bows-out-of-ufc-125

60 http://www.bjjgroundfighter.com/article_002.html

61 *Renzo Gracie: Legacy*, 2008

62 *The Ultimate Fighter: Season 5*, Episode 1 'It's Like Anarchy Here' 04/05/07

63 http://sports.yahoo.com/mma/news?slug=dm-pulver103108

64 http://www.youtube.com/watch?v=NAz_pwT8bMA&feature=relmfu

65 *The Montreal Gazette*, 03/04/06

66 *FIGHT! Magazine*, May 2008

67 http://www.youtube.com/watch?v=vXWL7eFOWqs

68 http://sportsillustrated.cnn.com/2009/writers/josh_gross/02/02/penn-st-pierre-post-fight/index.html

69 *ESPN: The Magazine*, 04/05/10

70 http://www.bjpenn.com/forum/topics/q-and-a-about-marinovich 03/23/11

71 http://www.youtube.com/watch?v=eXoqfIU0C6Y

72 http://www.mmaforum.com/ufc/63318-does-winning-tuf-mean-anything-any-more.html

73 http://www.fiveouncesofpain.com/2008/02/09/2102/

74 http://mmajunkie.com/news/17176/ufc-107-play-by-play-and-live-results.mma

75 http://mmaweekly.com/diego-sanchez-%E2%80%93-once-surrounded-by-alcohol-drugs-thieves-%E2%80%93-is-back-on-track

76 http://www.mmaweekly.com/diego-sanchez-falling-down-to-learn-to-pick-himself-back-up-again

77 *Why I Fight*, BJ Penn and Dave Weintraub, William Morrow, 2010

78   *Why I Fight*, BJ Penn and Dave Weintraub, William Morrow, 2010

79   *Why I Fight*, BJ Penn and Dave Weintraub, William Morrow, 2010

80   http://sportsillustrated.cnn.com/2010/writers/josh_gross/04/14/edgar.penn/index.html

81   http://weinish.blogspot.com/2010/04/book-stuff.html

82   http://sportsillustrated.cnn.com/2010/writers/josh_gross/04/14/edgar.penn/index.html

83   http://www.sherdog.net/forums/f2/bj-penn-book-comments-me-his-co-author-1192381/index14.html

84   http://sports.yahoo.com/mma/news?slug=ycn-10321189

85   http://www.openmatradio.com/2012/03/05/episode-9-bj-penn-pt-2/

86   http://www.mmaweekly.com/rory-macdonald-is-bj-penns-shot-at-redemption

87   *New York Times*, "Foreigners Follow Money to Booming Brazil, Land of $35 Martini," 8/12/11

88   *Like Water*, 2011

89   *FIGHT! Magazine*, February 2009.

90   http://www.youtube.com/watch?v=soOXgmvIdAI

91   http://pvtmag.portaldovt.com.br/en/06/

92   http://www.nationsencyclopedia.com/economies/Americas/Brazil-POVERTY-AND-WEALTH.html

93   *UFC Magazine*, February/March 2010

94   *Anderson Spider Silva*, Anderson Silva, Sextante, 2012

95   http://pvtmag.portaldovt.com.br/en/03/

96   http://www.youtube.com/watch?v=rZKLy7CsHrU

97   http://www.pridefc.com/pride2005/index.php?mainpage=news&news_id=997

98   http://punchdrunkgamer.com 09/25/09

99   http://sportsillustrated.cnn.com/vault/article/web/COM1148675/index.htm

100 http://www.sherdog.com/news/news/Dominican-Disaster-28866

101 www.boxingscene.com/forums 01/02/2011

102 http://fightsport.net/?p=3660

103 http://fightsport.net/?p=3657

104 http://www.fightersonlymag.com/content/news/8915-anderson-reignites-wanderlei-feud--?quot;you-will-get-yourself-hurt="=

105 http://www.fightersonlymag.com/content/news/16590-chute-boxe-owner-sues-anderson-silva-for-damage-to-reputation

106 http://www.bodybuilding.com/fun/anderson_silva_interview.htm

107 *FIGHT! Magazine*, February 2009

108 http://www.youtube.com/watch?v=_NhqU8ARL3Q

109 *FIGHT! Magazine*, February 2009

110 http://www.bodybuilding.com/fun/anderson_silva_interview.htm

111 http://latimesblogs.latimes.com/sports_blog/2011/04/ufc-middleweight-champion-silva-like-water.html

112 http://tiffmidnightmadness.blogspot.ca/2011/08/submit-ufc-champion-anderson-silva.html 8/31/11

113 *Sugar Ray Robinson: The Bright Lights and Dark Shadows of a Champion*, 1998

114 *Total MMA: Inside Ultimate Fighting*, Jonathan Snowden, ECW Press, 2008

115 http://sports.yahoo.com/blogs/mma-cagewriter/anderson-silva-says-didn-t-finish-thales-leites-140210592--mma.html

116 http://www.usatoday.com/sports/mma/2010-01-11-abu-dhabi-ufc_N.htm

117 http://www.mmafighting.com/2010/04/13/greg-jackson-really-enjoyed-anderson-silva-at-ufc-112

118 http://www.youtube.com/watch?v=FSqJESKeILw

119 http://www.oregonlive.com/west-linn/index.ssf/2011/10/west_linn_mixed_martial_artist.html

120 http://www.youtube.com/watch?v=VcVYanprziA

121 http://hosteddb.fightmetric.com/fighters/details/235#

122 http://sports.espn.go.com/extra/mma/news/story?id=6563904

123 http://sports.espn.go.com/extra/mma/news/story?id=5986635

124 http://www.break.com/usercontent/2010/12/15/anderson-silva-at-x-gym-1968926

125 http://www.youtube.com/watch?v=_NhqU8ARL3Q

126 http://www.mmamania.com/2010/3/8/1362683/here-we-go-anderson-silva-vitor

127 http://www.fiveknuckles.com/mma-news/Anderson-Silva-wears-a-mask-to-weigh-ins,-Vitor-Belfort-not-intimidated.html

128 http://mmajunkie.com/news/22367/silva-credits-seagal-for-ufc-126-win-eyes-brazil-or-las-vegas-for-gsp-showdown.mma

129 http://www.mixedmartialarts.com/news/403606/Anderson-Silva-Vitor-Belfort-is-a-coward-everyone-knows/

130 http://www.mmafighting.com/2012/11/29/3702500/george-st-pierres-return-estimated-at-doing-680-700000-buys-for-ufc

131 http://blogs.telegraph.co.uk/sport/garethadavies/100015839/ronaldo-brazilian-soccer-legend-signs-ufc-star-anderson-silva-as-first-client-in-new-management-agency/

132 http://bleacherreport.com/articles/593920-anderson-silva-scores-a-100000-pay-day-before-ufc-126

133 http://www.sherdog.com/news/news/Anderson-Silva-Lands-Nike-Corinthians-Sponsorship-Deals-34480

134 *UFC Magazine*, February/March 2010

135 http://www.pridefc.com/pride2005/index.php?mainpage=news&news_id=507

136 http://www.vancouversun.com/sports/champion+Maurício+gets+kicks+cage/4458698/story.html

137 http://www.ufc.ca/fighter/Maurício-Rua

138 http://prommanow.com/index.php/2008/08/31/new-interview-with-Maurício-

shogun-rua/

139 http://www.vancouversun.com/sports/champion+Maurício+gets+kicks+cage/4458698/story.html

140 http://www.youtube.com/watch?v=Tup4Sy_0Q28

141 http://www.pridefc.com/pride2005/index.php?mainpage=news&news_id=88

142 http://www.sherdog.com/news/articles/The-Brazilian-Notebook-PRIDE-GP-Edition-2716

143 http://www.sherdog.com/pictures/event/PRIDE-Opens-Weigh-Ins-to-Press-Shogun-Only-Fighter-Over-Limit-2722

144 http://www.bloodyelbow.com/2011/5/19/2179279/ufc-130-rampage-vs-hamill-conference-call-live-updates#comments

145 http://www.mmamania.com/2012/3/20/2888182/rampage-jackson-shogun-rua-prove-fight-knee-surgery-ufc-mma-rematch

146 http://www.411mania.com/MMA/video_reviews/107951/The-History-Of-Pride-FC:--Pride-FC-Final-Conflict-2005.htm

147 http://www.pridefc.com/pride2005/index.php?mainpage=news&news_id=474

148 *FIGHT! Magazine*, January 2009

149 http://www.boxingscene.com/mma/shukan-gendai-yakuza-owner-problematic-employee--747

150 http://www.pridefc.com/pride2005/index.php?mainpage=news&news_id=1035

151 http://mmaweekly.com/dana-white-discusses-pride-plans-fighters-2

152 http://mmajunkie.com/news/2385/dana-white-were-working-on-fedor-right-now-news-from-the-ufc-71-post-fight-press-conference.mma

153 http://www.mmaweekly.com/dana-white-discusses-pride-plans-fighters-2

154 http://mmajunkie.com/news/2357/report-Maurício-shogun-rua-signed-by-ufc-may-debut-at-ufc-72.mma

155 http://www.fightopinion.com/2007/05/09/thursday-trash-talk-boxing-is-cash-money/

156 http://www.fightopinion.com/2007/10/04/pride-office-in-tokyo-shut-down-all-workers-fired/

157 http://www.fightopinion.com/2008/02/05/playing-with-fire-zuffa-sues-dse/

158 http://www.sherdog.com/news/articles/Former-Pride-Owners-Sue-Zuffa-Holding-Companies-Fertittas-12187

159 http://www.fightlawyerblog.com/2010/08/sakakibaras-lawsuit-against-spectrum.html

160 http://fandaily.info/celebrity-couples/renata-ribeiro-rua-is-mma-Maurício-shogun-ruas-wife/

161 http://www.cagepotato.com/shogun-sidelined-indefinitely-after-undergoing-his-third-knee-surgery-past-three-years/

162 http://bleacherreport.com/articles/520845-ufc-123-lyoto-machidas-10-career-defining-moments/page/3

163 http://prowrestling.wikia.com/wiki/Antonio_Inoki

164 http://www.usadojo.com/biographies/mma/lyoto-machida.htm

165 http://fiveouncesofpain.com/2008/07/11/shoguns-possible-return/

166 http://www.torontosun.com/2012/05/03/st-pierres-knee-surgery-a-modern-marvel

167 http://www.youtube.com/watch?v=nTqqR-y-CPE

168 http://www.sherdog.com/news/articles/The-Machida-Puzzle-Box-17612

169 http://www.mmafight.com/2009/07/shogun-on-machida-he-comes-from-the-karate-school-and-i-come-from-the-muay-thai-school/

170 *Sport Science*, 03/13/10

171 http://www.tatame.com/2010/04/07/Karate-coach-analyzes-Shogun-x-Lyoto

172 http://www.heavy.com/mma/mma-previews/2010/05/shogun-machida-ii-a-pound-for-pound-star-returns/

173 http://www.tatame.com/2010/01/19/Maurício-Shogun 1/19/10

174 http://www.fightersonlymag.com/content/news/12325-shogun-had-appendix-removed-eight-weeks-ago

175 http://www.realpain-mma.com/en/events/view/60/interview-with-Maurício-shogun-rua

176 http://www.mmafighting.com/2010/05/05/lyoto-machidas-father-talks-urine-drinking-then-does-it-himsel

177 http://www.abs-cbnnews.com/sports/10/30/11/marquez-ive-stopped-drinking-my-own-urine

178 *Boku*, Kazushi Sakuraba, Tōhō Shuppan, 2007

179 http://www.mmaweekly.com/gary-goodridge-diagnosed-with-ctepugilistic-dementia-says-no-regrets-about-his-fighting-life

180 http://www.thestar.com/sports/mma/ufc/article/983272--the-high-cost-of-living-dangerously

181 http://www.aan.com/press/index.cfm?fuseaction=release.view&release=1060

182 http://sportsillustrated.cnn.com/2011/writers/jeff_wagenheim/01/11/liddell.interview/index.html

183 *New York Times*, "A Russian Warrior Who Doesn't Battle for Acclaim," 01/20/09

184 *FIGHT! Magazine*, October 2009

185 http://russiatrek.org/stary_oskol-city

186 http://www.themmanews.com/translated-interview-with-aleksander-emelianenko/

187 http://www.youtube.com/watch?feature=endscreen&v=7d0bzX40tR8&NR=1

188 http://www.sport-express.ru/newspaper/2008-03-21/16_1/

189 http://efedor.ru/index_eng.shtml?id=35

190 http://www.fightersonlymag.com/content/features/14539-Aleksander%27s-Ink--The-secret-story-of-Russian-tattoos

191 http://www.valetudo.ru/exclusive/interviewseng/3387-sergey-kharitonov-alex-

emelyanenko-is-a-mistake-of-nature

192 http://www.sport-express.ru/newspaper/2008-03-21/16_1/

193 http://fedor.bel.ru/index_eng.shtml?id=131

194 http://fedorfight.com/bio/

195 http://www.sherdog.com/news/articles/2/Finding-Fedor-10538

196 http://www.youtube.com/watch?v=5sc5FzzZHLc&feature=player_embedded

197 http://www.mixfight.ru/mma/publications/2007/9/18/fedor/

198 *TIME*, "How to Dodge the Draft in Russia," 03/30/09

199 http://efedor.ru/index_eng.shtml?id=146

200 http://rt.com/sport/medvedev-emelianenko-putin-council-411/

201 http://efedor.ru/index_eng.shtml?id=8

202 http://efedor.ru/index_eng.shtml?id=80

203 http://fedorfight.com/bio/

204 http://mma.sbnation.com/2011/7/29/2302951/volk-han-the-man-who-brought-Sambo-and-fedor-to-japan

205 *FIGHT! Magazine*, October 2009

206 http://www.pridefc.com/pride2005/index.php?mainpage=news&news_id=106

207 http://www.youtube.com/watch?v=vmAFFvdGc_o

208 http://www.youtube.com/watch?v=ozQVBlQsPvM&feature=relmfu

209 http://www.nokaut.com/?id=12&lang=e&solo_news=2102

210 http://www.sherdog.com/news/interviews/Devils-in-the-Details-Says-Fedors-Striking-Trainer-8331

211 http://fiveouncesofpain.com/2009/01/08/fedor-emelianenko-responds-to-andrei-arlovski-freddie-roach-and-dana-white-in-exclusive-interview-with-5-oz-of-pain/

212 http://fedor.over-blog.com/article-263528.html

213 *FIGHT! Magazine*, October 2009

214 http://www.bloodyelbow.com/2011/2/16/1997863/ufc-leaning-towards-toronto-over-dallas-for-future-mega-matches

215 *Boku*, Kazushi Sakuraba, Tōhō Shuppan, 2007

216 http://www.fightopinion.com/2012/03/01/miro-mijatovic-pride-yakuza-ownership/

217 http://www.mmafighting.com/2011/02/20/nippon-weekly-former-pride-fc-president-nobuyuki-sakakibara-bac

218 http://www.mmaweekly.com/the-head-kick-heard-round-the-world-the-legacy-of-mirko-cro-cop

219 http://www.mixfight.nl/forum/showthread.php?49275-een-lekker-lang-splinternieuw-Heath-Herring-interview-inside 06/15/12

220 http://sportsnavi.yahoo.co.jp/fight/pride/column/200311/1107sn_01.html

221 *PRIDE FC Secret Files*, Kamipro Books, 2008

222 http://www.nokaut.com/?id=12&lang=e&solo_news=2262 05/14/12

223 http://sportsillustrated.cnn.com/2009/writers/josh_gross/01/02/arlovski-roach/

224 http://sportsnavi.yahoo.co.jp/fight/pride/column/200312/1228sn_03.html
225 http://www.mmafighting.com/2012/8/23/3261416/olympic-gold-medalist-rulon-gardner-1-million-pride-fedor-emelianenko-mma-news
226 http://efedor.ru/index_eng.shtml?id=37
227 http://www.imdb.com/title/tt0445777/
228 http://www.sherdog.com/news/interviews/Devils-in-the-Details-Says-Fedors-Striking-Trainer-8331
229 http://bleacherreport.com/articles/1074589-gary-goodridge-90-percent-of-early-pride-fights-were-fixed
230 *A Fighter's Heart*, Sam Sheridan, Grove Press, 2007.
231 http://efedor.ru/news/424.html
232 *A Fighter's Heart*, Sam Sheridan, Grove Press, 2007
233 http://www.guardian.co.uk/sport/2007/sep/07/smalltalk.sportinterviews
234 http://mmacollector.com/moreinfo.html?rec=ZIPZANGPRIDE
235 http://fightsport.net/?p=10313
236 http://fcfighter.com/post/the-name-game
237 http://www.fight-j.com/archives/200502/14-0252.php
238 http://www.nokaut.com/forum/viewtopic.php?f=1&t=9482&start=0 07/12/12
239 http://www.fightopinion.com/2010/09/02/toshiro-igari/
240 http://www.tokyomango.com/tokyo_mango/2010/08/jake-adelstein-remembers-crime-lawyer-toshiro-igari-after-his-suicide.html
241 http://www.sherdog.com/news/news/PRIDE-Judge-Matt-Hume-Defends-Nog-vs-Ricco-Decision-1157
242 http://www.mmanews.com/news/85014
243 http://web.archive.org/web/20070910000923/http://www.sportsline.com/mmaboxing/story/10263227/4 10/05/12
244 http://thewrestlingpress.com/the-death-of-pride-fighting-championships-part-one/
245 http://mmaweekly.com/dana-white-discusses-pride-plans-fighters-2
246 http://www.bloodyelbow.com/2011/7/27/2296557/fedor-emelianenko-vs-matt-lindland-fight-video-mma
247 http://www.fightopinion.com/2007/10/22/m-1-global-hires-monte-cox-signs-fedor-emelianenko/
248 http://www.youtube.com/watch?v=-LOvFdUx6oY&feature=player_embedded
249 http://www.sherdog.com/news/news/Fighting-Fedor-Reality-Show-in-Works-14810
250 http://mmajunkie.com/news/15625/affliction-folds-mma-promotion-will-sponsor-ufc.mma
251 mmapayout.com/2011/06/details-involving-affliction-trilogy-cancellation-and-ufcaffliction-deal-emerge/
252 *FIGHT! Magazine*, October 2010
253 http://k1legend.wordpress.com/2009/10/02/bas-boon-of-golden-glory-on-

overeem-fedor-k-1-m-1-and-more/

254 http://mmajunkie.com/news/18820/m-1s-vadim-finkelchtein-addresses-boons-rubbish-apologizes-for-overeem-comments.mma

255 http://www.5thround.com/6020/affliction-tragedy-timeline/

256 http://www.youtube.com/watch?v=VZPurAmZrIU

257 http://www.sherdog.com/news/news/Update-Fedor-to-Strikeforce-UFC-Responds-18883

258 http://mmajunkie.com/news/17296/fabricio-werdum-likely-to-meet-fedor-emelianenko-at-strikeforces-april-cbs-event.mma

259 http://usatoday30.usatoday.com/sports/mma/post/2010/02/fedor-emelianenkos-next-bout-reportedly-delayed-to-may/1

260 http://mmajunkie.com/news/17416/ufc-and-m-1-reopen-talks-white-hopeful-for-emelianenko-and-mousasi-in-the-ufc.mma

261 http://sports.espn.go.com/extra/mma/news/story?id=4634640

262 http://www.mmarocks.pl/alexander-emelianenko/profile-alexander-emelianenko/

263 http://www.sherdog.net/forums/f61/fedors-coach-fedor-loss-overeem-lesnarx-carwin-1269311

264 http://www.tatame.com/2010/01/19/Werdum-vs-Fedor-99-confirmed-in-April 05/07/11

265 http://pvtmag.portaldovt.com.br/en/08/

266 http://www.sherdog.com/news/news/M-1-Global-Fedor-To-Attend-June-16-Strikeforce-Open-to-Overeem-Bout-24694

267 http://www.fightopinion.com/2012/03/12/dan-diaz-tapout-lawsuit/

268 http://www.sherdog.com/news/news/M1-UFC-Trying-to-Ruin-Fedors-Sponsorships-25329

269 http://www.cbsnews.com/2100-18560_162-585049.html

270 *Fighting Politics*, 2010

271 http://www.youtube.com/watch?v=SYRoW4vf-r4

272 http://www.mmafighting.com/2011/03/12/zuffa-purchases-strikeforce

273 http://www.bloodyelbow.com/2011/12/15/2638503/strikeforces-show-time-contract-extended-officially

274 http://bleacherreport.com/articles/665660-dan-henderson-wants-fedor-emelianenko-at-heavyweight-not-catchweight

275 http://thegarv.com/Ryo-Chonan-Reports-of-Fedor-Ending-Ishii-s-Career-are-False.html

276 http://lowkick.blitzcorner.com/Other/Fedor-Emelianenko-Its-not-a-fact-that-the-fight-Pedro-Rizzo-will-be-my-last-16087

277 http://sports.yahoo.com/news/fedor-emelianenko-officially-retires-no-221405300--mma.html

278 http://www.huffingtonpost.com/2012/06/07/nfl-concussion-brain-trauma-lawsuit-players_n_1577497.html

279 http://www.youtube.com/watch?v=fc2oIIEv20E

280 http://www.hd.net/blogs/dennis-alexio-the-last-bastion-of-a-teenage-memory-michael-schiavello/

281 http://www.sherdog.com/news/news/FTC-Closes-Investigation-of-UFC-Parent-Company-Zuffa-39817

33225712R00210

Made in the USA
Middletown, DE
12 January 2019